CH

D0759058

Athens

James H. S. McGregor

Athens

THE BELKNAP PRESS OF HARVARD UNIVERSITY PRESS

Cambridge, Massachusetts, and London, England • 2014

Library of Congress Cataloging-in-Publication Data

McGregor, James H. (James Harvey), 1946–
    Athens / James H.S. McGregor.
        pages cm
    Includes bibliographical references and index.
    ISBN 978-0-674-04772-3 (alkaline paper)   1. Athens (Greece)—Description and
travel.   2. Athens (Greece)—History.   3. City planning—Greece—Athens—History.
4. Athens (Greece)—Buildings, structures, etc.   5. Historic buildings—Greece—
Athens.   I. Title.
    DF919.M35 2014
    949.5'12—dc23   2013037579

Contents

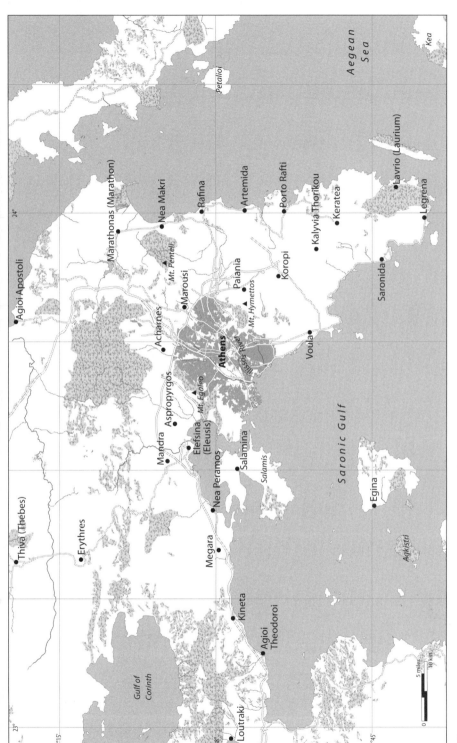

Attica

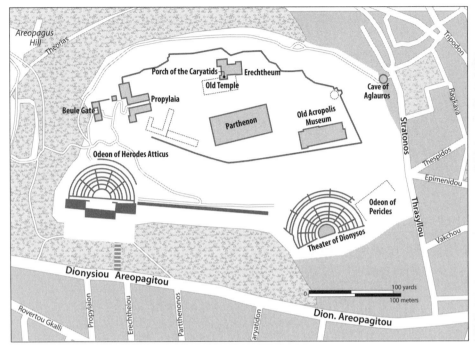

Acropolis

Acropolis and Syntagma Square

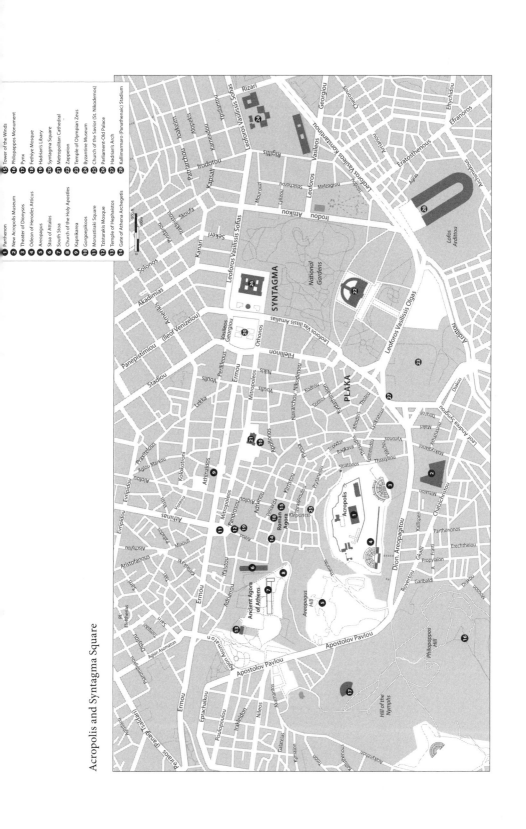

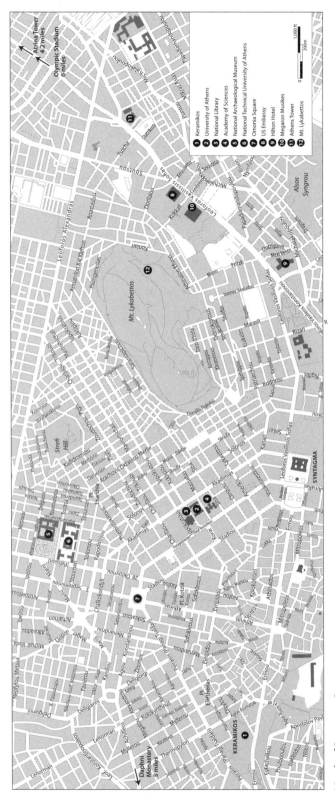

North of Syntagma Square

Athens

Introduction

Athens, Greece, is the hometown of Western thought, the birthplace of democracy, and the starting block for the modern Olympics. This city's art, architecture, and literature have risen from the ground not once but time after time to transform painting, writing, sculpture, and city planning. We honor Athenian thinkers for their exploration of law and justice, for their philosophical theorizing and their logical grounding of assertion, and for their deeply felt and complexly articulated conclusions about what is good and what makes for a good life. It is harder, however, to get a handle on Athens itself, as a city physical and present on the landscape. Hidden from the outside world behind its current economic and political crises, like the great and powerful Oz behind his curtain, this modern city seems out of patience with everything, including its own classical reputation.

The sources of the city's unease are multiple. For one thing, all this foundational acting and thinking was just that: a foundation laid down long ago that lingered, sometimes no more than a ghost, through the millennia. Most of its celebrated events and creative pioneers were already old news or fast approaching extinction back in 339 BCE, when Alexander the Great took possession of the city. History—with a big *H*—rested its attention on Athens for more or less the entire fifth century BCE, focusing on events that Athenians themselves had brought about. But stoking the fires and polishing the marble in the shrine of classical Athens these last hundred or so generations must often have been a burden while so much else was going on.

Over those generations—and with increased rancor, starting sometime in the late eighteenth century—there were plenty of outsiders who could not resist telling a contemporary Athens that it would never be the man its grandfather was. An early instance of this occurred in the twelfth century, when Michael Choniates, dispatched from Byzantium to serve as bishop of Athens, expected his audience to appreciate the flowery rhetoric of the imperial capital. When they did not, he wondered what had become of the descendants of those who had admired the brilliance of Pericles and Demosthenes.

Cudgeling postclassical Athens with the grandeur of its past might seem like a cheap shot, but that has never stood in the way of the self-righteous or the self-interested. Lord Elgin could be the poster child for that attitude. When Francesco Morosini's cannon blew up a Turkish powder magazine one September evening in 1687—taking a good part of the Parthenon along with it—at least he had the grace to be embarrassed by what he had done. Unlike Morosini, Elgin never seemed to realize that the people of Ottoman-dominated Athens might have a personal stake in the sculptures that survived Morosini's attack. Envious of Napoleon's archaeological fieldwork in Egypt, and fearful that the French would somehow scoop him in Athens, Elgin, who was then English ambassador to the Ottoman court, took advantage of his position to secure a loosely worded permit to take the sculptures away. From his point of view, the only relevant issues were political rivalries and his success at getting around the usually intractable and frequently hostile Ottoman government. There is no reason to believe that he considered how Athenians might feel about the looting of their heritage. If he recognized a connection—ancestral or otherwise—between the Athens of 1800 and the Athens of Pericles and Plato, he never acknowledged it.

At various times, of course, scholars argued that there was no connection between the two. Nineteenth-century historians maintained that modern Athenians were descendants of Slavic invaders who settled in the land of Pericles during the waning years of the Roman Empire and gradually replaced not just its cultural but its civic DNA with an unrelated and, it goes without saying, inferior product. For some German scholars, the idea that those fifth-century preinvasion Greeks might have been *Aryans* was too attractive to pass up. Even scholars without obvious race prejudice or racialist agendas could be fellow travelers, though their argument was more disinterested and high-minded: the heritage of the Greeks belongs to all mankind, not just to the people who happen to live there now. Still, the consequences were about the same, for the contrast of past and present weighed inevitably and unmistakably against the present.

A view of the Acropolis from the North, taken by polymath William James Stillman in 1869. (Fine Arts Library, Harvard University)

In practical terms, Athens has long outgrown its origins, and the megalopolitan sprawl of the modern city—one that contains about one third of the Greek population today—dwarfs the vestiges of the ancient city patiently resurrected from the region's rich soil and obtrusive limestone. On a daily basis the average Athenian has little direct contact with the confined zone around the Acropolis that contains most of what matters to world history and archaeology. This does not mean that Greeks or Athenians repudiate their classical heritage—not at all. Every Greek schoolchild knows an enormous amount about the monuments of ancient art, architecture, and literature that represent that heritage, and takes great pride in them. But that same child knows, as every Greek adult knows too, that the classical past is not the only point of reference in Athenian history. There are other great epochs and other grand events both triumphant and tragic that make up the history of Greece and its modern capital.

Cohabitation with the past was, in fact, structured into the very foundation of the modern city; it survives in the confined part of Athens typically visited by tourists, and it anchors—to the minimal extent that remains possible—the sprawl that constitutes the city in its current manifestation. By the time sovereignty came to the Greeks, Athens had been badly mangled in the birth trauma of a new nation. Ottoman Turks occupied mainland Greece in 1456, three years after the fall of the Byzantine Empire. In the 1820s, Greek heroes and European volunteers known as Philhellenes steered the country to independence through a bloody revolution that managed to include within it a free-for-all among rival factions in the never-before-united Greek peninsula.

Athens was not the administrative center of the Ottoman occupiers. Thessaloniki, located in the country's northeast and closer to the center of government in Anatolia, played that role, but after liberation, Thessalonika remained in Ottoman hands. Athens, chosen for the new capital, had been a significant battleground in the prolonged war for independence, and the old houses spilling down from the Acropolis were badly damaged. The job of building a new capital was a formidable one, and the first generation of town planners adopted a strategy that had already shown great adaptability in their era. At the end of the eighteenth century, medieval cities like Edinburgh found it impossible to modernize. Rather than attempt to improve conditions along the overburdened streets that crowded the historical city, Edinburgh's designers set their sights on the next hill over and started fresh. Separated by a deep ravine from the old town, and laid out on rolling hills a bit less strenuous in contour, the new Edinburgh had all the amenities of rational planning: square blocks, wide streets, public sculpture, open squares, light, fresh air, and easy access. As the colonial empires of European powers expanded, and as European administrators replaced local satraps in ancient capitals across the globe, this same strategy provided appropriately European settings for new administrations. New towns with wide boulevards, plazas and circles, statues and fountains, fresh air, and clean water were grafted to the old.

The capital of the newly formed Greek nation fell somewhat short of the rational-planning model. A bit late for the Edinburgh experiment, the newly designed city nevertheless made for a precocious colonial capital. But colonial it was, in the important sense that the structure of government and the city that would house it were a composite of contradictory and arguably foreign ideals. On the one hand, the era in which the nation was created—the decade of the 1830s—was one in which European powers were still fighting their last war. That war was, in this instance, the final one in a series of Continental conflicts brought on by Napoleon's campaigns to change the map of Europe. In triumph, the older European powers did everything they could to cancel out the radical tendencies of the French Revolution that Napoleon's campaigns had armed and unleashed. Monarchs were the victors, and monarchy, even in France, was the inevitable choice for a responsible government. Therefore the government of Greece would be a monarchy, even if Athens was the widely acknowledged "cradle of democracy." Since Greece had no ruling family of its own, the monarch would need to be an import, and European powers settled on Otto, son of King Ludwig I of Bavaria.

The layout for his new city was developed in Bavaria: Munich-based architects who had designed neoclassical buildings for King Ludwig contributed to plans for Greece's new capital, and their design grafted a new town onto the old. Their city affirmed what international powers wished to emphasize: that new Athens was firmly anchored in old Athens (meaning, of course, the Acropolis), not the intervening buildings that separated the two like an architectural no-man's-land. This new city would draw its strength—and the new nation its purpose—from the great wellspring of the fifth century. The jumble of architecture separating the two might represent the profit and loss of two and a half millennia of intervening history, but that was of little immediate consequence. Nineteenth-century Athens conspired with this founding agreement. Remnants of the postclassical millennia were given short shrift. Where known classical sites like the Athenian Agora lay underneath, the city did not hesitate to sacrifice its "marginal" history to its foundational one.

Had history ended in 1840, Athens might have remained in forced cohabitation with its fifth-century past. But history continued after the founding of the new Greek nation, and that history was turbulent and contentious. Most cities have an insider's narrative that fails to engage and may even contrast with the version of history accessible to a visitor. Athens is no exception, but in Athens the bitter aftertaste of events entirely unknown to outsiders is sharper and more persistent than elsewhere. What has happened in the centuries of independence has marked the city and its inhabitants as deeply, as viscerally, and more fatefully than its classical past. The bywords of Athenian and modern Greek history are enigmatic ciphers to outsiders. Every Greek knows what "the Great Idea," "the National Schism," and especially "the Asia Minor Catastrophe" were all about. Those key words, along with a further handful of bitter phrases like "the battle of Athens," "the White Terror," and "the Colonels," sum up for Greeks a uniquely grueling struggle to realize their nation's particular character.

From the era of Greek independence to the aftermath of the First World War, "the Great Idea" was the dominant theme of foreign policy and an anchor of domestic policy. In some sense, this idea was more a question than an answer; it carried with it a persistent ambiguity. This question was a seemingly simple one: "What, in territorial terms, constitutes Greece?" Since Greece had for millennia been a province in someone else's empire, uncertainty made sense. The answer, however, depended very much on which historical precedent was invoked. Ancient Greece included the mainland, the islands, portions of the West Asian coast, scattered settlements on the Black Sea, and colonies in Sicily and Southern Italy. The Hellenized empire of Alexander the Great was far larger than this; and so was the territory of the Byzantine Empire. The acreage handed over to Greece at independence offered narrow boundaries by comparison. For a hundred years, Greece campaigned diplomatically and militarily to acquire land it argued, believed, or hoped might somehow belong to it. As successive governments got into trouble at home, they pressed claims on territories embraced by the Great Idea, hoping to save themselves from domestic criticism by pushing a nationalist goal.

From time to time "the National Schism" got in the way of achieving the Great Idea or, in fact, anything else. This schism was an enduring fracture in a body politic that, like a chameleon, displayed itself in a variety of different garments. No matter what the political landscape might look like, sooner or later a substantial fissure opened within it. The founding split was between monarchists and antimonarchists, but this fracture pitted right against left, or liberals against conservatives. A version of the schism led to outright civil war in the aftermath of Nazi occupation. Persecution of the left by the right was the theme of the events known as "the White Terror." Conservatives in an unstable postwar government sponsored campaigns of reprisal against anyone with liberal or left leanings. The bitterness of the split has led to repeated political assassinations on both sides, as well as two significant periods of dictatorship. The National Schism caused its greatest damage through its hold over the Greek military: the colonels who seized dictatorial power in 1967 were the most dramatic expression of its malevolent power.

The Great Idea came to a head in the decade following the First World War. Throughout the nineteenth century, European powers agreed to support an ailing Ottoman Empire rather than risk going to war with each other over the Ottomans' substantial territory. But when the First World War concluded, the victors finally agreed to divide the spoils. France held most of North Africa in its portfolio already; after the Ottoman breakup, the French added Syria and Lebanon. Britain gained Palestine and Iraq, along with confirmation of special British interest in Egypt and dominance in the Arabian Peninsula. In the end, Greece, which was sharply divided over what side to support during the war (the National Schism at work again), joined the victorious side and was encouraged by France and Britain to secure territory in Anatolia once governed by the Byzantines. Greece responded by sending its army to invade Turkey, intent on securing control over a territory based around the port city of Smyrna, or Izmir. Once this Greek force was thinly spread across the countryside, the Turkish army turned, split, and devastated the invading troops. The Treaty of Lausanne in 1923 decreed an end to this struggle; with a stroke of the pen, it proposed to annul the ethnic intermingling that had served as a repeated casus belli and, during the First World War, provoked extreme ethnic violence in Turkey. Most of the Muslims of Greece—some four hundred thousand people—and the roughly 1.3 million Christians of Turkey, would be exchanged. No other population movement on this scale had ever taken place. All combined, the loss of the war, the extinction of the Great Idea, and the influx of impoverished and exhausted refugees had a staggering effect on Greece. This magnified population brought new opportunities as well as new problems. While many skilled workers joined the national labor force, many destitute and needy people came to Greece as well. The city of Athens suddenly found itself struggling to house refugees. While the work of assimilation continued, the Great Depression struck, making it even more difficult for Greece to provide for its people throughout the country and the world. The massacre

The Acropolis sits amid the surrounding city, with the sea in the distance.

of Greeks in Turkey during the First World War, the disastrous military intervention in Turkey in 1921, and the population exchange that began in
1923 together make up "the Asia Minor Catastrophe."

Greece and Athens are in the international news today for reasons that
seem entirely contemporary, financial or fiscal in origin, and endemic to the
euro zone in general. But the turmoil that unites Greece with other European countries on the brink of financial disaster has its particular roots in
the internal conflicts of the past century. State ownership of industry, generous pensions for those lucky enough to be employed by that industry, and
endemic political corruption have all contributed to the current crisis. Each
of these practices and habits has its origin in the particulars of twentieth-
century Greek history. Addressing or reversing them may be of pressing international concern, but their solutions lie within the sphere of domestic
policy and indigenous history.

This book looks at the long span of Athenian history, from the earliest
settlements on and around the Acropolis through the second modern

Olympics and the current debt crisis. It pays full credit to the artifacts and achievements of the ancient world, while it also chronicles the entire Athenian experience. The long years between the end of the classical era and the age of independence have left comparatively few traces on the ground, but many monuments and artifacts may still be seen. Landmarks that define that history are, in many cases, still in use today, and they serve as important markers of events that demand to be acknowledged and understood. The chapters are arranged at once chronologically and topographically. This makes the book not only a coherent narrative about the city's history and development, but also—with the help of the maps included—allows it to serve as a guide for visitors to the city.

1

On the Rock

Like much of the coastal Mediterranean, Athens is, at heart, recycled ocean floor. The city's raw materials slowly filtered through and settled beneath the shallow waters of an ancient pre-Mediterranean sea named Tethys. Sand, broken down from continental rock, and mud from flatlands and marshes surged with floodwaters or drifted offshore on the wind. In those same shallow waters, tiny sea creatures with calcium-rich shells lived, bred, and died. Their soft bodies decomposed, but their shells remained, and over unimaginable generations these shells consolidated and petrified to produce layers of limestone hundreds of feet thick.

Tethys happened to occupy a patch of shrinking real estate at the intersection of continents. The tectonic plate that carries Africa has, for millions of years, narrowed the gap between itself and the plates that support Europe and Asia. Along the western edge of the Italian peninsula, where the African plate is sliding under the European plate, its movement has created a line of volcanoes. Further east in the Balkans, these plates appear to have butted against each other rather than slipping one under the other; here there are no volcanoes, but the region has a long history of earthquakes. In Greece the steady thrust of the African plate has both lifted and compacted the former sea bottom. It has pushed petrified mud and shell above water level and simultaneously squeezed it into a series of parallel ridges. These ridges pile up along the leading edge of the plate; their direction, northwest to southeast, is perpendicular to the northeast thrust of the African continental mass.

These two primitive geological events—the sea floor deposits in Tethys and the ramming action of the African plate—pared down by the long-term effects of erosion, more or less account for the Greek landmass. Within that mass, Attica, the subregion to which Athens belongs, is a fairly good small-scale representation of the national geological dynamic. Rather than a mountain ridge that runs northwest to southeast, Attica is a peninsula with the same orientation—the geological forces that pushed up other regions failed to lift Attica far above the waterline. And while its few mountains are more shattered and eroded than others farther north, they are equally effective in blocking the peninsula from its neighbors. In essence, Greece is fragmented by mountains and especially by mountain ridges, and that fragmentation has been a fundamental political and cultural fact throughout much of the country's history.

Athens is close to the sea but not on it. It sits near the banks of the Ilissos River, but that river, like the majority of Greece's rivers, is seasonally dry. Athens's greatest resource is the Attic plain. From time to time during the prehistoric era, Athens and the Attic plain were joined economically and politically. Whenever that happened, Athens flourished. In other periods, the links were broken and the city's power, wealth, and influence collapsed. The importance of this intermittent interdependency between Athens and Attica rests on the nature of the particular historical period during which Greek life began.

The earliest known settlement in Athens dates from the Neolithic period. That period began in Greece in about 6500 BCE. Before that time, Greece's few occupants were foragers; hunting animals and gathering wild plants, fruits, and nuts were the basis for their survival. More than eight thousand years ago, settlers began to arrive in Greece from the coast of Anatolia. These migrants were probably few in number, but they brought with them the constituent parts of what prehistorians have recently begun to call the "Neolithic package." This was an interrelated suite of technologies and forms of social life that had been developed thousands of years earlier in various parts of the Levant. It included cultivation of cereal grains, legumes, fruits, nuts, and other crops. This "package" also incorporated domesticated sheep and goats, as well as a few larger animals like cattle and oxen. Along with the animals and vegetable crops, these settlers brought a few other novelties: they were skilled in making pottery, and they were accustomed to living in villages and towns.

Historians have long argued about the number of settlers who came to Greece in this era. Contemporary prehistorians tend to think that their numbers were quite small, but they also believe that, for a variety of reasons, their impact far outweighed their size. Interaction between the newly arrived settlers and the indigenous people was likely slight. Hunter-gatherers needed to be mobile, and they tended to follow their prey from one seasonal camp to another. These new arrivals were looking for agricultural land, which they were most likely to find in low-lying river valleys and along the coast. There was probably little immediate competition between the two groups for land or resources.

Over time, however, significant differences developed between the two groups, and those differences always worked to the advantage of the settlers. Hunter-gatherer populations were limited by the availability of prey; since they had no control over the productivity of the herds, grasses, and wild fruits that they depended on, their populations probably remained small and close to the upper limit of what their range could sustain. By contrast, the Neolithic people living in the valleys and along the coast grew their own food, and they could produce more by intensifying cultivation and expanding the land they farmed, so they were able to sustain bigger communities. When migrants married with hunter-gatherers, the farmers easily integrated them into their growing community, while the hunter-gatherer community was less able to reciprocate. Over a few generations, the many descendants of these few immigrants would form a much larger community than the descendants of the foragers. Farmers would control the most productive land, and the shrinking bands of hunter-gatherers would be pushed to the edges of their old domains, where resources were scarcest.

At a certain point, the farming community would begin to exceed the limits of its resources. Then a portion of it would break off and travel to new lands. Migrants from Greece moved northwestward into the valley of the Danube River, near its junction with the Black Sea. There they established a productive agricultural society that flourished in the fifth millennium BCE. Among historians, this community has been the focus of a great deal of interest and controversy. It appears to have been a peaceful, egalitarian society sensitive to its environment and one in which women were well-regarded if not in fact dominant. The connections between the Danube valley communities and the first agricultural communities in Greece suggest that those two cultures might have shared important characteristics. The earliest Greek communities might also have been relatively nonviolent, egalitarian ones in

which women had highly valued social roles. These societies are also assumed to have worshipped a pantheon of deities with similar characteristics. Typically, their religion is associated with a mother goddess linked to
the earth and the reproductive cycles of both the ecological and the human
communities.

An artifact representing this culture was found near the slopes of the
Acropolis and dated to the fifth millennium BCE. Discovered in 1938, the
figurine (pictured on page 67 of Hurwit, referred to in the Further Reading
list at the end of this book)—like many others collected in areas all around
the borders of the Mediterranean—is clearly female, with corpulent thighs,
buttocks, and belly. Figurines of this kind are typically labeled as images of
a goddess; their characteristic emphases and exaggerations are taken to be
evidence of a culture's respect for the reproductive power of women and the
fundamental role fecundity played in early Neolithic societies. Though not
directly related to agriculture, the figure's dimensions suggest a woman who
has been well nourished on the fat of the land. The emphasis on sexual characteristics suggests that her reproductive capacity, like that of the fields and
flocks that have nourished her, is of primary importance to her society.

The worship of the goddess—if that is what we are seeing in these figurines or, more generally, in the archaeological remains of early Neolithic
societies in the Eastern Mediterranean—eventually came to an end. The societies we know historically, from a written record that began in the early
third millennium BCE, are not matriarchal. In Greek history, art, and literature, which began much later, we see little reflection of the worldview
or the social structure of the earliest Neolithic period. The historical societies of Greece and other cultures of the ancient Mediterranean were male-
dominated ones in which warriors held power and commanded prestige,
while women and those who worked the soil were socially inferior. These
societies worshipped a pantheon of sky or mountain gods who had, according to their own mythologies, achieved power and dominion over earlier
generations of earth gods.

What happened to change this picture so dramatically? What happened
to the goddess and the cultures that reflected her earthbound values? How
did patriarchal, warrior societies come to be dominant not just in Attica but
throughout the region? These questions are particularly puzzling because
the patterns of Neolithic life remained unchanged between the ninth and

third millennia BCE, the period when these sweeping social changes would have taken place. Societies became more diversified, but they remained agricultural. The crops and many farming techniques remained constant, and all societies in the region continued to depend on agriculture for their survival. Still, early Neolithic mythology and social structure appear to have died out, to be replaced by something distinctly different.

In the nineteenth century, dramatic changes of this kind were always linked to one common cause: migration. The peace-loving, matriarchal farmers of the Danube valley appear to have been replaced by nomadic herders from the steppes of southern Russia sometime in the mid-fourth millennium BCE. Marija Gimbutas, a leading theorist of matriarchy in the twentieth century, argued that these nomads brought with them an entirely new kind of culture. Based on the mobility of the horse, this new culture substituted violence, masculine dominance, and a pantheon of sky gods for the older culture of the indigenous agriculturalists. In other words, an invading minority imposed its will and its value system on an agricultural majority. This also suggests that the warrior class imposed its worldview and its gods on an agricultural class at least ten times its size. It suggests that coercion rather than persuasion was the glue that held primitive societies together. There is evidence to support the notion that horse-riding invaders from the Russian steppes entered the Danube territories at the end of this most vital period. There is no evidence, however, to tell us whether these newcomers took advantage of existing political instability in a society collapsing under its own weight or whether they created the disaster themselves.

Ian Hodder, a leading prehistorian, has suggested that the transformation of Neolithic societies from their earliest egalitarian, woman-centered formations to those where men dominated may not have been the result of hostile invaders but part of the dynamic of agricultural development. When agricultural communities or colonies were small and had abundant resources available to them, it was the scarcity of labor that limited their ability to exploit the resources at their disposal. In that era, anything that increased the labor pool was precious. The reproductive capacity of women was sacred, because it was the only pathway toward increasing this resource. When a population reached the maximum that its agricultural base could sustain, the limiting factor changed from labor to land. Even in matriarchal societies, it seems to have been the case that men typically controlled land and trade while women controlled the household and the family. When land became a scarce resource, the power of the men who controlled it grew dramatically. Hodder's argument explains a great deal. The transition from matriarchy to patriarchy would not have been the result of invasion and the violent imposition of an alien value system on peasants too weak to resist; instead, it would have been the story of a crisis in faith brought on by changes in the most fundamental part of the social order, its agricultural base.

The Attic plain undoubtedly experienced a similar transformation from the cult of fecundity and fertility represented by the Acropolis figurine to something much more familiar from history and mythology. We can safely discount the notion that significant cultural change necessarily means invasion and the violent imposition of new values. We can also continue to appreciate the intimate connection between whatever social formation governed among the elite powers and the agricultural base that sustained them. Attica was an agrarian region, and Athens was the prime beneficiary of its productivity. The relationship between the city and its hinterland was not a coercive or exploitative one, but one that continued to reflect shared values and a universally recognized interdependency.

In Greek myth the linkage of multiple villages and power centers is called *synoikismos,* and its accomplishment in Attica is attributed to the mythical King Theseus. Ancient historians and Greek mythmakers both thought of this unification as a onetime event, but archaeology suggests that through its earliest history Athens was periodically united and intermittently severed from the surrounding region. In the modern world, a city is a largely independent political structure defined by its dense population and its close-knit fabric of houses and businesses. Modern Athens, which has spilled out of its historical confines and flowed over most of the Attic plain, is a prime example of a modern city.

In contrast to this modern view, writers from Homer through the time of Aristotle recognized a close relationship between the densely packed city and the countryside that surrounded it. Aristotle thought that all social life depended on the family and that the family was fundamentally a labor cooperative focused on farming. Villages were created by interdependent families, and urban centers, which Aristotle saw as the optimal environment

The Acropolis as seen from the country from the southeast, 1869. William James
Stillman, photographer. (Fine Arts Library, Harvard University)

for human beings, were one notch higher in organization and development.
In Aristotle's mind, as in the minds of most ancient Athenians, the city
never lost its links with the productive agricultural land that surrounded it.
Powerful Athenians may have enjoyed a particularly sophisticated lifestyle
that was well beyond the reach of rural folk, but the city remained rooted in
the villages and dependent upon them for survival—at their most successful, Athens and Attica were partners. What the plains of Attica produced
was consumed by the city of Athens. The pottery, scythes, and plows that
Athenian craftsmen made were essential to cultivating the fields and bringing in the harvest. The gods that the city worshipped ensured the welfare of
the entire community. *Synoikismos* in this sense meant the political recog-
nition of the interdependence of city and region.

Indeed, despite the brilliance of its intellectual and artistic life, life in ancient Attica was organized around agriculture. Eight or nine out of every ten men and women were directly involved in agriculture, so land was the most important source of wealth: taxes on wealthy landowners were the key to the city's military power as well as its religious and social culture. Athens was a major commercial center, and Attica had some mineral resources, especially silver. The bulk of its trade, however, like ancient trade in general, was in agricultural products. Olive oil, wine, and wool were probably Attica's biggest commodities. In key eras of its commercial success and influence, Athens also traded in pottery. Even this precious and highly sought good retained its links to practical life and, especially, to agriculture.

A striking example of the pervasive influence of agriculture even in this luxury market comes from Athens's Panathenaic games. Victors in those games received as prizes urns handcrafted in Athens and painted by skilled artisans. While we might assume that the urns were sufficient trophies of success, it turns out that they were awarded in quantity rather than one to a victor, and arrived filled with olive oil from the sacred grove of the Athenians. The urns were an enduring symbol of the victor's triumph, but the forty quarts of select oil that each urn contained was a precious commodity. The city's wealth, like its food, was grown almost entirely in Attica by farmers closely linked to Athens. Without this unusually rich agricultural surround, Athens could not have been the political and commercial powerhouse that it became.

The region's geology of rock, not just its soil, also played a fundamental part in shaping the city. For twenty-five centuries, the most prominent landmark in Athens has been an architectural monument elevated on a natural pedestal. Long before the Parthenon was built on top of it, the Acropolis outcrop was this city's most prominent feature and the core of repeated settlements. It is only one among a cluster of linked hills that have played significant parts in Athenian history. The Acropolis outcrop is not even the biggest hill in the immediate vicinity; that distinction belongs to Lykabettos, which has never played much of a role in civic life. Structurally, all of the hills of Athens, including the largest, are shattered remnants of one eroded limestone ridge, a bit of Tethys pushed up by the African plate and eroded by millions of years of storm and wind. And it is limestone that the Acropolis has relied on to power its long and significant civic history. The particular

Mount Lykabettos rises high above the surrounding blocks.

limestone of the Acropolis is a light blue-gray, and it is relatively hard, which has slowed its erosion and altogether prevented the wearing away of softer rock layers beneath it. This durable elevated platform has served the city in two widely recognized ways over its long history. During the thirteenth century BCE, the limestone mesa was home to a leading, if not ruling, family. Near the end of the era when the Greek city-state Mycenae dominated the Greek peninsula and much of the Eastern Mediterranean, sometime around 1250 BCE, their palatial residence was shielded by a massive wall.

From the mid-eighth century until the end of the classical era, the Acropolis was home to the city gods and the shrines that sheltered them. In that era, the ability of Athens to unify and lead the region depended on the religious authority of those shrines. In the centuries of postclassical occupation, the Acropolis reverted to its earliest role. Later, in the Middle Ages, it became a castle that could be cut off from the town below to shelter occupying powers. Beginning in the mid-fifteenth century, a Turkish military authority was based on the Acropolis, though civilian government was centered below. Storing gunpowder in the Parthenon, which came to be ignited by Venetian cannon fire, was one reflection of the site's military role.

The long-playing role of the Acropolis as a place to shelter power or to host divinity is easy to appreciate, but the Acropolis and, especially, its limestone cap have played less visible, though still important, roles. Despite its resistance to erosion, the Acropolis limestone is subtly porous. Rainwater sinks into the stone and filters slowly through it. At any given moment this limestone is saturated with the accumulated rainfall of several Athenian autumns. The rock layer beneath the limestone is more susceptible to weathering, but it is impermeable. When the water slowly seeping through the limestone cap reaches this layer, it cannot continue to fall. The result is a little like what happens when a wet sponge is placed on a granite countertop: water held in the sponge flows downward, then spreads out on the counter. When water leaching through the Acropolis limestone reaches the impermeable layers beneath, it also begins to flow sideways. At the seam between the two rock strata, the Acropolis leaks water in the form of seeps and springs.

This seepage was the source of water in the deep well of the Mycenaean era, but it was exploited long before—and after—that time. Some of the earliest evidence for occupation in Athens is provided by shallow wells dug into the Acropolis at mid-slope. Broken pottery from these wells suggests that they were in use around 3100 BCE. Wells from that era are clustered below the northwest corner of the Acropolis near a spring called the Klepsydra that remained important during antiquity. The location of these wells suggests that a Neolithic village was somewhere nearby. It was probably not located on the top of the Acropolis, but it might have stood somewhere adjacent to its sides. Historically then, one of the least conspicuous but most significant roles played by the Acropolis was to serve as a natural water tower in the midst of a seasonally dry landscape.

Trace amounts of acid in rainwater dissolve limestone. This process has accelerated in the modern era, when pollutants captured by raindrops produce extra acidity. Even in the absence of man-made pollution, though, there is enough acidity in most rain and groundwater to erode limestone. On the Acropolis, the boundary between limestone cap and underlying rock is pitted with caves carved by naturally acidic rainwater. These caves have been used by men and women for millennia. Some of the most important

ones are close to the Klepsydra spring, and it is possible that Neolithic settlers used them as shelters or homes. Throughout antiquity these caves also
served as shrines. Those at the base of the Acropolis, like the springs, are
natural features that have enhanced the usefulness of the rock and condi-
tioned the character of the city for many generations.

Probably the most elusive functional feature of the Acropolis is its shadow.
The hill is wider on its east-west axis than on its north-south axis. It presents
its long south side to the sun, while its equally long northern side stands in
shadow. Neanderthals and the anatomically modern humans that followed
them into Europe preferred to settle in shelters or caves facing south and
commanding a wide view over the landscape. It is hard to imagine that they
would not have been drawn by the south face of the Acropolis, but no evidence has been found of any occupation of the site in their era. Throughout
the city's long history, Athenians have almost always preferred the sheltered
north face of the hill. There is indication of primitive settlement on the south
of the hill, where caves and springs also exist, but modern Athens, like its
ancient predecessors, has its nucleus in settlement on the north side. The
shadow of the Acropolis—rather than its exposed southern flank—has been
the city's historical preference.

The first occupants of the Acropolis who left significant traces were men
and women of the Mycenaean era, which extended from 1600 to 1100 BCE.
They built extensively on the hilltop, and sufficient if subtle remains of their
work still exist. From these bits and pieces, archaeologists have been able to
draw a picture of some of the principal features of their settlement. The Mycenaean realm extended through much of Greece and Crete, and their ships
traded throughout the Eastern Mediterranean. Mycenaean remains, which
are much better preserved in many other Greek sites than they are in Athens, suggest a culture dominated by rich and powerful warlords. The great
archaeological pioneer Heinrich Schliemann, an excavator at Troy, proceeded
from that city in search of the palaces of powerful chieftains who, Homer
said, had participated in the great siege. Schliemann's first goal—and his
greatest success—came in excavations at the city of the warrior Agamemnon, Mycenae, on the Peloponnese south of Athens, from which the era took
its name. Excavations at Pylos, the home of the hero Nestor, have uncovered
one of the most completely preserved palaces of the Mycenaean era. At
Mycenae, Schliemann uncovered massive city walls with a monumental

entrance, a sprawling royal palace, and not one but a series of tombs that had remained undiscovered and unlooted for more than three thousand years. Wealth accumulated by the Mycenaean rulers through their periodic raids and steady trade was well represented in the grave goods found among these royal tombs.

During the era of Mycenaean dominance, Athens was not a significant city. It lay at the periphery of Mycenaean trade and power politics, and it even had Mycenaean rivals within Attica itself. Late in the life span of the Mycenaean power system, the city seems to have come up in the world. Either a local family gained sufficient prominence to build visibly and dramatically on the Acropolis, or a Mycenaean chieftain from outside came in to take control, establishing himself and his family on the hill. What remains today is mostly substructure. Parallel walls built into the north side of the sloping rock top allowed builders to create a flat platform as the foundation for a multiroom palace. Archaeologists know, through more extensive evidence found at other sites like Pylos, what kind of building this would likely have been. It would have featured multiple rooms to shelter the ruling family as well as their slaves and servants. It would also have included rooms for craftsmen who worked with bronze to forge weapons as well as precious metals to make the ornaments that wealthy Mycenaeans admired. There would have been some kind of shrine, or a series of shrines, dedicated to the deities that looked over the household and the city.

Mycenaean kings may have been powerful warriors, but their role as leaders typically combined both political and priestly functions. At the center of any Mycenaean palace was an area called the *megaron*. This was the principal ceremonial space of the palace, combining throne room and central hearth. The megaron at Pylos, which is one of the best preserved and most widely published, was probably a good deal more elaborate than the one in Athens, but its main features were no doubt similar. The megaron is a large and tall room with an elevated circular fire pit at its center. The fire pit is surrounded by four columns that reach to the ceiling and support a raised section of roof that admits light and draws smoke from the fire. The floor, columns, and walls of the Pylos megaron were plastered, and traces of elaborate decorative paint have been found on all surfaces. Reconstructions reveal an opulent, colorful chamber with the throne of the city's leader at its innermost core.

While the megaron was the center of the palace complex, it was one of a suite of rooms that were arranged along a long axis that led from an exterior plaza to the throne room. These rooms combined porches, interior spaces, and atria in a rhythm and combination that have been associated with the form of the later Doric temple. Though no trace of the Acropolis megaron now exists, it might well have been in place long enough to influence subsequent structures on the site. Some archaeologists imagine that the Mycenaean palace sheltered a primitive wooden statue that later Athenians would identify as an image of Athena and give pride of place in their much more elaborate Acropolis.

Bits and pieces of other Mycenaean structures on the Acropolis survive to this day. These include traces at various points of the large wall that surrounded and defended the hilltop. This wall was erected suddenly sometime around 1200 BCE, and it was made of locally quarried limestone blocks of large dimension fitted together without mortar but with smaller rocks as shims and infill. This is a kind of masonry typically called Cyclopean, as if the large rough-hewn stones that it comprises were the natural building materials not of humans but of one-eyed monsters like the giant Polyphemus whom Odysseus encountered and blinded in *Odyssey* 9. The best preserved and most visible portion of this wall lies at the base of the Propylaia, at the western entrance to the Acropolis. A second substantial stretch is visible in a trench on the south side of the hill near the Parthenon. Remains seen today near the Propylaia probably belonged to a bend in the wall that led into a massive gateway, like the famous Lion Gateway at Mycenae. In front of that gateway and a bit downhill from it are other remains of the Mycenaean defense of the Acropolis—these seem to be the foundation of a bastion or watchtower.

Other surviving features of the Mycenaean era are two stairways and a deep cistern. The stairways are both on the north side of the hill and connect the top with the caves and springs on the slope. Both entrances would have been unusable in the case of siege or attack on the fortified hilltop, so the Mycenaean defenders added another sheltered access to water at the base of the hill's limestone cap. This hidden access made use of a deep cleft created when an earthquake dislodged a massive piece of limestone at the top of the north slope but failed to propel it down the hillside. The piece rests with its upper edge leaning back against the hilltop and its lower edge pushed away from the central mass. Between it and the undisturbed cap is a cleft that runs the full thickness of the limestone. By digging down from the top, Mycenaean excavators gained access to the widest part of that cleft. There they built or carved stairs into its sides, which gave them secure, sheltered access to water collecting in a pit, which they also excavated, some forty or more feet below the entrance.

Protected by their massive wall and assured of a continual supply of water, the Mycenaean lords of Athens were well prepared to survive an attack. Whether that attack ever came is anyone's guess. The collapse of Mycenaean civilization was dramatic in other places, where fires typically destroyed their palaces. There is no trace of fire or any likelihood that such traces would have survived on the Acropolis, where multiple generations of builders have repeatedly erased most of what came before them. The cause of Mycenaean collapse is uncertain and widely debated. When invasion was a common answer to mysterious and dramatic social change in the past, it was also the answer to questions about collapse. Now, with the theory of invasion losing its adherents, the cause remains unknown. This collapse was followed by a long period that left little trace in the archaeological record—a period usually referred to as the Greek Dark Ages, but the darkness may be more a gap in the record than a period of cultural blight.

The next time the Acropolis comes into view is sometime around the eighth century BCE, when Athenians began to establish the site not as a regional stronghold, but as a powerful shrine. The prominence of the Acropolis, its incorporation of caves near the summit, and its long history all made it a good candidate for this role. It was a spot picked out by nature to play an unusually prominent part in the landscape, and that certainly endowed it with power in people's minds and imaginations. It reached toward the sky, but it also descended into the earth through caves. This meant that it had visible connections not just to the heavens and the Olympian deities living there, but also to the interior of the earth, which was home to earth-based gods. While the history of the ancient world has typically given prominence to the sky gods and their myths, the gods of the earth played a highly important role in worship. The ability of the Acropolis to house both kinds of gods must have given it great power and significance.

For every thousand visitors who explore the top of the Acropolis, probably only two or three visit the caves that surround it, although this is not a difficult thing to do, and the rewards are substantial. A hundred feet above, throngs of visitors bake in the unrelenting sun, while the caves remain uncrowded, cool, and silent. An ancient path called the Peripatos once ran around the Acropolis, and a paved version of it is still there today. At its western end, near the main entrance to the site, the path offers not just a view but access to many of the principal shrines of antiquity. Three caves sacred to three different gods are clustered near the western end of the path. There is a relatively small cave sacred to the god Pan, and two larger caves sacred to gods typically associated with the sky, rather than the earth. Pan, a god of wilderness, was often worshipped in caves and grottoes. Zeus and Apollo seem unlikely gods to have been honored within the earth, so the deities first worshipped in these shrines may have been quite different ones. Like most Olympians, Zeus and Apollo both acquired names and attributes over their long and important cultural lives, and these epithets brought them into association with a wide range of activities and locales. Zeus Melichios, for example, was a name given to the chief god when he was worshipped as an earth god. Under that title, he might be represented as a serpent or as a composite of human and snake. Apollo may have been the most Olympian of the Olympians in his association with the light of the sun and with reason, but his famous reputation as a predictor of the future depended on very different powers. The Pythian priestess of Apollo, who delivered the famous enigmatic prophecies at the god's chief shrine in Delphi, drew her inspiration from gases escaping from a cleft in the rock. Her powers came from the earth, not from the sky. The cave worship of these gods highlighted their connection to the earth. In any case, there is substantial evidence that the gods were invoked by generations of worshippers and that at least some of these worshippers gained something from their devotion. The rock face at the mouths of all three caves is marked with shallow indentations that are mostly rectangular in outline. These indentations were carved to hold votive plaques on which ancient worshippers acknowledged the gift they had received from the god.

Farther along, the path passes caves sacred to Aphrodite and Eros. While both these gods were Olympians, too, their associations with the earth are especially strong. Aphrodite and her son, Eros—the name simply means "desire"—have close ties to fertility, a cause dear to earth gods in general. The fertility of soil was not their concern; instead they oversaw human

Two of the many caves that surround the Acropolis.

fertility and the forces of attraction and desire that guaranteed it. Worshippers turned to these gods for help winning the lovers they desired. The number of niches around the shrines of each suggests that they were often successful.

A large inaccessible cave overlooks the path from the east end of the Acropolis. This is the cave of Aglauros. Aglauros was one of the daughters of Cecrops, a mythical founder of Athens who was worshipped on the Acropolis (his legend is described in some detail in the next chapter). Associating this cave with one of his daughters suggests that it played an important, if obscure, role in the religious life of the city itself, not of individuals. Because Cecrops was a founder of the city, his cult is always associated with the earth.

History also played its part in making the Acropolis sacred. The ruins of the Mycenaean palace and the very prominent Cyclopean walls would have contributed to its air of mystery. It is hard to imagine what the shrine builders of the eighth century thought they were seeing when they looked at the ruins on the Acropolis, which would have been five centuries old at the time. These ruins would have represented the remains of a culture that had evidently been powerful, and one that had passed entirely away. The shrine builders might have thought that the ruins dated to the time of the Trojan War and the era of the great heroes of Homer's pan-Hellenic epic poem that was taking shape at that time. They might also have thought that the walls were the work not of men but of giants who once roamed the earth. Without a doubt these notions would have made the hill seem especially impressive.

Any visitor to the modern Acropolis knows what a jumble it has become: getting a sense of what's what as you wander the site is challenging. Of course, a visitor might assume that this confusion is the result of the near destruction of everything there, but the facts are very different. In its heyday, the Acropolis was equally disordered, if not more so. Pausanias, who described the monuments as they existed in the second century CE, gives a confused and confusing sense of it. So this jumble is an authentic part of the character of the site in its heyday. Oddly enough, this confusion is yet another representation of the great religious power of the site.

Our experience of religious shrines is apt to be based on what has become of them during an era when faith is waning. Visiting the important churches of Rome, for example, which have been objects of devotion for millennia, the visitor is unlikely to see much hint of the fervor of popular faith. A parish church in Trastevere, on the other hand, may boast a plaster Madonna decorated with jewelry and surrounded by gifts glued to the wall. Active shrines are messy because people want to make contact with them. They want to touch them, and when they can no longer touch them, they want to put parts of themselves or representations of themselves nearby. Their gifts, called votive offerings, represent their faith in the god of the shrine and also act as effigies of the donors themselves. Gifts are permanent, if indirect, ways for the donor to stand in the presence of the gods.

What is true of donors is also true of gods, especially minor ones; they want to bask in the celebrity of more prominent deities, and for the Acropolis, at least, this was the case. This site primarily honored Athena, but it also revered Poseidon, and the legendary human Erechtheus, who was the first Athenian ruler, as well as a host of lesser gods and heroes. The power of the place itself, which was already enormous when it housed nothing but Mycenaean ruins, was magnified over centuries by the power of the great gods worshipped there. Lesser deities clamored for space on the Acropolis, which in time they gained. Eventually the Acropolis was crowded with shrines, altars, and votive gifts that together created a cacophony of devotions that anyone would have been hard-pressed to keep straight, but keeping them straight was not at all the point: the point was to accumulate, embellish, and enrich the shrine, bringing more holiness to it in order to draw more holiness from it, and creating a carnival of gods, heroes, demigods, priests, prophets, devotees, and donors. This clamor would not have appealed to the austere and philosophical Athenians who have retroactively given the city's reputation a rationalistic, disciplined cast, but at least in the eighth century when all this activity had its start, no one had ever heard of a philosopher.

Greek shrines really do not require architecture, though we do associate architecture with the Acropolis in its fifth-century form. Most people today would think of the Parthenon as the centerpiece of Athens, but historically, the Parthenon was only one more embellishment of the Acropolis, which was the real focus of both human and divine attention. There may have been some architecture on the Acropolis in the eighth century—perhaps a building that sheltered the old Mycenaean image of Athena, if that object really existed. Yet in the absence of clear evidence of architecture, how is it possible to say that the Acropolis began to rise to regional prominence as a shrine? The answer may be found not in remains of temples, but in the abundant evidence of devotion. Broken bits of pottery dating from that time are plentiful in the archaeological record. Some bear the etched names of donors or perhaps devotees (Hurwit, 90–91). Much more impressive and suggestive are the remains of bronze tripods found on this site.

Victors in Greek athletic and poetic contests might have received urns filled with oil, but if their triumph was an important one, the prize might have been a bronze tripod. And the appropriate thing to do with such a valuable prize was to give it away to a god. This act of re-gifting enhanced the value of the prize by putting it on permanent display in a shrine, where it would serve as a reminder to the god and to every visitor of the victor's identity and achievement. Excavations at the Acropolis have uncovered a large number of fragments from bronze tripods produced in the mid-eighth century, and archaeologists infer that these were all dedications to gods worshipped—if not necessarily housed—on the Acropolis. The accumulation of valuable gifts during this period shows that the shrine was gaining ground.

What happened on the Acropolis also happened more generally throughout the country: it was a period when the *polis,* from which we get our word "politics," was born in Greece. A polis is not just a city and certainly not what we call a state, though that is the common modern translation; rather, the polis was an interlocked city and countryside—a more focused version of *synoikismos.* During the mid-eighth century, political unions of this character with very different social structures and systems of interdependency developed all over Greece. Their "constitutions"—meaning the particular terms of their coming together and their means of sharing power and determining policy—were collected in the fourth century BCE by Aristotle and his followers. Only one of the nineteen or so constitutions they are known to have described has survived, and that is the constitution of the Athenians.

The rise to prominence that the Acropolis experienced in the eighth century slowed and may even have been reversed in the seventh century. It is not until the second quarter of the sixth century BCE that significant development begins again. In the meantime, the Athenian constitution went through several crises that ended with the reforms of Solon, the great political negotiator. These reforms restricted enslavement for debt, a condition that had been threatening Athenian agriculture, but in doing so, they also left the wealthiest citizens in charge. Oligarchy was the order of the day, and powerful families were able to impose their rule on the city and pass it along to their sons. It was evidently the policy of these tyrants to increase the power and majesty of the Acropolis, and their first step toward that goal was to create a monumental entryway for the site.

The gate of the Cyclopean wall stood on the western side of the hill protected by its bastion, and it was here that sixth-century builders aimed to transform the narrow, well-protected entryway of this fortress into something entirely different. Its narrow gate and twisting path, once valuable for a stronghold, were replaced by a project that increased access to an area that served crowds of devotees. This work included constructing a ramp nearly three hundred feet long and almost thirty feet wide, with a substructure of pounded earth supported by stone retaining walls. If their goal was only to make it easier for devotees to reach the Acropolis, then the project was over-engineered. This wide ramp gave access to masses of people all at one time, yet the principal occasion when crowds of people would all have gone to the Acropolis together was during the Panathenaic procession. And although that processional had been held annually for some unknown length of time, in 566 BCE, right around the time that the new ramp was ready to use, the celebration of the Panathenaia gained a new wrinkle. Every fourth year, a Greater Panathenaia was celebrated, which meant that this augmented festival required more participants and drew bigger crowds who might well overfill the ramp as they climbed toward the altar of Athena on top of the Acropolis.

The creation of this new ramp did have a dramatic effect: by increasing access on the western side of the hill, it dragged the center of Athenian commercial and political life away from its earliest center northeast of the Acropolis. The Agora that Athenians knew at the city's height—the one visitors know from the extensive modern excavations—is located where it is because of the attractive force of that new ramp ascending the western slope of the Acropolis. Before the ramp was built, the space that became the classical Agora was a residential area with a few scattered graves at its edges.

At about the same time that the ramp was completed, the bastion was leveled and its top crowned with a small temple dedicated to Athena the Victor. The greatest improvement to the site was the construction of a temple called the Hekatompedon. Nothing of it can be seen on the Acropolis itself, although substantial remains of that temple are on display in the New Acropolis Museum, and many details of its construction are well known. What is, surprisingly, not known today is its location. The betting is that it either occupied the site of the old Mycenaean palace on the north side of the Acropolis, or that its foundations are buried beneath the Parthenon. Judging from surviving pieces, the temple measured approximately 60 by 120 feet. This temple would have been bigger than any shrine to stand on the hill before its time, but it was not particularly large by comparison with contemporary temples elsewhere.

The Hekatompedon temple was built in an architectural style called the Doric order. Like all Greek temples, it featured a central walled enclosure, probably divided into separate rooms where the image of the deity and stores of votive gifts were housed. The building would have been surrounded on all sides by columns, not unlike the Parthenon. These columns would have been fluted and crowned with very simple rounded capitals shaped like the bottom of a wineglass or an inverted mushroom cap. The colonnade supported an entablature that ran around the entire building, and the bottom third of this entablature was a band of squared-off stone that as a whole resembled a roof beam laid on top of square pads above the columns. Many people have argued that Greek stone buildings were based on patterns originally built of wood. The lowest band of the entablature is a stone version of what would have been, in some earlier period, a squared-off beam of wood. The second portion of the entablature rests on a shallow decorative cornice at the top of the beam. Called a frieze, this middle section is made up of an alternating system of blank squares and incised blocks. The blocks are divided into three parts, from which they derive their name, "triglyphs." In a wooden building, these blocks would be the projecting ends of roof beams perpendicular to and resting on the beam that the columns support. The spaces between the triglyphs were like blank canvases to be decorated by shallow carvings that were painted. Unlike other temples, the Hekatompedon offers no continuous story on the panels of its frieze; rather, its panels were decorated with geometrical designs, leaf patterns, and reliefs of lions and leopards.

The uppermost section of the entablature, or "cornice," jutted out beyond the plane of the lower two sections. Wooden buildings often have cornices of this kind to protect the beams and beam ends from rainwater, which causes rot. Stone, especially carved and painted stone, benefits from similar protection. Rainwater washes away paint and erodes limestone, the material from which the Hekatompedon was built. The underside of this cornice bears a curious form of embellishment that looks like pure decoration but actually serves a function. Flat plates with rows of raised dots inscribed along the underside of the overhang appear for all the world like carved dominoes or Lego blocks, but they are not architectural fantasies or oblique evidence of time travel; rather, they are tools for capturing and shedding water. Rainwater falling on the top of the cornice has a way of sticking to its surface, sliding around to its underside, then onto the vertical surface beneath. When surface water meets these curious features, it collects into drops and falls to the ground, adding further protection to the exposed stone below the cornice. These blocks with their raised dots are called *guttae,* which is the Latin word for "droplets."

The cornice supports a pitched roof typically covered in flat marble tiles. The roof is like a tent with its sloping sides attached to the long side of the building and its openings at either short end. The corners of the roof are often decorated with sculpted or cast figures. While figures below these are usually decorative or tell a story, figures at the roof corners play a special role: they are meant to ward off evil influences from the building by looking scary. The image most commonly used—a Gorgon mask or a running Gorgon—comes from Greek mythology: the Gorgons were three sisters with the power to turn to stone anyone who looked at them. Best known among these three sisters was Medusa, who had snakes instead of hair. The hero Perseus was able to kill Medusa by looking at her reflection, never directly at her. Gorgon images on temples appear more or less alike. The face of the Gorgon is round and always shown head on. Her nose is broad and flat, and her tongue sticks out between her fangs. The running Gorgon is a little paradoxical, because she runs sideways but faces forward. Gorgon images are related to Mesopotamian images of the forest monster Humbaba. Though he is male, he looks the same way and, more significantly, he is depicted in the same unrealistic style, running one way but facing the viewer.

Pediments, the triangular spaces located at each end of the temple, were typically decorated like the blanks between the triglyphs below them, and sculptures accommodated to these spaces filled them. The main surviving elements from the Hekatompedon are sculptures from the two ends of the building, and one of the most striking things about them is that, like the Gorgon images, they are clearly based on Mesopotamian models. Crouched in the corner of one of the pediments is the image of a very muscular lioness. Beneath her, embraced by her powerful arm, is a dying bull, which she is beginning to tear apart. Homer described a similar scene on the mythical shield of Achilles in book 18 of the *Iliad,* but the scene is a repeated motif in Mesopotamian art, reaching back millennia before Homer. Art of every kind and on every scale—from monumental sculpture to cylinder seals and signet rings—featured scenes of this type. Its presence on this sixth-century temple affirms the connections between early Greek art and the art of older civilizations in West Asia, although later generations of Greeks denied such influence. Over time, Athenians, for reasons that were very important to their political and cultural self-image, portrayed themselves as sprung from the soil of Attica. Any notion that their culture and art might have foreign roots became abhorrent to them, and the mere suggestion was vehemently denied. And yet the Hekatompedon clearly reflects a period when the art of Mesopotamia was acknowledged through imitation.

It is somewhat ironic that images linked to this theory of Athenian origins also have their place on the pediments. A huge serpent with coiled tail fills one corner, while a composite figure with three human heads and torsos ending in three twisted, serpentine tails fills the opposite corner. Because snakes live underground, traditional Greek worship connected them with the gods of the earth and with buried ancestors who were worshipped because of their continuing influence on the lives of their descendants. The figure that combines human and serpent-like characteristics is more puzzling, although it may be connected to Cecrops, the mythical founder of Athens. If this is true, it would mean that the temple combines a paradoxical mix of images associated with the Athenian myth of self-creation alongside representations whose styles and themes suggest foreign influence.

A number of smaller buildings were constructed on the Acropolis in the same era, but their remains are puzzling even to experts. Off the hill, on flat land to the south of the Acropolis, the tyrants began to erect a temple to Olympian Zeus, an exceptionally grandiose project. Their plan, however, required more political muscle than the regime could muster; when the tyranny collapsed, the temple remained unfinished. Succeeding governments left it that way, not as a rebuke to the god, but as a reminder of the titanic ambition and consequent failure of a system of government that they repudiated. The Roman emperor Hadrian finally completed the temple during the second century CE.

At the end of the sixth century, Athens reorganized itself as a democracy. By modern standards the democratic character of the city was equivocal. Slaves, who did much of the work of the society, were not allowed to vote, though they could be given their freedom and might under special circumstances gain citizenship. Women had no political rights, though they did participate in ritual life and could hold important priesthoods. Children were under the control of their fathers until they reached age eighteen. Resident foreigners, of whom there were many, could not vote and could not participate in most of the city's religious festivals. And yet a man did not have to live inside the limits of Athens to be a citizen. While early in its history Rome disenfranchised people living outside its city boundary, Athens endorsed a different sort of political structure: Athens remained a political union of city and countryside, so its citizenship extended beyond the physical boundaries of the urban center.

Athens established a host of elected offices and positions filled by lot that were held for relatively short periods of time by qualified citizens. It had a popular assembly that met at the Pnyx, a hill to the west of the Acropolis, as well as a small group of elected officials, called archons, who lived and ate at public expense in a special building at the marketplace. One of the distinguishing features of Athenian democracy was the large number of citizen juries that decided important cases. Like a supreme court, decisions from a number of these cases brought about constitutional changes, many of which came into effect on the cusp of the fifth century BCE.

The Acropolis was a key place where this new democratic social order made its presence felt. Some archaeologists believe that this was accomplished first by destroying the Hekatompedon, since, like the incomplete Temple of Olympian Zeus, it was associated with a history of tyranny. If the temple was indeed torn down, its sculptural decoration was presumably reused on another building. Whether or not the builders of the early democratic era destroyed the old temple, they certainly built a new structure at the very center of the Acropolis, between the site of the Mycenaean palace (and perhaps of the Hecatompedon) and the present Parthenon. This building was known as the Archaios Naos or Old Temple, and little survives but its foundations and a few sculptures. It was surrounded by columns, and judging from the excavated foundations, it had two entrances positioned at each end of the building and leading to two different kinds of interior rooms. The larger room held an image of the deity, while the smaller suite of rooms protected treasures and served other ritual functions. The deity worshipped in the Old Temple was Athena Polias, which means "Athena of the city." Many archaeologists believe that the image of Athena preserved in the temple was the crude wooden figure that may have been first worshipped more than seven hundred years earlier in the Mycenaean palace.

The most interesting remains of the Old Temple are sculptures from the temple's pediments exhibited on Level 1 of the Acropolis Museum, which featured depictions of an event in mythical history called the Gigantomachia—an epic battle between the Olympian gods and a race of giants. The Greeks believed that Zeus and the other Olympians had come to power by overwhelming

an earlier generation of gods whose leader was Kronos. Even after they defeated these gods (who were their own parents) and established themselves
as rulers of the cosmos, they still faced challenges. Semidivine giant children of this first generation of gods attempted to overthrow the Olympians.
One plot involved piling two Greek mountains, Ossa and Pelion, one on top
of the other, so that the giants could reach the heights of Olympus and
assault the gods in their home. Details of this war are very confusing—in
several accounts the gods were assisted by some of the giants, while in other
tales all the giants opposed them. In the end, the Olympians won the day
and the giants were imprisoned under mountains.

Surviving sculptures from the Old Temple include a fallen giant who re-
coils in one corner of the pediment and a second armless figure who appears
to be rising from the earth and springing to the attack. The central figures of
the pediment may have included images of Zeus and Apollo—perhaps rid-
ing in a chariot—but there is little physical evidence to confirm this. A remarkable image of the patron goddess of the city, Athena, is one significant
divine figure that did survive. This image of the goddess takes a long stride
toward the fallen giant in the corner of the pediment. Her right arm, which
is now lost, was raised and once held a spear. Her left arm reaches forward as
she walks, displaying a special shawl-like garment that the goddess wore.
This garment, which identifies and symbolizes Athena, is called the aegis. In
many representations of the goddess its distinguishing characteristic is a
Gorgon mask. As the striding Athena extends her arm, the aegis stretches,
and its elaborate lower border marked with square openings gives the sense
that her arm and her figure are in motion.

The story of the Gigantomachia is a significant event in the history of the
Olympians, and Athena's prominent role within it would seem to justify
selecting this story as the theme of the pediment on the Acropolis temple.
There is also, of course, the possibility that this scene held a more direct
message for Athenians of the late sixth century BCE. Given that the tyrants
were so recently defeated, allowing for an Athenian democracy to become
established, the odds are that contemporaries would have seen in the decisive action of the goddess some analogy to their own history. Just as Athena
destroyed the giants, the men and women of her city destroyed the tyrants
who oppressed them and threatened their sovereignty.

The greatest creation of this era came somewhat later, in 490 BCE, after an Athenian army defeated a much larger force of invading Persians at the battle of Marathon. Their victory gave the city a tremendous psychological boost, and it increased the prominence of Athens among its Greek neighbors. Though the war with Persia was far from over, this victory seemed to promise peace and prosperity. In its immediate aftermath, Athenians began an enormous building project on the south edge of the Acropolis. Creating an adequate foundation for their proposed new building was in itself an enormous job. Surviving substructures, required to level off the sloping site, are forty feet deep in some places. They consist of thousands of two-ton blocks of limestone transported to the site from quarries near the seaport town of Piraeus. The project was never completed, although the massive substructures now support the Parthenon. Marble for the project, which stood in various stages of finish, was brought to the Acropolis, all of which temporarily transformed the area into a gigantic construction site, though most of that marble was never used.

This incomplete building—the first Parthenon—was burned by invading Persians in 480 BCE. Just ten years after the victory at Marathon seemed to put an end to the Persian threat, they returned and devastated the city of those who had defeated them. Persian attempts at invasion—and Greek resistance to them—continued until a final peace treaty was signed in 449 BCE. By the so-called Oath of Plataea, sworn before the battle of that name, the allied Greek cities vowed to fight to the death against the Persian army and leave any temple destroyed by the enemy unrepaired as a perpetual memorial. The legend of the oath-taking was questioned as early as the fourth century BCE, and generations of scholars have argued that nothing of the kind ever happened. Whether or not such an oath was the reason, the Acropolis, whose dedications and architecture represented the cult of the goddess Athena as well as the growing power of Athens over four hundred years, stood in ruins for a generation. Exposed for thirty years to the repeated threat of Persian attack, Athens lay in the shadow of a sacred hill that represented outrage and defeat rather than triumph and exuberance.

2

The Acropolis in the Fifth Century

By the time any threat of Persian attack ended in the second half of the fifth century, preserving the ruined Acropolis as a war memorial had lost its appeal. Like other Greek cities that had suffered during the prolonged conflict, Athens was ready to move on. The task of restoring the Acropolis to its former glory and prominence was a formidable one. It is believed that no building remained intact on the hill. The Hekatompedon was evidently taken down early in the fifth century, its sculptures reused in other structures. The Old Temple was either gone or too damaged to be recovered. Drums intended for columns on the incomplete Parthenon project were never finished or erected and were instead set into the retaining walls that shored up the north side of the hill; these drums can still be seen today. Architectural sculpture did survive, and many of the votive offerings on the hill were also preserved.

The pathway of the Panathenaic processional was fixed, and the broad ramp leading up to the western edge of the hill still determined the entry point for the complex above. The city below had accommodated itself to that important pathway, so this western access to the site was a given. Also, a temple to Athena the Victor stood for more than a century on the remains of the Mycenaean bastion, near the top of that ramp. There was no good argument for rejecting this platform, which was still intact, so the temple at its top was rebuilt; the rest of the western entryway was dramatically reshaped.

Building a new Parthenon on the site of the old—rather than at some other spot—offered advantages. The old monument had been well secured on deep and solid foundations, which were still usable. The superstructure, however, could be replaced from top to bottom. While Athenians could argue that their new building was a fulfillment of their ancestors' intentions

William James Stillman captures the Acropolis in 1869. (Fine Arts Library, Harvard University)

to honor the virgin goddess, they were also free to build the monument in ways that appealed to them. They were able to combine the prestige of long tradition with the freedom to innovate, which is an unusual combination in any age. Of course, their freedom to innovate was hedged in not just by the contours of the site, but by historical styles. Greek temple architecture, indeed Greek architecture in general, was exceedingly conservative. So, while new buildings might be constructed, they were not going to be radically different architecturally from the buildings that preceded them. This was true of the Doric Hecatompedon when it was built in the early sixth century BCE, and it was true of the Archaios Naos, erected six decades later, as well as the Old Parthenon, constructed thirty years after that: all were structured in very similar ways. All were rectangular in ground plan, raised on stepped pedestals, and surrounded by an unbroken file of columns. Their continuous colonnades supported entablatures with spaces for painted bas-reliefs, and the narrow ends of the temples sheltered pediments under their pitched roofs where more sculptures could be placed. And in each, along the roofline of the central chambers inside the colonnade there was room for one more sculptural narrative.

While the new buildings on the Acropolis then reflected the novel point of view of the fifth century, they would not do so by rejecting the architectural vocabulary established by long tradition. Instead, innovation would be introduced in three quite subtle ways: first, there would be new sites for many altars and dedications; second, the buildings that housed these altars and cult statues would be grouped in a new way, and through this organization and the framing work of the Propylaia, the site would, for the first time, gain cohesiveness and an overall plan; and third, while architecture remained conservative, a dramatic shift in sculptural style and a new freedom in creating sculptural narrative evolved during the fifth century. Since sculpture was an important element in architectural decoration, this dramatic new style would give conservative architecture a different look.

It is interesting to compare the job of contemporary museologists with the task that faced the rebuilders of the Acropolis in the fifth century. The old Acropolis Museum—located on the site itself, just east of the Parthenon—was little more than a glorified storeroom and display area for objects found on the site—it was intended to supplement the preserved buildings on the Acropolis, filling in their backstory and adding circumstantial detail that would flesh out the monumental history that the site embodied. Installations in the New Acropolis Museum, located on the flat plain south of the Acropolis, near the Temple of Olympian Zeus, do a better job of chronicling the history of the hill from the sixth century through the era of its greatest development, but that is not the limit of its role. The new museum, as its name ironically implies, is a New Acropolis, where the principal monuments on the hill are preserved and represented in a setting that is more conducive to their preservation, more comfortable for visitors, and entirely modern in form. From the museum itself—and from its extensive Parthenon installation—the visitor is likely to gain a much greater understanding and appreciation of the hilltop that is, in any case, visible through its glass walls. There are strong arguments for the museum, just as there were strong arguments for the new Acropolis of the fifth century. Most people will not question that the new projects were, in both cases, inevitable and unimpeachable; others will see a balance sheet of losses and gains.

While the new Parthenon was raised on the site of the old with, in many cases, materials still usable after the Persian devastation of the site, there were from the start significant differences between the two monuments. The new building was larger than the old one; it had two additional columns on its narrow ends, and one more column on each long side. This not only made it bigger, but it changed its proportions in a slight yet meaningful way. These modifications in themselves would have made the new building and the old foundations somewhat incompatible; however, the builders also shifted the new structure about fifteen feet to the north, so they had to create new foundations while covering the old, exposed foundations on the south side. These were just minor adjustments, but they illustrate the builders' sense that they were free to improvise as long as they didn't go too far.

Two writers in the first century CE record the names of the Parthenon architects—sadly, they disagree. Both writers name Iktinos; but Plutarch, who wrote biographies of famous Greeks and Romans, named Kallikrates as Iktinos's partner, while Vitruvius, a contemporary Roman writer on architecture, mentioned Karpion. The betting is that Kallikrates is the right name, since he was known from other sources to have worked on architectural projects in Athens during the late fifth century. Vitruvius does say that the architects of the building wrote a book together describing their design. Perhaps it would have detailed how the two split the tasks of design and management of construction, especially since it seems to be true that a certain amount of improvisation and change of plan took place as the building was going up. This book might also have explained the rationale for and the means of creating some of the famous refinements that are built into the Parthenon. Any visitor to the site who looks down the three-step platform supporting its colonnades can see the gentle curve that rises and falls from one end to the other. This subtle uplift in a long horizontal increases the dynamism of this dimension. The contours and pitch of the columns were also manipulated for similar effect. The columns are not vertical, but tilt inward to a small degree, and each vertical shaft expands a bit at its center. The columns at the corners are silhouetted against the sky and thicker than the other columns.

The eastern façade of the Parthenon, 1869. William James Stillman, photographer. (Fine Arts Library, Harvard University)

Except for the curve in the building's platform, which is visible to any visitor who knows to look for it, the tiny modifications in the building go unrecognized. That does not mean, however, that they do not achieve their desired effect. Without being aware, the viewer responds predictably to these modifications. The columns appear solid, rectilinear, and straight; those at the corners are dramatic in silhouette. What the builders of the Parthenon recognized, articulated, and provided for in their structures was the contribution that the human eye and the optical processors in the human brain make to what we see. They knew that vision has its own logic, and they were prepared to accommodate their work to that logic.

Inside the great colonnade that surrounded the new Parthenon, builders constructed a curious sanctuary. The Parthenon had two disconnected interior rooms of very different sizes set back to back, and entered from opposite

The Parthenon today.

ends of the building. The room on the west was smaller, its main feature a cluster of four columns at the center of a square space. These columns stretched to the coffered ceiling of the room but were probably not necessary to support it. The room was filled with votive gifts to the goddess and also with the treasury of the Athenians. While we might expect there to be some separation of worship and the housing and protection of a city treasury, in the Greek world these functions were often combined. Temples were sound, solidly constructed buildings that were hard to break into and relatively easy to secure. The surviving columns in front of the Parthenon's two doorways are marked by grooves and indentations that suggest an iron grillwork was set between them to guard access to the building. The Parthenon doors were large and impregnable, probably cast in bronze or plated in bronze. Temple doors were traditionally locked or at least capable of being locked. In Greek art, a large and elaborate door key was the symbol that identified a priest or priestess.

Temples were protected by traditions that defined them as sacred and inviolable. In a way, the temple was a little like an oath: people swore oaths in pragmatic legal and commercial settings, but these oaths were always underwritten by invocation of a god's power to punish those who swore falsely. The temple as a repository of secular wealth probably enjoyed the god's protection in a similar way. No one could steal the gold without offending the god. However they understood the connection, it was common not just among the Greeks but among the Romans as well to use temples to store wealth on behalf of the city and its citizens. Roman temples often had secured vaults in their foundations for just this purpose.

The eastern room in the interior of the Parthenon was about twice as big as the room for worship and treasure. Like the smaller room, this one also had interior columns. The columns stood in two superimposed ranks all around the room. They served little purpose except to isolate and frame the center of the long room, which housed a colossal and immensely valuable image of the goddess Athena. Some scholars have imagined that there was an opening in the roof of the Parthenon to let in light that would illuminate the sculpture. Others imagine that light coming in from the wide door and small windows on the east end of the building was the only source of direct illumination. There is evidence that a shallow basin for water—some scholars say olive oil—was set into the floor immediately in front of the image. Light from outside reflected upward by this shallow pool would increase the illumination of the statue and change the nature of the shadows that played across it.

Unlike the majority of Greek sculptures, this famous statue was not cast from bronze, or carved from marble; instead, it was a construction that bore some resemblance to the much larger Statue of Liberty. At the core of Athena's image was a wooden framework that supported the visible surface of the statue, which was a carefully fitted assembly of carved panels of ivory and castings of gold. Ivory represented the skin of the goddess, and contoured gold plates covered the rest. The overseers of construction "published" their expenses annually on stone pillars so that citizens could keep an eye on their accounts. According to these lists, the amount of gold used in the statue weighed between forty and fifty talents. The modern-day equivalent of any ancient measurement is always hard to estimate, but to give this some context, in the fifth century BCE, an average Greek worker expected to earn

The eastern portico of the Parthenon, looking northward, 1869. William James Stillman, photographer. (Fine Arts Library, Harvard University)

one drachma per day. There were six thousand drachmas in a talent of silver.
The Athenian overseers paid for the gold they needed with silver coins at a
ratio of about fourteen to one. So each gold talent would have cost them
fourteen silver talents or about eighty-four thousand drachmas. At the rate
of one drachma every day, a laborer would need to work 230 years to earn a
single gold talent. By any standard, the expenditure just for the raw material
to make the statue was staggering. It is widely believed that the money spent
on the statue equaled or exceeded the cost of the building that sheltered it.

Nothing of the statue survives today except for parts of its pedestal on the
Parthenon floor and bits of the rim of the basin that illuminated it. This
statue was important, however, and it lasted for hundreds of years, during
which time tens of thousands of people saw it. Ancient descriptions survive,
and ancient reproductions on all scales exist. If the Statue of Liberty were
suddenly to disappear, restorers would have thousands of facsimiles of all
sizes and qualities on which to base a reconstruction. The problem would
be choosing among them, since the absence of detail or the presence of
contradictory features would obscure the issue. Those same uncertainties
face scholars and artists who have worked to reconstruct the monument
through the visual and literary arts. The best known reproduction of the
Athena stands in the Parthenon reconstruction located in Nashville, Tennes-
see. It is roughly the same size as the original and reproduces those details
that are generally believed to belong to the original. Rather than make the
statue of plates of gold bolted into place, the Nashville reproduction was
made of much less expensive materials, then gilded.

The Parthenon Athena was huge, somewhere around forty feet tall. She
wore a typical Greek woman's garment called a *peplos* that reached from her
neck to her feet, folded at her waist, and was belted beneath her breasts.
Around her shoulders she wore her aegis with its Gorgon mask at the center
surrounded by a network of writhing snakes. She wore a helmet with a high
central crest and ornaments to either side. According to Pausanias, who saw
the statue in the first century CE, the images on the helmet represented two
mythical beasts. The central image was a sphinx—half woman, half lion—
flanked by griffins, which are composites of lions and eagles. A small replica
of the Athena Parthenos in the New Acropolis Museum has griffins on the
cheek pieces of the helmet and winged horses on either side of the sphinx.
These mythical beasts, like the Gorgon on her aegis, are expressions of the

goddess's dominance. Through use of her powers, she has tamed these creatures and made them serve her will.

The goddess holds out her right arm, where a winged figure of nearly human size appears to perch like Tinker Bell on the outstretched palm of a monstrous Peter Pan. Her extended hand and arm have been a conundrum for specialists and restorers: in the New Acropolis Museum example, a pillar supports the arm, but many other representations of the original, including the Nashville version, lack this support. The fairy-like figure represents Victory, so it is usually assumed that she personifies the victory of the Greeks over the Persians at Marathon in 479.

At her left, Athena held a spear and an enormous round shield that stood ready at her side. The outer surface of the shield featured carvings in low relief of Amazons scaling the Acropolis. Amazons were legendary female warriors believed to live in the East somewhere. Generically, these carvings represented Athenian civilization pitted against the forces of barbarism; specifically, they represent a similar, real-life invasion by the Persians, whom the Greeks viewed as barbarians. A battle between the gods and the giants (the subject of pediment sculptures on the Old Temple) was represented on the inner surface of the shield. Athena's right knee was flexed, and her right foot was visible behind a break in her skirt. She wore a thick-soled sandal, and tiny figures carved on the outside of the sole represented a battle between centaurs and Lapiths. Like the battle of the Amazons, this, too, represented civilization versus barbarism and indirectly alluded to the Persian war. A huge serpent rested its upright coils against the inner surface of the shield. In Athenian mythology, the serpent was particularly tied to Erechtheus, the founding hero of Athens.

Scholars argue over the question of whether the Athena Parthenos was a cult statue and received sacrifices or a votive gift that did not, and this controversy also affects how the Parthenon itself is defined. If the statue it held was not the focus of sacrifice, then the building was not a temple but a structure that sheltered and protected an extraordinary votive gift. This unusual function could account for the atypical layout of the Parthenon's interior. Reports from the building's overseers mention an ivory offering table, which makes sense if the statue were a cult image. But how the building was used and even how its interior rooms were named (which also comes up in overseers' reports) are very confusing. It is unlikely that we will ever be certain of just how Athenians conceived of the image and the building that housed it.

There is little doubt that Athenians admired the statue and the sculptor who supervised its creation. Pheidias, one of the great names in Athenian sculpture, who is mentioned in many ancient documents and treatises, was thought to play a role in creating the Athena Parthenos, though, not surprisingly, in recent years that role has been reevaluated. Writers in the first century CE described Pheidias not only as the sculptor of the Athena, but also as the designer and overseer of all sculptural projects on the Parthenon. Contemporary scholars are skeptical and tend to believe that Pheidias designed the Athena and supervised the workshop that constructed it, but they do not cast him, as Plutarch did, in the role of *episkopos panton*—the "supervisor of the whole."

Just as Pheidias was demoted from project manager to subcontractor, Pericles was uprooted from his historical connection with the Parthenon and the fifth-century remake of the Acropolis. Books still speak of the architectural and artistic refashioning of the hill in this era as part of a "Periclean building program," but that notion, too, is being reassessed. The tendency to attribute large and complex projects to the instigation and oversight of a single powerful individual has been a constant for centuries. It may be true in this instance, but it seems more likely that in fifth-century Athens, the Acropolis renovation was a popular project with broad appeal. The builders of the oligarchic sixth century might have needed projects of this kind to boost their prestige and shore up their questionable legitimacy, but the fifth-century situation was different. Though participation in civic life was restrictive by modern standards, it was very broad by comparison with both earlier and later political regimes. The Periclean building program makes sense if we understand Pericles as the identifying label of an era, rather than the solitary prime mover of the rebuilding.

The Athena Parthenos was an extraordinary achievement. And it propelled Pheidias toward an even more important commission—to create a colossal gold and ivory image of Zeus, the chief god, for his temple in Olympia. What ancient people seem to have admired about it, however, was not its ingenuity, nor its artistic qualities, but the awe it inspired. Since we don't believe in the Greek gods, we find it hard to believe that sophisticated people like the ancient Greeks could have believed in them either.

We know that some Greek philosophers were skeptics, and that others felt free to critique the gods and dismiss their legends, but that was not the general attitude. Through their actions, the Athenians revealed themselves again and again to be staunch partisans of Athena and enthusiastic supporters of her cult. She embodied the city for them in ways that no other figure could. The city and the goddess shared a long history, during which she repeatedly served as its benefactor and protector. An Athenian could not love or admire his city without also reflecting that love in honor of its patron and protector.

The Athena Parthenos is not at all the sort of artwork that specialists have admired over the last two centuries; it lacks many characteristics that classical scholars revere in Greek bronze and marble sculpture. The Athena may have been designed by Pheidias, but it clearly was not made by him single-handedly, so it lends no support to the ideal of an individual artist's transcendent vision and superior ability; instead, it is the work not precisely of a committee, but certainly of a multitude of individuals. Some would have been responsible for shaping particular materials, while others would have used a variety of skills suitable to different small tasks. Pheidias, who has traditionally been celebrated for his artistic genius in the Romantic or heroic sense, was necessarily a skillful promoter, negotiator, and team manager. More familiar examples of these differences come from the Renaissance: Michelangelo is a prime example of the lone, titanic creator, whereas Filippo Brunelleschi, architect of the Duomo of Florence, is an example of the skilled negotiator and manager. Modern art historians have typically cast ancient Greek artists in the Michelangelo mold, but the Athena Parthenos suggests that the reality was different, and that skills admired in a great sculptor might have been similar to the ones that characterized a great architect—the ability to envisage a project, to modify it as needed, to mediate between the client and the job, and to supervise a diverse workforce.

Because it is not austere or economical in means, the Athena Parthenos is also at odds with the conventional aesthetic views of Greek sculpture. It is made of rich materials that demand to be noticed and appreciated as much for their intrinsic qualities and value as for their artistic adaptation. In this case, the drama of the artist triumphing over and dwarfing his material does not apply. Ivory and gold continue to assert their preciousness despite the work of the transformative imagination. The Athena does not showcase the human body in motion or exalt the human scale. It marks a clear divide between the human and the divine, reveling in the fact that the divine dwarfs the human. It is too big to present the human form as "the measure of all things"—its very size declares that humans and gods exist on a different scale and in a different order of being.

The Athena is complicated; instead of representing a simple and pure divine image, the sculptural assembly unpacks a suitcase full of legends, all designed to highlight aspects of the goddess's nature and her relationship with her beloved people. The Athena is like a Brueghel painting filled with busy figures doing a variety of strange things. Tiny beings swarm around her head, her shield (inside and out), the soles of her sandals, and the front edge of the pedestal on which she stands. All are allegorical representations that have to be decoded; they cannot simply be seen and immediately understood. Nothing is more foreign to the common portrayal of Greek aesthetics than allegory.

The allegories of the Athena Parthenos—those multiple overlapping legends that make clear what is so important about an otherwise voiceless and enigmatic image—are not only essential features of this one statue, but they are the foundation of the sculptural decoration of the Parthenon as a whole. Pheidias's work and the work of the multiple crews responsible for the sculpture on the building harmonized. This does not mean that Pheidias supervised the entire program; rather, it means that the underlying theme of the building and its principal contents were thoroughly understood by all contributing artists.

One of the largest and most ambitious sculptural programs on the Parthenon is the series of carved panels that ran around the entablature of the building. (Though some of the panels remain, most can no longer be found on the Acropolis.) These panels, called metopes, were separated by triglyphs—which were probably painted bright blue—so that instead of one continuous, unbroken frieze, the metopes presented a series of interrelated discrete scenes. The four sides of the building created further divisions among these scenes, and, in fact, four separate legendary sequences were depicted in the metopes on each of the building's sides. These sequences had important connections with allegorical figures on the Athena Parthenos. Following clockwise, these metope scenes are:

EAST

The eastern side of the Parthenon—the side away from the Propylaia, where the doors lead into the chamber that housed the Athena Parthenos—features a scene from the battle of the gods and the giants. It is a scene from the pediment on the Old Temple, and is also found on the inside of the shield of the Athena.

SOUTH

The south side of the temple, the side facing away from the city, offers the story of the conflict between the centaurs and the Lapiths. This conflict is also represented on Athena's sandal sole.

WEST

The western end of the building describes mounted Greek soldiers at battle against the Amazons, a scene also depicted on the outside of Athena's shield.

NORTH

The sequence on the north side of the Parthenon faces the center of the ancient city, and it is the only one of the four not represented on the Athena. This long sequence of metopes depicts the war at Troy.

If we knew nothing of the Athena Parthenos and its iconography, we would be hard-pressed to understand why these particular scenes were chosen to decorate her temple in such highly visible locations. With the exception of the pediment sculptures, these scenes are the most prominent ones on the monument, yet their connection with the legend of Athena is far from clear. Their presence as supporting players on the Athena Parthenos, however, shows that in the mind of Athenians, these stories were relevant to the character of their goddess. In a broad sense, the metope narratives depict Athena as a goddess of conflicts. This trait is also apparent in the story of the war at Troy. Homer's *Iliad* represents all of the gods as active participants in the fighting at Troy and as strong partisans of one side or the other. Athena is an active and aggressive supporter of the Greeks. The other scenes of conflict suggest a theme consistent with what Athena stood for. She was not just a partisan protector of the Greeks or the Athenians, but also a comrade who stood with civilization in its conflicts against barbarism and with the Olympians in their struggle against usurpation. These metopes portray the goddess as the principled warrior whose power and divinity support what is good and right.

Surely the artists and artisans who interpreted the sculptural program of the Parthenon agreed, as did the interpreters of the Athena, that the Persian war was an inescapable memory in the minds of their city. Every scene offers some hint or echo of that war, including scenes from Troy that can be read more broadly as a war between Greece and an Asiatic enemy. How Athenians chose to understand and interpret that war, however, has been more elusive. It is clear that the sculptural programs took an ideological slant on the war: they do not begin to imagine it as a conflict between equals; instead, they cast it as a battle between the civilized and the barbarous, with strong overtones of impiety. Monster centaurs battle against human Lapiths, and Greek male warriors battle against females, who, by becoming enemy combatants, denied the natural order of things as Greeks understood them. These are the scenes that best engage the theme of civilization versus barbarism. But the metopes take a step further by implicitly comparing the Persian attacks on Athens to the giants' attempt to storm Olympus. This comparison makes the Acropolis Olympus and the Persian invaders enemies of the divine order. By portraying the Persian invaders in this way, the Athenians define themselves. If the Persians represent barbarism, then Athens must be the home of the civilized. If the Persians are giants intent on destroying the divine order, then Athens must be the force that upholds that order.

These metopes have not been treated well over time and circumstance. Though they were high above the temple's colonnade, they were the most exposed and most accessible sculptures on the building. There is ample evidence that they were painted in ways that accented the difference between bare flesh and drapery and between the appropriately pale skin of sheltered women and the sunburnt skin of active men. Spears and shields, bridles and other objects made of bronze were fastened to the sculptures to heighten their realism. Weathering and vandalism removed most of these details, though hints of color survive, and holes where metal objects were once anchored cannot be erased. Earthquakes have periodically shaken the Acropolis, and Germanic tribes swept through Athens during the era of Roman control, apparently damaging all monuments in the city. The Venetian shell that exploded the Turkish powder magazine in 1687 severely damaged the midsection of each long sequence.

The greatest damage endured by these very visible metopes was deliberate, and it came about when the temple of the goddess Athena was converted to a church honoring the Virgin Mary. It may be clear why images of the gods in the Gigantomachy and the war at Troy could not to be tolerated on a Christian basilica, but it is less clear why battles between centaurs and Lapiths, or between Greeks and Amazons, might be found offensive—but evidently they were. Whatever their exact motives, Athenian Christians, in iconoclastic fervor, defaced and damaged the sculptures of the Parthenon metopes, which were particularly susceptible to such damage because of the way they were sculpted. In their original state, these metopes would have appeared very three-dimensional; in fact, some figures would have jutted beyond their frames. From directly below, a visitor would have seen hands and arms projecting out from the frame of the entablature. This three-dimensional character made the sculptures that much more fragile and all the more vulnerable to attack.

In contrast, a far more famous and contentious Parthenon frieze was much less vulnerable to the hammers and rocks of Christian zealots. This frieze, which is represented in its entirety in the New Acropolis Museum, stood in the best-protected position on the temple exterior. Running along the top edge of the outside wall of the inner chamber, it was always sheltered from the weather. And because it was carved in low relief instead of the dramatic high relief of the metopes, this frieze was structurally much stronger. A hammer and chisel might erase some of its features—and individual faces have been carved away—but it would take a seriously dedicated, strong and skillful vandal to do extensive damage. And while the themes of this frieze might have been every bit as offensive to Christians as those of the metopes, it was less visible. It was hard to damage and easy enough to ignore. Judging from the state of its preservation, that is precisely what people did.

Unlike the metopes of the Parthenon, which tell four different but related stories, this frieze describes a single event. Images on each of the temple's four sides create a continuous narrative. The absence of triglyphs, which divide the metopes into discrete, free-standing scenes, increases its unity. The frieze narrates an enormous processional involving not just men and women

The interior of the Parthenon from the eastern end, 1869. William James Stillman, photographer. (Fine Arts Library, Harvard University)

walking, but riders on horseback, charioteers, musicians, cattle and sheep, the dead, heroes, gods, and goddesses. The images of animals along with the gods marks the processional as one that involves blood sacrifice.

The installation of the frieze in the New Acropolis Museum, like the exhibition of the metopes, makes them visible to more visitors than could ever have seen them at the Parthenon itself. This is certainly a good thing in many ways, but it does not represent a neutral change. The surviving pieces that remain in the museum in Athens are preserved and integrated with casts of pieces that were removed from the building long ago and dispersed to various European nations. The best-preserved blocks from the frieze have been moved to the British Museum, where they are joined with the pedimental sculptures that Lord Elgin was able, by means now deemed illegitimate, to secure for his own. Greece has long been adamant in its demand that the blocks be returned to their homeland.

It might be argued, however, that the museum has weakened any argument for restitution, given that it, too, removed sculptures from their architectural setting and installed them in a new building off site. While the Parthenon cannot be seen through the windows of the British Museum as it can from the New Acropolis Museum, in other ways both installations are questionable. Both depend on the common act of stripping the Parthenon of its architectural sculptures. This was not a deliberate act of vandalism but an effort at preservation; all the same, both acts entail a bold assault on what the building represents, a redirection of its character, and an unmistakable blow to its integrity. Why bother to walk on the Acropolis when the important bits have been transferred to a comfortable and accessible indoor setting?

The relocation of the frieze and the metopes to the New Acropolis Museum presents them as sources of information; it highlights their didactic content as well as their roles as objects of aesthetic worth, and it encourages art appreciation. These are modern ideals that have little to do with what the builders of the Parthenon intended. Creating easily visible sculptures was not their purpose; rather, they placed them in a way that suited the conventions of temple building and which, not coincidentally, offered them the best chance to escape weathering. Their preservation and their integration with the architecture that supported them were prime considerations. Given the sacredness of the Parthenon, both must have been created to serve the divinity honored within. The sculptures were tied to the religious and civic function of a unique building. In the museum they become beautiful objects that teach lessons about Greek artistry, history, and mythology—the very aspects of ancient art that seem meaningful to us today, but not what the Parthenon's architects and sculptors had in mind.

The frieze depicting an enormous processional was celebratory. It did not offer information; it rehearsed ritual. It was placed on the building to trace the procession moving from its point of origin near the western gates of the city toward its goal on the Acropolis. The start of the processional, which began in the ceramic-producing area of the city, near its western gate, is represented on the western end of the temple. In two parallel paths, it marches along the long sides of the temple until it reaches its goal above the eastern door. On the frieze, there are no hints of actual Athenian places encountered by the real processional as it passed through; instead, the geography of the processional—and with it the geography of Athens—are represented by placing the frieze on the east-west axis of the Parthenon.

The Panathenaia was an annual ritual observed with greater pomp every fourth year, when a Great Panathenaia was celebrated. While citizens playing important roles in this quadrennial event varied with each celebration, the processional was very old, and its route was deeply ingrained in the experience of every man, woman, and child who lived in Athens. The Parthenon presented the Panathenaia as occurring not just annually but perpetually. In an idealized Athens, represented by the Parthenon, the processional was always about to begin; it was put in motion by every visitor who followed its trajectory from one end of the temple to the other.

The Parthenon was not the goal of the processional, which ended instead at the Erechtheum. Neither the building nor the giant statue of Athena it housed played any part in the ritual. Enshrining the processional on the Parthenon looks like an effort to update the venerable ritual so that it embraces on a purely symbolic level a new goal and a new object of devotion. This also offers further evidence of the degree to which the creators of the fifth-century Acropolis felt justified in modifying tradition. While those designers might not have liked the New Acropolis Museum, they would certainly have understood what it meant to take firm hold of a venerable tradition and bend it to new purposes.

A substantial portion of the frieze on three of the Parthenon's sides is devoted to the activities of horsemen. It is not clear that riders played such a significant role in the actual Panathenaic processional, but their presence does bring a sense of dynamism to the frieze. Men and women parading one after another easily turn into a static colonnade like a sentence filled with nothing but the letter IIIIIIIIIIIII. Riders on horseback present more complex shapes, and the gait of the horse and its posture can vary. The horses and riders on the Parthenon frieze are further complicated and enriched on both the long sides by a striking and ingenious system of overlapping representations that create an illusion of depth. The horse and rider groups on the western end of the temple are different from those on the other two sides. Some riders are mounted, while others stand beside their horses. One figure appears to be jumping onto his rearing horse while another holds its reins.

On the eastern end of the inner chamber the scene is considerably less agitated. There the Olympian gods are seated in small groups on backless chairs. Only Zeus, the chief of the gods, sits in a throne-like seat with a backrest. Though the gods are seated, they fill the whole width of the frieze, a space that a human standing up would fill. Gigantism is one of the few traits that separate humans from gods, and, of course, the giant Athena inside the temple showed this difference of scale in an even more dramatic way. The gods depicted on the frieze—gods who will receive the sacrificial victims that are led in the processional—are shown at not quite double the size of a human. Otherwise, they are indistinguishable from humans; they dress in the same way, their bodies are the same, and they hold themselves in relaxed and casual postures that are thoroughly human.

The central scene on the east side of the temple, directly above the door leading to the Athena Parthenos, is where this processional culminates, although the scene that most directly signals the goal of the processional is insignificant in itself. A single block carved with two figures alludes to, but does not represent, the ritual act that served as the focus and rationale of the Panathenaia. Every four years a new garment, a peplos, was woven to clothe an ancient statue of Athena that had been enshrined in a succession of Acropolis temples. In the fifth century, this image was kept in the Erechtheum. Some scholars believe that the statue may have been venerated much earlier, in the Mycenaean palace on the hill. No one knows how old it was, where it was created, or what it looked like; unlike the Athena Parthenos, which was represented in all sorts of media, this ancient image of Athena does not appear to have been copied or depicted in any way.

At the culmination of the Panathenaic processional, this image was draped in the newly created peplos, and the old peplos that covered the image during the preceding year was folded up and taken away. The scene that serves as the endpoint of the Parthenon frieze also appears to show this ritual afterthought: on the block, a tall, middle-aged man hands the folded blanket-like peplos to a young boy. The old man is usually identified as the *archon basileus,* a chief magistrate whose duties included some of the ritual functions once carried out by Athenian kings (*basileus* means king). Though the figure who receives the peplos has sometimes been identified as a young girl, since it bares a thigh and buttock the odds are it is a boy rather than a girl. It seems anticlimactic for the centerpiece of this frieze to be little more than an appendix to a great annual ritual, but this approach is typical of Greek representations of very sacred things. It is permissible to allude to them, but it would be improper to depict them. Anyone familiar with the ritual would know that the folded peplos means that every part of those obligatory actions of the solemn rite had been carried out. The viewer who did not know the details of the rite would learn nothing about its most sacred moment from this frieze.

Women are not part of the hurly-burly of the bareback riders and charioteers that dominate the friezes on the west. As the procession reaches its goal, the mood of the representation shifts from the dynamic and unruly surge of the horsemen to the measured steps and pious solemnity of women who carry baskets and bits of ritual apparatus. Women played a significant part in many Greek public rituals, and the Panathenaic processional was no exception. But, even in a sphere where their contributions were valued, women and men lived separate lives, and they were subject to distinct rules of behavior and decorum. Just as men and women are differentiated on the frieze by their carriage and function, the female goddesses are easily distinguished from their male counterparts by their garments. Men wear loose clothes with multiple folds that look to be loosely bound around their waists and sometimes folded over their arms. Women wear garments that cover all but their heads and hands in most cases, though some female figures have bare arms. The most solemn act depicted on the frieze—folding the goddess's garment—is carried out by men rather than women. Despite the fact that weaving was an important cottage industry in ancient Athens, mostly carried out by women rather than men, it is not entirely clear from the historical record that women wove the peplos for the goddess.

The greatest and most prominent stages for architectural sculpture on any Greek temple were the two pediments under the pitched roof at each short end of the building. Among such monuments, the pediments of the Parthenon have come to be seen as the greatest stage in the world, and the remnants of the works that once filled them suggest that the artists who created them were equal to their formidable commission. These sculptures have, unfortunately, suffered repeated damage during their long history, and most of that damage was inflicted not by earthquakes or weathering but by human beings. The Christians who converted the Parthenon to a church were responsible not only for defacing the metopes and friezes, but also for inflicting significant damage to the pedimental sculptures. They were not in this case trying to erase the images of pagan gods; the Christian remodelers were restructuring the building to accommodate a novel form of worship.

Greek and Roman temples were not well-suited to Christian worship, and few of them were converted from one cult to another. At first the Roman rulers of Athens and the rest of the Mediterranean insisted on the preservation of ancient temples more or less as historical monuments. Christian churches were typically installed on new sites and in new buildings. By the sixth century, however, the attitude of the empire changed: temples still standing were made available for conversion to Christian use. The Pantheon in Rome, which had survived the pillage of barbarian invaders and major earthquakes that destroyed or damaged many other buildings, was finally converted to a church dedicated to the Virgin Mary in the sixth century CE. At the same time, the Parthenon in Athens was made available for conversion to Christian worship.

Rome's Pantheon was an atypical building for which little structural change was required to adapt it to a new purpose, whereas the Parthenon, like most Greek temples, was very poorly suited to the rituals of Christianity, so it required much structural change to make it useful. The wall dividing the two inner chambers was removed to accommodate a single large nave. A balcony was added, its outer edge resting on the lower order of the double colonnade in the original building. The biggest change—and the one that caused damage to the pedimental sculpture—took place on the eastern end of the building, where an apse was built. An apse is a semicylindrical projection typically found on one narrow end of a Roman building type called a basilica. The apse was used to frame a judge or magistrate, because of its ability to focus and amplify his voice in a building that served the Romans as law courts or administrative halls. This same building type served the early Christian community. The apse was adapted to frame the altar and channel the voice of the celebrant toward the congregation. The Parthenon had no apse, so when an apse was added it projected into the porch beneath the pediments, damaging or forcing the removal of the sculptures above it.

Though most of the damage caused by the Venetian bombardment in 1687 was to the long sides of the building, the shock of the explosion dislodged some of the remaining pedimental sculptures. Morosini, the Venetian admiral in charge, attempted to remove some of them, with the aim of sending them back to Venice. Had he been successful, these sculptures might have joined the Byzantine horses on the façade of San Marco, or the Greek lions in front of the Arsenale, as trophies representing Venetian conquest. Unlike the metopes and frieze, which were solid rectangular blocks of building stone with artwork applied, the sculptures in the pediment were free-standing. They were anchored in the shallow floor of the pediment by brackets and braces of iron and bronze. To heighten their effect, they were positioned well forward in the pediment. This made them easier to see from below, but it also meant that their weight was not solidly anchored in the building. Their forward position made them more vulnerable to damage from shocks to the building as a whole, and it also made them seem easier to remove from their settings and transport. Unfortunately for all concerned, they were not quite as ripe for the picking as they seemed. Morosini's men were energetic in their attempts to remove them, but they came away with no sculpture, and the pediment suffered additional damage in the process. Lord Elgin's men were more successful in dislodging the sculptures, but both they and the building suffered in the process of extraction. Pieces were broken as they came free from their settings, and an entire statue fell to shatter to the ground.

Though their sculptures are free-standing and their pediments are oddly shaped, both ends of the Parthenon tell stories. Narratives with beginnings, middles, and ends are best suited to long narrow spaces that can, if necessary, be chopped up into discrete scenes like panels in a graphic novel—both the metopes and the frieze are common settings for sequential stories of this type. A pediment, however, is less receptive, because its outline imposes a particular shape on the events that it can accommodate, and a story cannot run uniformly from one side to the other. The pediment has a musical dynamic; it moves between diminuendo and crescendo; quiet little things belong in the corners of the pediment, while big things happen in the middle. For this reason, stories depicted on pediments tend to show a single climactic moment at its centerpiece, with matters of secondary importance pushed off to either side. Both patterns, curiously, are represented in Greek drama, which offered a continuous narrative—a frieze—punctuated with moments of intense and significant action—a pediment.

Climactic moments narrated on the pediments were not included on the Athena Parthenos, though they were very important and familiar events in the life of the goddess. The west pediment, which is the first a visitor would see as he or she passed through the Propylaia, tells the story of a mythical contest between the god of the sea, Poseidon, and the goddess Athena. The more important scene, narrated above the east entrance to the temple, where the Panathenaic frieze ends, describes the birth of the goddess Athena. Like the peplos, which is depicted immediately below this pediment, the birth of Athena was closely associated with this processional. Though this story of the contest is given pride of place on the Parthenon, it was not a myth that carried much weight outside Athens, so few ancient authors mentioned it. The best source for the legend comes from the Greek writer Apollodorus, who lived in the second century CE. His work is a collection of Greek myths that even in his day had the status not of religious or theological texts but of learned curiosities and strange stories. Apollodorus seems to have regarded the works he collected and transcribed as fictions, myths more or less in the modern sense of the word. The story of the contest as he tells it begins in the reign of the half-man half-serpent King Cecrops or Kekrops.

> It is said that in his time the gods decided to take possession of cities in order to establish their own cults. Poseidon came to Attica first and struck his trident on the Acropolis producing a salt spring now called "the sea of Erechtheus." Athena came after him calling Kekrops as witness of her taking possession; she planted an olive tree, which is still to be seen [on the Acropolis]. And when the two gods fought for possession of the country, Zeus parted them appointing as judges . . . the twelve gods. Their verdict gave Athena the land thanks to Kekrops's testimony that she planted the olive tree first. Athena then gave her name to the city, Athens. (Neils, 243)

This myth is set in the time of the legendary king who, like Athena, had a shrine on the Acropolis, an important cult, and an annual festival. Other versions of the myth make Cecrops himself the judge between the two gods, but here he plays the lesser role of witness. Since he offers perjured testimony in the case, and because the gods believe what he says, he remains an important figure in the founding of Athena's worship in Athens. According to the myth, the worship of Athena was established during the "time the gods decided to take possession of cities." This seems to refer to a period of city consolidation throughout seventh-century Greece, which in Athens corresponds to the first era of dramatic growth on the Acropolis following the Mycenaean decline.

The west pediment has been reconstructed on the basis of the story Apollodorus told, but its cast of characters does not fully mesh with the names he lists. Cecrops is almost certainly present, as is Erechtheus, another Athenian hero worshipped on the Acropolis but absent from Apollodorus. The Olympian gods he names as judges are not on the pediment; instead Hermes and Iris, messengers of the gods, have been identified, along with a collection of nymphs. At the center of the pediment, the two competing gods lean away from each other. Athena is on the right dressed in her peplos and stepping toward two rearing horses. Poseidon moves in the opposite direction toward a pair of horses rearing on his left. Both gods turn their faces away from the direction they are moving to look back at one another. The contest says a great deal about the way the city thought of itself and its relationship with the victorious goddess. Rather than humans vying for her favor, it is the gods themselves who fight for the privilege of Athenian worship. The prize was a valuable one, and the long history of building on the Acropolis shows that Athenians were willing to put enormous effort into the worship of their patron.

The east pediment, depicting the birth of Athena, is both better preserved and easier to understand. The central figures on the pediment disappeared at the time the building was converted to a church, so only portions of one of them survive. Marks on the pediment floor suggest that the central figure was Zeus, flanked on his left by Hera and on his right by the newborn goddess. Many vase paintings of the birth of Athena exist, but they show the scene differently. Athena is the child of Zeus and Zeus alone, and she is usually shown popping out of the top of Zeus's head. On vases she is a tiny figure, but she is not a baby. She is a miniature adult dressed in her peplos and helmet, carrying a shield and lance. On the east pediment of the Parthenon, Athena was fully mature at the moment of her birth and full-size as well. She stood to the right of her father, directly opposite his wife and sister, Hera, who is her aunt but not her mother.

The birth of Athena occurred at sunrise on a summer day that was also the day of the Panathenaic processional. The east pediment faces the sunrise, and given its position near the top of the building, it would have been illuminated before any other part. The differing heights of the figures in the pediment, which are fixed by the angles of the pediment roof, mean that the sun would have shone first on Zeus's head, from which Athena was born, then on the figures of Athena and Hera who stood beside him. As the sun rose further, it illuminated the other gods and goddesses who witnessed the birth. Of course, with the sculptures no longer on the building, no one has been able to see them lit by the rising sun in this way for many centuries, yet it must have been one of the great moments to visit the Parthenon.

This important moment was commemorated on the pediment itself. In the far left corner, Helios, the sun god, is just about to drive his chariot across the sky. On the far right, Selene, the goddess of the moon, is just visible as her chariot sinks below the horizon. All too often, the pediment was an inconveniently shaped display space for sculpture. The figures in its corners are often bent or cramped in ways that suggest a lack of imagination. The figures on the west pediment suffer from this, and the two outermost figures there look very ill at ease. On the east pediment, the designer has translated the pediment floor into the horizon line. Rather than squeeze the horses and the gods who drive them into these tiny spaces, Helios is shown as his head and shoulder rise through the floor pulled by four horses whose heads and necks are also just beginning to emerge. In the opposite corner the heads of Selene's horses and the torso of the goddess are all that remain aboveground. The rest have plunged into darkness.

The god directly in front of Helios's horses is Dionysos, who is nude and reclines on a seat or rock that is covered with his peplos. Three goddesses sit beside him, and like Dionysos they have links with death, the underworld, and rebirth. The first two are Demeter, goddess of agricultural productivity, and her daughter Persephone, also called Kore—which means both girl and daughter. In Greek mythology, Kore was abducted by Zeus's brother, Hades, god of the dead, who carried her down to his underworld kingdom. Her mother searched the world for her and eventually found her, but since Persephone had eaten the seeds of a pomegranate while in the kingdom of the dead, she could not be completely liberated. Every autumn she must return to the underworld. The third goddess is Hekate, who stands next to Demeter and is a goddess of crossroads, the moon, childbirth, and death. Placing these figures on the Helios side of the pediment with its crescendoing action suggests the triumph over death and darkness. With the birth of the goddess,

The remnants of the sculpture on the east and west pediments of the Parthenon.

all things come into the light. On the right side of the missing central figures are sculptures of another group of gods and goddesses who have been identified as Leto, Artemis, and Aphrodite. A seated figure of Apollo may also have been present, and the head of the god Eros may have been visible behind the seated goddesses.

Given the gods and goddesses most commonly identified, the themes of the pediment are complex and interesting ones. Clearly the play of light and darkness is central to its meaning. The pediment floor, which as a symbol of the horizon line implicitly distinguishes the realms of light and darkness, may also suggest the boundary between the realms of light and life on the one hand and death and darkness on the other. Certainly the presence of deities with underworld associations is very strong on the Helios side of the pediment. On the opposite side the theme is more complex. Given the emphasis on light, it would be entirely appropriate for Apollo, god of both light and enlightenment, to be present. Apollo's twin sister, Artemis, and their mother, Leto, belong to this same thematic grouping. Artemis is like Athena in many ways. She is a virgin and remains unmarried, and she is militant, though hunting rather than warfare is her primary occupation. But unlike Athena, she is especially associated with young women before the age of marriage. Though female herself, Athena had no special interest in women or association with women's activities. Aphrodite, the goddess of beauty and of desire, is present along with Eros.

Aphrodite is the outermost of the goddesses portrayed. Her part of the pediment offers little headroom, and her posture had to be adjusted to fit the shrinking space. While the rest of the female deities sit upright, Aphrodite reclines. Her elbow rests on Artemis's thighs, and her right shoulder leans against Artemis's left breast. The contrast in posture between the two goddesses tells a lot about their characters. The virgin goddess sits primly upright, while the goddess of love uses her as a backrest and stretches out in a relaxed and comfortable pose. Representations of gods and goddesses in the frieze directly below show a similar contrast between decorous upright seating and relaxed sprawling, but in this instance the contrast is uniformly between males and females. Aphrodite refuses to obey the rules defining how proper women should display their bodies in public. She acts with the abandon of a man, and the figure on the pediment who most clearly echoes her is the nude, sprawling Dionysos in the corresponding place and posture on the opposite end of the pediment.

Aphrodite is paired with Dionysos not just in terms of posture, but in terms of meaning as well. Those two gods on opposite sides of the pediment belong together, and the mother-son pair of Aphrodite and Eros might also relate to the mother-daughter pair of Demeter and Kore on the opposite side. All these figures have something to do with the cycle of birth and death and the mystery of renewed fertility both in the soil and in the human community. In Greek tragedy these Dionysiac elements are put in dialogue with light and intellect, the attributes of Apollo. In one of the rare tragedies in which Athena has a significant role, the *Eumenides,* the third play of Aeschylus's cycle called the *Oresteia,* Athena moderates between these two realms. If that example is relevant here, then the grand theme of the east pediment of the Parthenon may be something like the goddess as arbiter between the realms of life and death, darkness and light. The Parthenon sculptures, then, like the multiple figures that swarm over the sandals and battle-gear of the Athena Parthenos, work together to tell the complex story of who she is and what she can do. They are all offerings of praise to the goddess that the Athenians sometimes seem to rank above Zeus himself.

The style of the pedimental sculptures is similar to the style of the frieze, and in significant ways distinct from the slightly earlier style represented on the metopes. These parts of the Parthenon program are the leading examples of the distinctly classical style in Greek sculpture, with the human body as its common denominator. Bodies in a variety of naturalistic poses are represented in all the sculptural programs of the Parthenon. Looking at these bodies for a while, one begins to notice not so much what is represented among them, but what is not. There are many fewer women than men; there are many fewer old men than young men or boys. The young men who predominate are much of a type; none are shorter than average, nor are fat, and there are none who are deformed or disfigured by injury. Like the horses with which they are paired in the frieze, these young men are muscular and athletic; their poses emphasize strength and agility. The older male gods in the frieze are equally strong, equally well proportioned, and equally free of imperfections, but they are presented not in activity but at rest. They are supremely relaxed and supremely at ease, yet clearly strong and agile enough to spring into action at a moment's notice. While their bodies are expressive, the heads of these figures are more than a little disappointing; there is no representation of personality, but instead a mask-like uniformity among perfectly proportioned faces unmarked by emotion or experience.

The classical style is one that rests most firmly on representations of the male figure, for when the female figure is represented, social conventions demand that it be fully clothed or very nearly so. Classical drapery is among the most sophisticated and influential sculptural themes. What Greek sculptors did became a model not just for the plastic arts but for painting and drawing well into the nineteenth century. Clinging, intricately wrinkled and folded drapery that captures the light in interesting ways and suggests dynamic movement in a static figure is one of the most significant attributes and legacies of this art. It has had little place in modern art, but that is an aberration in art history. The human body in purposeful motion, whether revealed directly in athletic poses or indirectly through the play of light and shadow across draped figures, is the most stunning achievement of Greek classical art.

The classical style is not only about bodies, but about perfect bodies. The characteristics of perfection—as this style represents them—are an ideal that the style publicizes and perpetuates. The simplest thing to say about this style is that it represents value judgments: men more than women, young men more than older men, the active body rather than the inactive, the able as opposed to the disabled, the flawless as opposed to the body marked by experience, and the serene and unemotional as opposed to the stressed or anxious expression. By its preferred subjects and its manner of representation, this style asserts its preferences.

What this style meant to ancient Athenians, however, is elusive. In their day, emphasis on the unblemished and the perfectly formed may have had religious rather than social implications. Disfigurement could disqualify a man or woman from participation in certain rites, just as a blemish of any kind disqualified an animal from being sacrificed to the gods. It may not help to realize that imitation of this style was encouraged by Augustus Caesar, who made it a staple of his official art. He encouraged its use in representations of himself, of Roman heroes, and of men and women in power. The style contrasted very markedly with native Roman sculptural traditions, and that contrast pointed to a new era and a new kind of ruler who was secure in power, unmoved by events, vital, and eternally young in face and body. Fascist ideologists used a similar style to represent the Aryan ideal, eternally young, active, and strong, not given to disfiguring emotion and unblemished by age, disease, or ethnicity.

Neither of these overtly political agendas seems appropriate for the fifth century BCE, but they do point to the exclusive rather than inclusive character of the classical ideal. That ideal fitted a society where men outranked women and preferred to keep them close at home. It suited a society in which there were clear lines between Athenian and foreigner, too, but it was less representative of a society where mature men had more power and prestige than younger men. Forty-year-old men were the leaders of society, but the majority of the men represented on the Parthenon appear younger than that. Was this artistic convention, or wishful thinking? One of the easiest ways to get a clear sense of the attributes of the classical style is to compare these sculptures from the Parthenon with examples of Greek sculpture from earlier periods. Fortunately, this is very easy to do in the New Acropolis Museum, where the chronicle of stylistic development in Greek sculpture is exemplified by the many votive statues from the Acropolis collected there.

The earliest widely represented style that precedes the fifth-century classical style is called Archaic. The example of the Archaic style that many scholars turn to is the Moschophoros—the calf bearer—a votive sculpture carved around 570 BCE. It stood on the Acropolis for more than a hundred years before the Persian invasion. The sculptor is unknown, but the man who sponsored and paid for it was called Rhombos, and presumably he is the figure represented. Though the figure is striking in itself and represents substantial skill in the handling of the material from which it was carved, there are marked differences between the way it looks and the features of the much later Parthenon style. Rhombos is a bit like a plinth or a column. His body is contained in a space that must once have been defined by a tall and broad but relatively shallow rectangular prism of marble. He steps forward on his right foot, but the rest of his body fails to respond in any way to that motion. His hips are at equal height above the ground, and there is no twist or torsion in his upper body to carry through the movement of his legs.

He wears a sheer, clinging garment that molds to his body and accentuates the fusion of his arms to his torso, a feature that increases the sense of

The entrance to the New Acropolis Museum.

stolidity and the slight distance that the figure has traveled from stone yard to sculpture. The lines of abdominal muscles are incised on the body. Only the muscles of the forearms suggest actual power, rather than a stylized representation of what is supposed to be there. The figure carries a calf on his shoulder. It is a sacrificial animal that Rhombos once dedicated to Athena and which his effigy continues to offer to the goddess. The calf is naturalistically proportioned and carved; its head and eyes are beautifully expressive. Rhombos's own head is highly stylized. As a glance around the collection will confirm, the convention for representing human heads and faces in Archaic sculpture was absolute. Huge, wide-open eyes, a characteristic so-called Archaic smile, braided hair, and beards as smooth as chin straps are universals.

If the defining anatomical feature of Rhombos is his thinly veiled body, the most noticeable feature of women in sculpture from the same period is clothing. The all-purpose drapery of the pediments and frieze were definitely not in fashion during the Archaic period. The votive figure of a woman, called, like the daughter of Demeter, Kore, is very clearly identified by the clothes that she wears. The Peplos Kore of about 530 BCE seems to be wearing a simple belted gown topped by a cropped shirt. Chances are, though, that the sculptor meant to represent the double fold of a peplos that is cinched at her waist and under her breasts, hanging in a deep fold in front and back. Because the sculptor refused to give the fabric any volume of its own, the garment appears more form-fitting than in reality. A few pleats are indicated in the same shallow relief that defines the abdominal muscles of Rhombos.

Continuing from that relatively early point, the expansion in wardrobe and the dynamism of its representation increase exponentially. Many korai wear a shirt with deep puckers in parallel rows close to their bodies. These garments were first woven of linen or fine wool, then teased apart with needles to make them loose textured. They were light and cool, but the labor involved meant they were also extremely expensive. Over these undershirts, women wore one, two, or more elaborately draped layers of clothes. Since many of the korai were painted, often borders of the clothes are colored and patterned. Garments hang in elaborate swoops and folds, carved in increasingly high relief as they become more independent of the bodies they cover. It is not unusual in cultures dominated by men for assertions of prestige and rank to be disguised or displaced. Men might choose to represent themselves without the trappings of wealth, but when their wives are on display—either in real life or in representations like these statues—the case is different. In this arena, wealth and power are openly displayed; it is less aggressive to show off through surrogates.

The heads of many korai are virtually identical with that of Rhombos. A woman's hair is always curled on her forehead and frequently covered with a band. Long braided locks frame her neck and hang down onto her breast. Women and men have large, wide-open eyes and fixed smiles so wide they flex the muscles in their cheeks and create a puff of flesh under each eye. The fashion in kore faces changed over time, while depictions of their clothing remained relatively constant. The conventions of the Archaic style are more relaxed in the figure known variously as "the kore with the almond eyes," "the melancholy kore," or "the kore with eyes of a sphinx," exhibited on the first level of the New Acropolis Museum and prosaically labeled with the acquisition number 674. Her smile is more subtle, and it inflects her face less.

Her almond-shaped eyes, though they are not precisely aligned, are if not more naturalistic at least less obviously stylized. Her braids outline not just her neck but also her face and create a bit of mysterious shadow. She seems to have a personality; she is not merely a type but an actual person. This softening of Archaic conventions is called, somewhat improbably, the "severe style." It marks the art of the early fifth century, a time when the Persian campaigns had not yet occurred, and when art began to gain a dynamism that would come to fruition in the classical period.

A statue attributed to a sculptor named Kritios reflects the transitional character of art in this period. Of course, artists rarely see the transition in real time; only objects arranged in a museum can demonstrate such a notion. The so-called Kritios Boy is in many ways similar to Rhombos. He, too, is plinth-like and easily imagined as emerging from a block of marble. His musculature is distinct, defined by subtle changes in volume or mass, and not by incising the outlines of muscles on the surface of the stone. While the well-developed muscles in the forearms of Rhombos were not represented, the Kritios Boy's torso has a more pronounced articulation. And unlike the earlier work, where different parts of the body show different degrees of development and different technical approaches, the Kritios Boy is evenly toned, with no emphases or exaggerations. This characteristic links him more directly with classical art than Archaic art. The artist's most striking and important innovation in depicting the body is the bend in the right leg that causes his hips to dip on the right, giving his body a gentle curve. This is the first step toward naturalistic motion carried through an entire figure, a trait that defines classical sculpture. It is the head and face of Kritios's work that take the longest step away from the conventions of the Archaic. While the eyes are still prominent and, like those in Archaic sculptures, ready to be inset with color or painted, the archaic smile is entirely gone, replaced by a somewhat indifferent expression of the mouth. With the smile gone, the face can relax, and the exaggerated musculature of the cheeks disappears.

An Athena dating from about 460 is another masterwork of this transitional style. The goddess's crested helmet is pulled up and rests on top of her head, and she leans on a slim staff, staring toward a plinth at the lower right. She wears a simple peplos cinched at the waist and falling in deep parallel folds to her feet. These folds suggest the fluting of a column, while the slight tilt of her figure, her expressive face, and her exposed feet combine to suggest energy and direction. She appears to be at a balance point between stasis and movement, between the material support of the columnar peplos and the illusion of support created by her slim staff.

Surrounded by a forest of ancient votive statues in many of the styles represented by the museum collection, the Parthenon was the main attraction of the classical Acropolis. One of the surrounding dedications, however, was a little disproportionate. Like the colossal statue of Athena Parthenos that stood inside the Parthenon, there was also a giant bronze statue of the goddess that stood against a sheltering wall just inside the Propylaia. Nothing of the statue survives—bronze was always valuable, and looters in every age were eager to get it. There are ancient descriptions of it and traces of its anchoring in the rock of the Acropolis. The statue was so tall that its head and shoulders reached above the other monuments; like the Statue of Liberty, it could be seen from a great distance and would have served as a landmark for travelers.

Other fifth-century structures have survived, including the Athena Nike temple, the Propylaia, and the Erechtheum. The Nike temple was built on the site of an earlier temple to the Athena of Victories, which the Persians had destroyed. It stood beside the ramp leading to the Acropolis and rested on Mycenaean foundations that once supported a defensive tower guarding the western approach to the Acropolis. This adopted site restricted the freedom of the builders, so rather than being surrounded by a colonnade, the building has columns only at the front and back. The walls of the sanctuary are exposed on both sides. There are no metopes, but a sculpted frieze ran around the building, and there were sculptures in both pediments. The scenes in the friezes described an assembly of the gods on Olympus and battles between various antagonists. While it is hard to guess the themes of the pediment sculptures, it is likely that they included depictions of the war between the gods and the giants and a battle between the Greeks and the Amazons. The figure of Athena worshipped in the temple was an ancient one carved of wood. The balustrade that guarded the sheer drop at the back of the Athena Nike temple was decorated with relief sculptures. One of the slabs of marble that served this purpose contains a beautiful representation of a woman who lifts her leg and bends to reach her sandal strap.

Unlike the Athena Nike, the Erechtheum was a religious and architectural catch-all. Built on several levels and with porches on both sides, the

The Erechtheum.

temple complex served the cults of a collection of deities. As a whole, it represents a side of Greek worship that moderns are most prone to forget: namely, that much of it was based on accumulated traditions that were poorly understood yet too venerable to neglect. We may prefer the dignity and decorum of the Parthenon, but the Erechtheum is an equally authentic representation of what mattered even in the nominally rationalistic fifth century. Like all authentic forms of worship, Greek religion was complicated and undisciplined.

Probably the most important cult served by the temple was that of Athena Polias, the goddess in her role as patron and protector of the city. The image of the goddess was an ancient one made of wood; in fact, it may once have been worshipped in the Mycenaean palace. This was the figure that received the peplos at the Greater Panathenaian festival. It was probably the oldest and most highly venerated object possessed by Athenians. An olive tree grew outside the eastern end of the temple, presumably the same tree that Athena planted in her contest with Poseidon. Poseidon himself, though he lost that crucial contest, was too important to be exiled from the Acropolis. He had made his mark there, and evidence of his epiphany—the presence of a god—required veneration. For this reason, the western end of the Erechtheum enclosed a salt spring that Poseidon had created or uncovered, along with another kind of relic that tradition labeled as some portion of his trident. The rest of the temple was dedicated to another key participant in the contest between the gods. Erechtheus, the temple's namesake, had witnessed the contest, but he had a story of his own that was both very odd and very important to Athenians.

At some time in the remote mythical past before Athens existed as a city, Hephaistos, the lame craftsman among the gods and husband of Aphrodite, felt a sudden desire for the goddess Athena. As he struggled in an effort to have sex with her, he became excited and ejaculated. From the ground where his sperm fell, Erechtheus was born. So while the child's father was the Olympian Hephaistos, his mother was in effect the earth, and he took on characteristics of his two parents. His upper, Olympian half was human, while his lower, earthly half was serpent-shaped. Serpents, like the one represented beneath the shield of the Athena Parthenos, represented earth, its fertility, and the underworld. Though Athena was not his mother, she was directly involved in his conception and so took responsibility for him. She hid the child in a box and turned him over to the three daughters of King Cecrops of Athens, giving them instructions not unlike those that Pandora ignored. When the box was opened, perhaps by all three daughters but certainly by two of them, Aglauros and Herse, they were driven to commit suicide by jumping off the Acropolis. The very ancient and important commemoration of these women was celebrated annually in one of the caves on the north side of the Acropolis. According to legend, Erechtheus, sometimes called Erichthonius, was either the founder of Athens or its first king.

This myth may seem absurd: why anyone would want to commemorate such a misadventure seems puzzling, and logic would have a very hard time explaining its appeal. The myth suited the Athenians, however, because it described a civic origin with significant political value for them. As Athens became increasingly prominent in the politics of the Greek mainland, it was eager to justify not just its equality but its preeminence among Greek cities. Part of what would determine preeminence was a city's origin story. In this context, rather than being an embarrassment, the Erechtheus story was a

The western flank of the Erechtheum, as captured by William James Stillman in 1869. (Fine Arts Library, Harvard University)

godsend. Most Greek legends of city founding involved colonists coming from one region and settling in another. Athens was not settled by colonists from somewhere else. Its founder had literally sprung from the soil on which the city was established. Among cities, then, Athens ranked as original rather than as an offshoot of some other city. So, the Athenians were happy to acknowledge Erechtheus as their founder, despite the circumstances of his birth. Erechtheus had a section of the temple complex devoted to his worship, and he shared this space with a shrine to his father, Hephaistos, as well as a shrine that honored his brother, Boutes.

The connections between the origins of Athens, the goddess Athena, and the hero Erechtheus account for a good deal of the worship combined under one roof in the Erechtheum. What appears to be left out is the shrine to Poseidon, but this is not in fact the case. While the origin story of Erechtheus makes no mention of the fact, this hero was also associated very directly with Poseidon. In some cases, the two were worshipped as the same deity, as if Erechtheus were one of the names or attributes of the sea god. This association binds all the dedicatees of the Erechtheum together and offers further commentary on the contest between Athena and Poseidon represented on the Archaios Naos and the Parthenon. The notion of a contest strongly suggests a winner and a loser, one deity who remains as a sponsor while the other one goes away. In a polytheistic system, it is never good when gods go away, so the best solution for the Athenians is for both Athena and Poseidon to remain concerned with their welfare. This dual guardianship may not be evident in the Parthenon image, but it is a major theme of the Erechtheum.

Porches projected from the north and south sides of the Erechtheum. The northern porch sheltered a sacred spot where a thunderbolt of Zeus had struck the ground. Spots where lightning had struck and left its mark were sacred to both the Greeks and Romans, and they often created little shrines to outline and protect such places. This shrine commemorated a particular bolt of lightning that Zeus had hurled at Erechtheus himself. It is important as a representation of the chief god's part in the Erechtheus story. It adds another god to the roll call of benefactors.

One of the building's best-known features, the Caryatid Porch, sits on the south side of the Erechtheum. Five of its six columns—designed as six women—have been removed to the safety of the New Acropolis Museum, and the sixth can be found in the British Museum; replicas now stand in their original place on the monument. This decision to move the sculptures from the Acropolis to the museum has liberated the women from their architectural burden and accentuated the characteristics that have always defined them as figures in motion. Their downturned heads and flexed knees suggest that they are walking forward in procession, like the women on the Parthenon frieze. Early interpretations of identity and purpose suggested that they were slaves weighed down by the roof they supported and consigned to perform a difficult and unending task. By contrast, contemporary interpretations suggest that these women bear offerings and are marching toward the grave of the mythical king Cecrops, where it lies sheltered within the Caryatid Porch. Like Rhombos, who perpetually brings a calf to Athena, these figures are always bringing gifts to the buried hero.

The Erechtheum, with the Porch of the Caryatids on the left.

The Propylaia is unusual among Acropolis monuments. In the strictest sense, it is not a religious monument, though its architecture is temple-like, and the building served as a key point in the Panathenaic processional. Here the architectural vocabulary is typical of the precinct and the period: there are Doric columns surmounted by an entablature with a frieze composed of triglyphs and metopes, and the main feature is a wide doorway, not unlike a temple, with four columns across its opening and two columns projecting from bits of wall like the ones that enclose the sanctuary of a temple. Still, the Propylaia only suggests sanctity; it does not embody it. At heart it is nothing but a gateway with a wide central area where the greater part of participants in the Panathenaic processional and the animals to be sacrificed could enter the sacred hilltop. Narrower passages approached by stairs on either side allowed access for others. The Propylaia marked a transition between the approach and the goal of the processional. It monumentalized the boundary between the city and the sacred place where the processional achieved its ritual climax.

The western façade of the Propylaia, with the Temple of Victory and the ancient steps, 1869. William James Stillman, photographer. (Fine Arts Library, Harvard University)

Architecturally, the Propylaia not only directs a worshipper's or visitor's feet, but also limits and shapes his or her view of the hilltop. It was admirably suited to the eclecticism and complexity of the historic Acropolis, as it offered coherence and focus, bringing a perceived if not quite actual order to things. As the visitor climbs toward the entrance, ramparts of the Acropolis block most of what is above from view. As she continues upward, the substructures and projecting wings of the Propylaia carry on the same role; rather than allow the eye to wander at will over the sacred landscape, the structure continues to block most of what lies beyond. The roof of the Parthenon would probably have been visible, and of course the head and shoulders of the great bronze Athena would also have been seen. These would have served to remind visitors of the main focus of the climb, the shrines to Athena. Once a visitor entered the Propylaia and stood between its columns, sight lines would still be restricted. More monuments would come into view, but the perspective would still have been controlled in a way that it is hard to imagine today, when the hillside is a largely undifferentiated agglomeration of bare limestone platform and scattered bits of broken monuments. In the fifth century, however, the view would have been highly selective and focused in significant ways on the dominant presence of the cult of Athena.

Two wings of different lengths open from both sides of the central passageway. Leading to the left, this wing opens to two rooms—a small antechamber and a large hall called the Pinakotheke, or "picture gallery." How this room was used is uncertain, and we do not know what pictures might have been exhibited there. It may have been a meeting or banquet hall, or perhaps just a place for visitors to be welcomed. The paintings may have been frescoed decoration or detachable artwork. Most of what we know about classical Greek painting comes from descriptions, from hints that vase painting offers, and from later works arguably influenced by it. Classical painters and their achievements were held in high regard throughout antiquity, so it is possible that this prominent and prestigious site may have displayed art of the highest quality. We are left to guess about the art and its purpose, as well as how the room was used. We can only speculate that the wing to the right may have been a sculpture gallery, or it may simply have served as passageway into the temple of Athena Nike.

3

The Athenian Agora

At its heart, the Athenian Agora was an all-purpose downtown open space where people could meet to buy and sell, to talk politics, and to make decisions about the affairs of their city. The Agora that has been excavated during the centuries of Greek independence is the city's second. Remains of graves found during the course of excavation revealed that it had once been a marginal area outside the town limits. As the Acropolis developed into a powerful shrine, and the Panathenaic processional grew in importance, a new pathway was created leading up the hill. The ramp prompted a major restructuring of early Athens. After its completion, the center of gravity for commerce and public business shifted westward, taking the Agora with it.

Rather than create the equivalent of a government center—a place where clusters of buildings dominate and open space is at a premium—Athenians took the opposite approach, creating an extremely informal central space in the Agora. Crisscrossed by pathways leading to various sections of the city, it may have been shaded by trees, and activities within the Agora's open space were probably more often than not temporary and fugitive. During the day, merchants and farmers set up booths sheltered by awnings to display and sell their products; at night they took them down and bundled them up or carried them away.

Despite its informality and its dominance by commercial activity, the Agora was also home to significant Athenian political institutions. Over time it came to be ringed by buildings that housed all kinds of public activities. Reconstructions of some of the principal finds from excavations of the past 150 years have revealed major buildings and spurred new research into their purpose. Assigning historically attested functions to particular buildings is difficult because Athenian public buildings looked much the same. Like the

The ancient Agora.

Propylaia, the architectural vocabulary of temples was applied to these civic buildings as well. This suggests both an underlying architectural conservatism and, more importantly, a cultural link between the political activities of the city and its religious life. Athens was in no sense a secular state—its worship of Athena was cultural, political, historical, and even legalistic. Its political activities could never be completely separated from the cult of the goddess, nor from the cult of the gods in general. Those gods looked out for the welfare of the city, guarded and secured the oaths that bound it to allies, and ensured the reliability of legal testimony and the security of legal contracts. In such a culture, it made perfect sense that civic buildings should be similar in style and construction to religious ones.

The dominant building form in the Agora was the stoa, a building that is typically longer than deep, with a colonnade on one of its long sides. The colonnade that defined this building supported an entablature less elaborate than those found on temples, and less often decorated with sculptural friezes.

It supported a pitched, tile-covered roof. The remaining sides of the building would have been made of limestone or marble block. The stoa's colonnades faced the Agora, so from the back this structure featured blank walls with a few unglazed windows near their rooflines. Like the much later Roman basilica, the stoa was a particularly apt kind of building to set along the edges of an outdoor space—in a sudden downpour, its colonnade could shelter buyers and sellers chased from the open air.

Interior plans for many of the stoas were simple and flexible. The roofed and walled spaces were broken up only by rows of columns that supported the roof. Clustered together at the narrow north end of the Agora, the so-called Painted Stoa, the Royal Stoa, and the Stoa of Zeus were buildings of this type. They were like little bits of the outdoors that had been broken off and roofed but otherwise left unmarked. Their interiors were suited to many different kinds of activities. The South Stoa on the opposite end of the Agora had built-in subdivisions, but this was unusual. The Stoa of Zeus was unlike the others in ground plan: though the typical stoa was a long shed, the Stoa of Zeus combined a center section with perpendicular wings.

The rationale for the stoa's shape came from a need to light its interior. We are so used to the ubiquity of electrical light that we might assume that some more primitive form of artificial lighting existed in important public institutions of the past. The meager light of an oil lamp, however, would have been insufficient to light any of these buildings, and lighting enough lamps to make a difference would have been very expensive. For this reason, even major public buildings like these were designed to maximize the reach of natural light. Most of the light that entered these buildings came through the colonnade, because tiny, high windows along the solid outer walls could contribute very little. This lighting issue also accounts for the general lack of internal divisions in buildings. An internal wall that blocked the light would do as much harm as good; for this reason, internal subdivisions in the South Stoa run parallel to the light source. With its perpendicular wings blocking the source, lighting in the Stoa of Zeus must always have been unequal. Heating was a related issue: portable braziers could be brought into buildings, but generally speaking, sunlight was the major source of heat as well as light. Stoas were almost entirely what are now called passive solar buildings.

There were other building types in the Agora more specialized in shape and function than the stoas. The Bouleuterion was one example, and there

Statues in the ancient Agora.

were in fact two buildings—an older one and its replacement or addition—with this same name in the Agora. The Old Bouleuterion, also called the Metroon, was a combined shrine, meeting place, and public archive. It was designed somewhat like an Athenian house with a central open courtyard, though its exterior was elaborated with decorative elements also found on temples. The building was a shrine to the mother goddess, and it held an important image of her. When this multipurpose building became too small to serve, a new Bouleuterion supplemented it and took over some of its functions. From the time of its creation in the fifth century, the new structure housed an important arm of the Athenian political administration, called the Boule.

In that era, Athens was divided into ten political subgroups known as tribes, and each took turns providing staff for the Boule. For thirty-six days in succession each tribe was responsible for ensuring that, twenty-four hours a day, there were a minimum of seventeen elected tribe members serving in the Bouleuterion. The members of this group could respond to public needs at any hour of the day or night, and they were also responsible for calling a public assembly about every nine days. The Bouleuterion must have worked more or less as a modern firehouse: three shifts of officials were on duty each day, and they were housed and fed at public expense. Though the duties of this office must have been onerous for its members, lifetime limits on service were strict: an individual could only serve two nonconsecutive terms during his entire adult life.

Next to the two Bouleuterion buildings was a round structure called the Tholos. (Tholos is not the name of a political body, like the Boule, but the generic name for a round building.) It appears to have been the dining hall for the Boule. It also operated as a bureau of standards. A uniform set of weights and measures was kept inside, to be used periodically to calibrate and ensure the accuracy of weights used in the market. Set against its outside walls were roof tiles of a standard size intended as guides for builders and their clients.

To understand the peculiar and plainly cumbersome characteristics of the Boule and other Athenian democratic institutions, it helps to know something about Athenian political history. Institutions of the fifth century were all created in reaction to politicians and political systems that had ruled in Athens during the centuries before. Every democratic institution was crafted by men who were looking over their shoulders and trying to build a government immune from some particular problem of the past. While hundreds of books have been written about Athenian political history and the rise of this peculiar democracy, there is one significant primary source behind them all. Sometime in the mid-fourth century, Aristotle's students (and many believe even the philosopher himself) studied the peculiar political systems—the constitutions—that the major Greek cities had evolved for themselves. Among some twenty original studies undertaken and written, only one survives, and its title is *The Athenian Constitution.*

The background to Athenian democracy, as this text describes it, is tyranny and oligarchy. The creation of democracy was a piecemeal process that depended on the innovations of public-minded leaders who were called on to craft political compromises in eras when tyranny collapsed. Athenians believed themselves to have been a monarchy in their founding era; their origin stories feature heroes like Erechtheus and Cecrops, who were known as the kings of Athens. The earliest surviving Athenian political offices, however, reflected a time when the kingship had already been abolished. In its place the Athenians created a series of magistrates called archons.

According to *The Athenian Constitution,* the city was at first governed by a group of nine magistrates, all with the title archon, but with different areas of responsibility. The *basileus* or king archon took over most of the religious responsibilities of the ancient monarchs. He was the chief priest of the Athenians' civic religion, and he also acted as presiding judge in one of the oldest Athenian law courts, the Court of the Areopagus. The *polemarch* was the commander in chief of the Athenian army. The archon, also called the eponymous archon, was the executive officer of the city. During some remote era, as Aristotle's text describes, all these magistrates were selected to serve for life. Over time their terms were shortened—first to a decade, then to a year. Later six additional and much less grand title holders joined the administration. Their terms were never more than a year, and when first instituted, these officers had no religious responsibilities, a fact that made them less important than their fellow archons.

The Athenian Constitution states that the archons were at first "elected according to qualifications of birth and wealth." In other words, a man had to be noble and rich in order to be eligible for these high offices. This limited eligibility for election effectively placed power in the hands of a few wealthy families who had been prominent in the city for many generations. Such narrow qualifications for election guaranteed that the magistrates would be similar in outlook and inclined to advocate the interests of families like their own. This was a recipe for oligarchy, if not for tyranny. Combining this limited eligibility with a lifetime appointment to office left nothing but a hereditary succession to create a monarchy in all but name.

Draco is said to have been the first political reformer in Athenian memory. Draco expanded the number and type of men able to hold political power by lowering the qualification for enfranchisement: anyone who had enough money to provide himself with the minimum equipment of a foot soldier—helmet, shield, breastplate, leg guards, and spear—was entitled to vote. This level of wealth also rendered a man eligible to be selected at random to hold one of the four hundred council seats or to hold a seat on one of the lesser magistracies. As an enfranchised citizen, he could go to court to take action against anyone who had violated his rights or the rights of his household. Despite this expansion of the political base, the wealthiest citizens continued to elect the archons, so real power remained in the hands of established, affluent families.

Expanding the franchise in these ways was meaningful, but the economic situation of the Athenian state was moving steadily toward a crisis that would eventually force far more sweeping changes. Wealthy landowners gave loans to others who were less well off. They also hired out their land to tenant farmers who were obliged to pay annual rents. Small-scale farming was uncertain, and the burden of debt was unforgiving. A few bad years could force a debtor to default. In ancient Greece, debt was, as *The Athenian Constitution* described, "secured upon the person of the debtor." Debtors who could not make their payments became, along with their families, the slaves of those who had lent them money. As this process continued over generations, the wealthiest families accumulated ever larger amounts of land and hundreds of enslaved workers to cultivate it. Enslavement brought disenfranchisement, which meant that as rich men accumulated slaves, they also gained political power.

The reformer Solon—a man secure enough financially to become a voting citizen, but not so well off as to be a member of the ruling elite—was able to work out a political compromise that both creditors and debtors willingly accepted. "Solon liberated the people once and for all, by prohibiting all loans on the security of the debtor's person: and in addition he made laws by which he cancelled all debts, public and private." Once this fundamental reform was accepted and debtors were released from bondage, Solon was able to put through a number of other long-term reforms:

> Solon drew up a constitution and enacted new laws. The elections to the various offices Solon enacted should be by lot, out of candidates selected by each of the tribes. Each tribe selected ten candidates for the nine archonships, and among these the lot was cast.

The old council of four hundred was retained, with one hundred of its members coming from each of the then-existing four tribes. A smaller body, like the later Boule but different in composition, served as its executive committee.

> The Council of the Areopagus acted as the guardian of the constitution in general. It kept watch over the affairs of the state in most of the more

important matters, and corrected offenders, with full powers to inflict either fines or personal punishment. . . . It also tried those who conspired for the overthrow of the state.

These combined legislative and judicial roles made the Council the most powerful body in the state and, unfortunately, also the one most likely to hamstring the legislature. This is more or less what happened in the years following Solon's reforms. In the mid-sixth century, Pisistratos managed to seize control of the government and to maintain himself in power for twenty years. Though he was regarded as a tyrant who seized and held power illegitimately, *The Athenian Constitution* described his rule as beneficial, and he was popular with the citizens of Athens. At his death, Pisistratos was succeeded by his sons, three men of very different character and ability. Hippias, who was most like his father, took control of the government; his brother Hipparchus became a patron of the arts. The third son, Thessalus, played the part of the tyrant's arrogant and willful child.

Thessalus fell in love with and pursued Harmodius, a young man who rejected him. In revenge, Thessalus publicly accused Harmodius's sister of sexual misconduct and had her barred from the Panathenaic processional. Other accounts suggest that he accused Harmodius of sexual misconduct and used that as a reason to exclude his sister from the rites. This public humiliation of his family was too much for Harmodius. He and his actual lover, Aristogeiton, organized a conspiracy to assassinate all three brothers and liberate Athens from their rule. The plot was timed for the Panathenaic celebration in which Hippias and Hipparchus had principal roles. While the procession was being organized, Harmodius and Aristogeiton saw one of their coconspirators in conversation with Hippias. They jumped to the conclusion that he was betraying the conspiracy. Rather than delay and lose any chance they might have to strike a blow, the two rushed to accomplish whatever they could before it was too late. They found Hipparchus, who was organizing the marchers, and together they cut him down. Hipparchus's bodyguards killed Harmodius on the spot and took Aristogeiton prisoner.

What happened after that is far from clear. There is no question that Aristogeiton was tortured in the cruelest manner imaginable. There is also no disputing the fact that under torture he named names. What remains unclear is whether the names he offered up to his torturers were the names of coconspirators or those of men from prominent families close to the tyrants with no part in the plan. From a political point of view, the rationale for giving false names was to lead the tyrants to destroy their own allies. From an Athenian point of view, however, Aristogeiton's strategy, if it existed, was even more subtle. Killing innocent men would make the tyrants murderers. The innocent blood on the killers' hands would make them ritually unclean and, like the character Oedipus, in Sophocles's play, create a pollution that the city must expel. Making them ritually impure would be a more powerful strike against them than anything else their opponents could have inflicted.

Aristogeiton's death also came about as a result of a forced ritual pollution. As he suffered under torture, he convinced Hippias that he had more information that he would reveal only if Hippias made a pact with him. Hippias shook hands with Aristogeiton to seal the deal. Once that was done, Aristogeiton accused Hippias of having willingly taken the bloody hand of his brother's murderer. Enraged at the trick and the taunt, Hippias grabbed a dagger and killed Aristogeiton, freeing him from further suffering.

Though Hippias had survived the assassination plot, it changed his character and the character of his rule. Within three years, he was so despised and his power so diminished that he was driven out of office not by the Athenians, but by their sometime ally and longterm rival, the city of Sparta. Sparta put a puppet dictatorship in place that lasted only a short while until Athenians under the leadership of Cleisthenes drove out the foreigners and their supporters. From his new position of power, Cleisthenes enacted a number of political reforms that cemented the long progress toward democratization.

Cleisthenes was the originator of the ten tribes. He took the original four tribes that had been the foundation of Solon's reforms and reorganized them. Rather than break them into twelve groups, which would have been easy to do, since each tribe was divided into three parts, he created ten groups without links to either of the earlier subdivisions. He added a further one hundred members to the council of four hundred; henceforth, fifty members of the council would be chosen by each tribe. He divided the city and the country into thirty political subdivisions called *demes*. There were ten demes in the city, ten in the agricultural lands of Attica, and ten along the coast. Each tribe was then allotted a deme from each region, assigned at random. Until this time, Athenians had been known by their family names,

but Cleisthenes substituted the name of the demes for this traditional identification and declared that all members of a single deme would be considered to be related. This process of reshuffling, renaming, and repatriating
was intended to destabilize the long-term alliances among powerful families that had underpinned the oligarchy. It would at the same time do away
with tribal allegiances that had anchored political factions.

Cleisthenes picked the tyrant slayers, Harmodius and Aristogeiton, to be
symbols of his reforms. He commissioned statues of the two men and had
them placed not on the Acropolis to honor the gods but in the Agora, as an
emblem of the new political order that was founded on their act of tyranni-
cide. The original statues were destroyed by the Persians when they attacked
Athens early in the fifth century. They were replaced in the postwar years
and once again removed during the occupation by Alexander the Great,
who eventually returned them, probably when he thought Athens no longer
posed any kind of threat to his rule.

To Athenians, the tyrant slayers represented a great deal more than the
historical record could substantiate or even suggest. They epitomized what
Athenians had come to understand as the arc of their political history, which
they conceived in retrospect as a struggle against tyranny that had led, step
by step, to the founding of a democracy. As political symbols, Harmodius
and Aristogeiton were updates of the founding kings, Erechtheus and Cecrops, mythical heroes who were venerated on the Acropolis and closely associated with Athena and Poseidon. Harmodius and Aristogeiton were not
kings, and they were not semidivine—they did not even have divine protection or sponsorship for their act. As far as it was possible within the context
of Athenian politics, they were secular and historical heroes.

A sculpture that strongly resembles the tyrant slayer group, not in appearance but in purpose, was created almost two thousand years later. When the
rulers of Renaissance Florence set Michelangelo's *David* in front of their
government center, they were using art to make a political statement. The
biblical David was a tyrant slayer, just like Harmodius and Aristogeiton. His
giant stature in Michelangelo's sculpture was intended to represent the people
of Florence, humble like David but powerful when they united to overthrow
Medici tyranny.

Reforms put into effect by Cleisthenes were important and long lasting,
but they did not solve the problem of Athenian oligarchy. Tribal allegiances
and rivalries that crippled the assembly had been addressed, but not the

forces that pulled the strings. From the time of Solon (if not before), the Council of the Areopagus, dominated by old wealthy families, held tremendous power. As *The Athenian Constitution* points out, this Council dominated the government for

> about seventeen years after the Persian wars, although gradually declining. But as the strength of the masses increased, Ephialtes, son of Sophonides, a man with a reputation for incorruptibility and public virtue, who had become the leader of the people, made an attack upon that Council. First of all he ruined many of its members by bringing actions against them with reference to their administration.

In other words, Ephialtes accused individual members of the Council of betraying the public trust while in office. His ability to do this came from the all-important provision in the reforms of Draco that guaranteed legal redress to citizens whose rights had been violated.

> Then, in the archonship of Conon, [Ephialtes] stripped the Council of all the acquired prerogatives from which it derived its guardianship of the constitution, and assigned some of them to the Council of Five Hundred, and others to the Assembly and the law-courts. In this revolution he was assisted by Themistocles.

The successful challenge to the entrenched Council of the Areopagus was one of the most significant reforms in the history of Athenian political organization. This group went from being an all-purpose committee with broad powers to "defend the constitution" to becoming a weaker insitution whose portfolio was broken apart and redistributed. Legislative responsibility passed to the Boule, and all but one of the Council's judicial roles were reassigned to other law courts. Archons were selected by lot from a slate of candidates.

Not far from the Bouleuterion and Tholos complex was a shrine that was sacred to the supposed founders of Cleisthenes's ten tribes. These tribes were named after famous men, and the shrine honored these men and, by extension, the individual tribes. This association gave the tribes a genealogical and religious character that they would have lacked as simple political divisions. The shrine was similar to those that a family would erect to honor not just its ancestors but more specifically its founding ancestor or its most powerful and prominent ancestor. This honored ancestor acted to some degree like an earth god. He (it was always a he) looked after the fate of his descendants, guaranteeing that they would continue to produce offspring (especially sons), and he also took care of the fields and the flocks. In gratitude for these gifts, family members offered sacrifices to nourish his spirit and that of their honored dead in general. The shrines of Cleisthenes's tribal founders were honored in a similar way. Like the worship of Athena that was always both religious and political, the cult of the tribal founders combined civic pride, political activity, and religious devotion.

The democracy of fifth-century Athens was direct rather than representative. That meant that most political decisions were debated and passed in a huge public assembly. In its earliest days that assembly—called the ecclesia— had met in the Agora, but over time the Agora's wide-open and undifferentiated area proved inadequate. Though even after the assembly meeting place was moved to a nearby hill, the Pnyx, the process of convening the assembly still took place in the Agora. Citizens gathered there at the appointed time—either on purpose or by accident—and were shepherded toward the site by sergeants-at-arms who carried a rope dipped in red dye. A citizen found outside the assembly after being marked with the dye was fined. Attendance was crucial because the assembly required a quorum of six thousand men to do its work—women, the underage, foreigners, and slaves were all excluded.

There was no building big enough to house the voters of Athens, who, like the Romans, may have taken pride in their willingness to meet outside and on foot in all seasons of the year and in any kind of weather. The meeting place of the assembly was a bowl-like structure built into one of the smaller hills that overlooked the Agora, which meant it was, in turn, overshadowed by the Acropolis. The Pnyx was just a few minutes' walk from the Agora. The assembly met in what might best be described as a piece of creative landscaping that resembled a Greek theater. The Pnyx hillside was carved out, with dirt piled up to create a rounded platform that rose toward its outer edge. A retaining wall uncovered in nineteenth-century excavations supported this outer edge and made a crescent-shaped trace on the hillside. Steps led to this upraised outer rim, and members of the assembly apparently entered by these steps. The focus of the assembly was at the structure's lower central point, where a speaker's platform stood. Backed by the excavated wall of the hillside and aided by the rise in the land, a speaker's voice could probably be heard for some distance. (Theaters were arranged in the opposite way: the slope of the hill held the audience and the actors addressed them from flat ground below.) Like the stoas of the Agora that made use of natural light, this assembly meeting place made use of the landscape to maximize the range of the human voice. Any citizen had the right to be heard, but it is hard to imagine that there were many with the courage and the vocal skills to be effective. Votes were taken by a show of hands.

Even after the assembly moved out, the Agora remained the scene of one peculiarly Athenian political activity. One of the safety valves in the Athenian democratic system was the community's right to exile any of its members. This allowed for a preemptive, extralegal strike against anyone disliked by the majority. From a constitutional point of view, this provision made it possible to remove anyone the community suspected of having ambitions to become a tyrant. Like so many other reforms, exile was a reaction to the tyrannies of the sixth century that had caused so much hardship. Though they were long past, those tyrannies remained the intellectual catalyst for what might easily be characterized as an overly complicated and excessively cautious form of democratic organization.

On an appointed day in winter, the Agora was enclosed behind wooden barricades. Ten gates, one for each of the ten tribes, opened into it. Access was strictly controlled, and only citizens were admitted and presumably only through the gates assigned to their tribes. Once inside the Agora, the citizens were free to scratch the name of any individual on a broken shard of pottery, called an *ostrakon*. If six thousand *ostraka* revealed the name of any single person, he would have ten days to remove his household from Athens and Attica—this exile lasted for ten years. Thousands of ostraka—from which the word "ostracism" derives—have turned up in the Agora excavations. Yet despite all its structural safeguards, the Athenian government still fell prey from time to time to the power of oligarchs and the ambitions of tyrants.

After the dismantling of the Council of the Areopagus, most of its judicial responsibilities passed to courts with different memberships and different responsibilities. The Boule heard cases of misconduct by state officials. Official misconduct of an especially serious kind, like treasonable activity while in office, was judged by the entire Athenian assembly in its meeting place on the Pnyx. All the other courts met in or on the fringes of the Agora. The Heliaia was the most general Athenian court. It is known from many ancient documents, but its exact meeting place in the Agora is uncertain. The betting is that its site was a large open-air enclosure next to the South Stoa, but there is no clear archaeological evidence to confirm this. This court heard every case that fell between official misconduct and murder. Such a broad-ranging jurisdiction meant that it was active in commercial, social, and private affairs.

Murder was the most troubling crime to Athenians, but not for the same reasons that make it consequential today. Taking a human life was as grave a matter for Athenians as it is for us, but murder trials involved more than deciding who was responsible for a death. As the case of Harmodius and Aristogeiton suggests, murder was a complicated crime that affected many more than those individuals directly involved. It reached into social and spiritual realms that were well beyond the limits of secular responsibility and retribution. Murder always created pollution in the religious sense of the word. This pollution, which was brought on by the private act of spilling human blood, ultimatedly involved the entire community.

Every Athenian murderer committed a double crime: one against the victim and his or her family, and another against the gods. It was the community's responsibility to identify the murderer and to expel him or her in order to annul the pollution that spilled blood had created. A case of murder required extreme diligence and also extreme seriousness of purpose. The venerable Council of the Areopagus, even after it was stripped of all its other powers, remained the high court that prosecuted murderers. One of the earliest surviving Greek tragedies, Aeschylus's *Eumenides,* focused its action on this court, and one of the play's purposes was to rehabilitate the diminished Council in the public eye by dramatizing its workings in a case that involved gods of the underworld along with Apollo and Athena. When it tried a murder case, the Council met on the hill called the Areopagus, a low limestone knob dedicated to the war god Ares, which, like the Pnyx, overlooked the Agora.

An unsolved murder created serious problems for the state, and there was a special court to deal with such cases. Its members were the king archon and the leaders of the ten tribes. When no human could be identified, this

The Areopagus.

court met and pronounced guilty either an instrument, such as the murder weapon, or a symbolic being—a scapegoat. The "guilty party," whether bloody ax or billy goat, was then sent into exile, thus cleansing the city and its people of the blood the murderer had spilled. The king archon had jurisdiction over pleas of justification or mitigating circumstances in homicide prosecutions. He could refer cases to a special court that he also presided over.

Trials in Athens were jury trails, and juries were typically huge. Again the aim was to break the stranglehold of the rich and powerful on the administration of law and justice, so a jury could vary in size from two hundred to two thousand, but it would never comprise those exact numbers. With an even number of jurors, a tie was theoretically possible, so Athenians always added one more to the pool. Political misconduct trials had the biggest juries of all—the assembly, with a quorum of six thousand citizen-jurors.

Because it is the basis of Plato's dialogue called *The Apology of Socrates,* the trial of that singular individual is well known. The dialogue describes the trial from only one point of view, that of the defendant, Socrates. "Apology" in this context means defense, not excuse, so the dialogue is really more of a monologue, and its aim is to portray Socrates as a heroic representative of Plato's philosophy. With these qualifications, however, it is possible to see in this fictionalized trial a lively representation of Athenian legal give and take. It is fairly clear that the prosecution was politically motivated. Socrates had managed to alienate both powerful members of the upper class and vast numbers of citizens. In his defense, he characterized this widespread antagonism as collateral damage caused by his unrelenting search for truth, but the causes were probably more mundane.

There was no state prosecutor to bring charges against Socrates or anyone else. A citizen taking advantage of his right to legal redress made the accusation, and this was not an activity entirely free of risk. If the accuser failed to persuade one-fifth of the jurors to cast a vote of "guilty," he became liable to prosecution himself. Certainly this provided some safeguards against frivolous accusations, but it also ensured that cases where the public already had formed an opinion about guilt and innocence or a prejudice against the accused were more likely to go forward. This appears to be the case in the prosecution of Socrates, which at least from the account we have looks like an attempt to use the judicial process to send into exile an annoying individual with powerful enemies.

The charges against Socrates were ones that had been leveled against other philosophers. The substance of the charges lay in the link that the city always maintained between its civil and religious life. The philosopher's accusers charged that he taught that the earth and moon were not divine but material; that he challenged belief in the state gods and that he corrupted young people. In his defense, which was lighthearted and ironic, Socrates pointed out the absurdities of the charges. He explained to the prosecution and to the jury that he had no interest in the physical composition of the universe and did not teach anything about it. Speculation about the planets and their raw materials, he reminded them, was the concern of "natural philosophers"—people we would call physicists or cosmologists today—and he had lost interest in their studies when he was still a young man. These charges were generic and apt to be brought up any time a person of intellect and education was on trial.

The other charges were either self-contradictory or absurd, at least in Socrates's view. He denied that he had repudiated the state's gods, and he proved his point, at least to his own satisfaction. On the charge of corrupting the youth of Athens, he replied that no intelligent man would corrupt those he lived among because this would put him in danger. He also asked the jurors to note the presence and support of the very youth he was alleged to have corrupted. All in all, Socrates had the better of the argument in Plato's version of the trial. Socrates expressed doubts that even his accusers themselves believed the charges; nevertheless, the jury, by a narrow margin, found him guilty. After this verdict, the penalty phase of the trial began. Death was the prescribed penalty for Socrates's crimes, but it was seldom imposed. Although the jury expected him to propose exile, a far more standard punishment, Socrates refused and then further antagonized the jury by proposing that instead of being punished he should be rewarded. In reaction, they voted the death penalty.

Before his execution, Socrates spent about a month in prison. Two of Plato's dialogues—*Crito* and *Phaedo*—describe the many friends who visited the condemned man, as well as their conversations after his death was a certainty. Prison conditions—at least for a man so prominent and with wealthy, powerful friends—do not appear to have been in any way harsh. A jail located in the southwest corner of the Agora was the site of his imprisonment. It was surrounded by a wall that enclosed an open courtyard, a series of other cells, and a suite of offices for the jailers.

Though it was an official structure, the architecture of the prison did not reflect the monumental buildings of the Agora—there is no sign of a colonnade, nor of dressed stone. Its closest models were domestic rather than official, and both its layout and the materials from which it was built echo the few fifth-century Athenian houses found in modern excavations. Because excavators' priorities have typically been the quest for official buildings with historical connections, the houses excavated are typically on the fringes of more valued sites. There are a few near the Agora, some near the Pnyx, and others a little downhill from the Areopagus, and though the houses are of varying size and organization, each appears to have both an enclosing outer wall and an inner courtyard. The simplest domestic space uncovered so far is known as the house-workshop of the sculptors Micion and Menon. Though their building is only partially exposed, its outline suggests a courtyard with a gate that leads in from the street, two connected spaces—

workshops, perhaps—abutting the open space, and a dwelling that may have had two stories to the rear of the courtyard.

A house on the Pnyx was adapted to its hillside site: its front gate opened at the lowest point of the slope, onto a small courtyard that was surrounded by rooms of various sizes. These rooms were built into the hill and buried in its slope. All remaining traces of their walls suggest that these rooms were grouped around the courtyard. One room ran the full depth of the house and was probably used as a ceremonial dining room for important guests. It seems likely that the house also had a second story. A similar floor plan is all that remains of two semidetached houses on the Areopagus. These houses are defined by enclosing walls that face the street, as well as a small interior courtyard that was overlooked by single- or double-storied suites of rooms. Though side by side, these houses were of very different dimensions: the larger one had eleven first-floor rooms; the smaller had only four.

Not every Athenian could afford a free-standing house; much of the population lived in buildings that were more like apartments. A housing block uncovered near the South Stoa has a multitude of different-size rooms grouped in curious ways within a very irregular ground plan. One side offers three apartments that are larger in overall area and feature spacious rooms within them. In contrast, the other side of the same building suggests four narrow units laid out in the style of American "shotgun houses," where a series of rooms open into each other and run the depth of the house, from front to back. The combination of generous living spaces and spare ones in a single complex suggests that the wealthy and the poor lived next door to each other.

Grander homes for the very affluent also existed—three of these, built side by side, have been excavated south of the Panathenaic Way, where it leads past the Agora. Like the apartment block, these linked houses are of different dimensions, but all suggest a level of comfort far beyond the ordinary. The main dwelling is the most luxurious; it surrounds a central courtyard with an internal colonnade that in all likelihood supported a balcony from which a second colonnade extended to the edge of a pitched roof. This roof was open at the center, allowing light and rainwater to reach the unsheltered midsection of the court below. One room in the house featured an elaborate floor mosaic. Similar residences excavated at other sites in Greece were plastered inside, their walls painted in red, yellow, black, or white applied in linear patterns, so the walls of this house may have had similar decoration, although no trace of it survives. Houses to either side of this main residence had fewer rooms and lacked colonnades in their open courtyards.

One room in the main residence was reserved for a rare form of entertainment known from Athenian history and literature: that room is called the *andron*. It is identifiable by its large size and by a raised platform against its outer walls—a platform intended to hold couches where men reclined during dinner parties. These parties, called *symposia* (banquets), were one of the few ways that Athenian men could display wealth and influence in a private setting. The normal channels of social competition included taking a prominent part in public ceremonies and the assembly, and giving costly votive offerings to the gods. Athenian homes were hidden from view behind anonymous walls, and even the wealthiest men dressed in what amounted to a uniform, a single sheet of cloth wrapped around the body in various ways. The symposium was a unique opportunity to display the interior of the house, its abundant stores of foods and wines, and the quality of its tableware. The wealth and status of the host would be revealed by these things, and confirmed by the prominence of his invited guests and the nature of the entertainment he offered during the evening.

The symposium was a form of entertainment restricted to men, although women played various parts. Family slaves—both male and female—served the guests, and female entertainers of various sorts were also likely to be included. Women who performed music on the double-shafted recorder or the lyre were a standard form of entertainment. Much information about symposia comes from the decorations on drinking cups used at the banquets, and many survive today. Images on these shallow, bowl-like vessels with twin handles and a pedestal base suggest the way that a party might develop. Flute-girls and female acrobats are often shown in transparent robes or stark naked. Sexual activity between the guests and the entertainers—or among the guests themselves—was often depicted. The evening ended with a sexually charged dance between male and female performers. Since drinking wine played a big part in these evening-long parties, some guests became so drunk they had to be carried home by slaves.

Erotic art, which the paintings that depict symposia sometimes are, is often more about fantasy than reality, so it is risky to assume that the cups represent the norm of Athenian banqueting. The situation is complicated by the fact that the symposium's feast honored the god of wine, Dionysos. The formal part of the evening began with each guest pouring a wine offering to the god. Drinking, euphoria, incapacity, and sex were all parts of his portfolio, and while scenes on these cups suggest that things got out of hand at real Athenian parties, those scenes may actually represent attributes of the god brought to life in ideal revelers. Customary worship of Dionysos may have mandated these seemingly extemporaneous and excessive elements of the symposium; in other words, rather than being unscripted, these parties may have been formulaic, their excesses more symbolic than real.

The most famous and complete representation of a symposium known was created by Plato in his dialogue the *Symposium*. It tells the story of a group of friends gathered at the house of Agathon, who has just won a very important prize in the annual Greek dramatic festival (see chapter 4). That festival, like the symposium itself, honored Dionysos, so the god's presence and influence is doubled in Plato's highly fictionalized description of events. At the beginning of the banquet, the waiting flute-girls are sent away, and the men agree not to drink to excess, in part because many of them are already hung over from revelry the night before, but also so that they can engage in a philosophical conversation about the nature of love. Their conversation includes a lot of flirtatious byplay among the various participants. Late in the evening, Socrates's pupil and the sometime Athenian traitor, Alcibiades, comes in already drunk. His arrival changes the tone of the party, deepening and complicating its conversation about love, as Alcibiades describes his own boyhood crush on Socrates and how the philosopher reacted to his attempts at seduction. What began as a discussion of love ends with a tribute to the philosopher, extolling the love of what is good, true, beautiful, and permanent. At the same time, Plato's dialogue becomes a more and more complex conversation about the character and attributes of the god Dionysos and his links to philosophy.

Greek religion, especially the worship of Dionysos, is very foreign to modern sensibilities, so it is hard to know exactly what representations of the symposia—whether on vases or in Plato's dialogue—might have meant to the Athenians who practiced them. Our view of key components of the Dionysian complex is markedly different from that of the ancient Greeks. First, we do not typically associate religion with eroticism or drunkenness, although scholars recognize that Judaism, Christianity, and Islam all share some traditions in which erotic writing and drunken ecstasy turn into mystical praise of God. For the Greeks, the drug of choice was wine, though opiates were sometimes available. Most moderns consider drug use, like sex, to be recreational—its purpose is pleasure, and the context of its consumption or use is typically secular. Among the ancient Greeks, the context of drug use was explicitly religious. The symposium honored Dionysos, so drinking—and the altered state of consciousness it could create—should also be considered under the rubric of religion. Again, skepticism might lead us to think differently, but it is worth considering the other options. Mind-altering drugs in ancient cultures were relatively scarce, so the experiences they produced were uncommon and more often ritualized and set in a sacred context. The experiences of euphoria and altered or transcendent insight were cultivated and valued. In this light, the drunken revelers in Plato's *Symposium* become far more meaningful. There the philosopher—who is usually a super-rational figure associated with the bright light of day—takes on a nighttime persona. Like the ecstatic worshipper of the god, his goal is knowledge hidden in darkness

The ancient Greeks had no difficulty remembering another connection that many moderns find hard to grasp, namely, the association of eroticism with procreation. Modern sexuality is often playful and typically seeks to avoid pregnancy. Ancient sexuality—and the gods like Dionysos and Aphrodite who presided over it—was linked not just to sexual pleasure but to reproduction. Gods with an erotic portfolio were always interested in the product of copulation, not just the procedure. That is why ancient symbols of love, like the Greek Eros or the Roman Cupid, were children. Sex and babies went together in ancient thought, and so young children could serve as sexual symbols. Like all ancient societies, Greece was well aware that success in every area of life depended on the fertility of both the human community and the fields and flocks. In ancient Mesopotamia and many other civilizations in West Asia, fertility was the responsibility of a female deity, called Ishtar or Innana, among many other names. For the Greeks, fertility in the guise of sexual potency was personified by males as well as females.

Dionysus was the god who looked after it, and the heroic founder of every lineage, community, or city was concerned with it. Its role was so important that the Agora, a political hotbed perhaps but not in any other sense a fertile place, featured an important area simply called the Herms, where male images represented only by heads and penises were clustered. Herms, with their accent on male potency, presided over all sorts of significant places.

The symposium was always the privilege of a few wealthy men in each generation. The scattered houses uncovered by excavators over the last two centuries show great variety in the domestic circumstances of Athenians, sometimes revealing great disparities of wealth and privilege between neighbors. Despite this diversity, Athenian housing as a whole reflects a few core principles: most houses had interior courtyards whose open spaces seem to be the focal point for structures that turned inward rather than out toward the street; their rooms come in a variety of shapes and sizes (the footprint for every house excavated today reveals some degree of irregularity); and there are few right angles in any of the plans—odd rooms and sharp corners are found in most structures.

If all of ancient Athens could be excavated like Pompeii or the Roman port city of Ostia, it would be possible to see how these scattered fragments fit together into an urban whole. That is impossible, of course, but from these common characteristics we can guess what the residential parts of the city were like during the fifth century. Houses fit into the urban grid like pieces in a puzzle, and so their internal structures typically reflect the organization of the whole. House building and urban planning share similar principles. During the first half of the nineteenth century, for example, American house plans were commonly rectilinear and symmetrical; they matched a street grid that was equally regular and geometric. At the end of that century, developers began to build asymmetrical houses, and street plans in new communities became more meandering.

A rectilinear house with square sides and a fixed structure suggests, though it does not require, a city of even blocks and uniform streets. Irregular floor plans like the ones revealed in the excavated dwellings of ancient Athens suggest something different. An entire city made up of buildings of this kind would probably be a hodgepodge. Since there is no hint of an organizing grid within the houses, there is little likelihood that the streets outside met at right angles, or that neighborhoods had any visible order, either physical or social. We know that rich and poor lived side by side; they shared the same streets, and sometimes the same apartment block, yet they enjoyed very different levels of comfort. Whether luxurious or humble, all Athenian houses lay along narrow and twisting streets with occasional straight stretches and random widenings.

Walking along these streets would have been dull, since there was nothing to see but featureless walls with locked doors that revealed little about the homes and courtyards inside. An occasional open shop might provide some variety. Streets with one-story structures would be bathed in natural light, but blocks with two-story buildings on both sides would sit in nearly perpetual shadow. It would have been easy to become lost in Athens, were it not for the fact that during the day the Acropolis was visible from almost anywhere. On a moonless night, of course, a stranger would have had little chance of finding his way. Wandering by chance into the Agora or suddenly stepping out into the wide Panathenaic Way might have been his only hope for orientation.

4

On the Perimeter

Just up the slope from the Agora—and visible from many places within it—was the Hephaisteion, a temple to the craftsman of the gods, the lame Hephaistos, husband of Aphrodite. Hephaistos played a major part in Greek literature. In the *Iliad,* Homer described him at work forging armor for the Greek hero Achilles. Excavations on the slopes of the little mound that elevates the temple have uncovered remains of the forges of metalworkers for whom the god of fire and craftsmanship held special significance. That association was reinforced by the temple's proximity to the craftsmen's quarters or Kerameikos. Hephaistos and Athena were both adept craftspeople. All proper females were expected to be skillful weavers, and Athena was no exception. The ritual that began the weaving of Athena's peplos occurred at the center of the Kerameikos, during the Chalkeia, a festival dedicated to both gods.

The cult of Hephaistos also held political importance, for while the clever, hardworking smith may have been the profile of the god known to every Greek, what especially mattered to Athenians was the role he played in the founding of their city. This role was celebrated on the Acropolis, of course, but the political power conferred by the myth of Athenian self-generation meant that the Agora was also a proper place to commemorate his role as founder. Like the statues of the tyrant slayers Harmodius and Aristogeiton, the Hephaisteion made a political statement.

The Hephaisteion was begun in the middle of the fifth century, but it remained unfinished until sometime near the end of the century. Though the sculptural decoration on the building was similar in placement and structure to that of the Parthenon, it was less interesting, and it was never finished. The sides of the building visible from the Agora were completely

The Temple of Hephaistos.

decorated with sculptures, while the sides turned away were not. On the east, ten metopes recorded the labors of the god Herakles; these were complemented by others representing the labors of yet another mythical Athenian hero, Theseus. These latter scenes are so prominent that the building has often been labeled as a temple of Theseus rather than one dedicated to Hephaistos. A frieze on one side of a high outer wall of the cult chamber shows the gods observing an epic battle; the frieze on the other side depicts the conventional battle of centaurs and Lapiths.

Though the pediments of the building are well preserved, the pedimental sculptures were removed long ago and have always been more a subject of archaeological conjecture than anything else. During the Agora excavations, scattered bits of recovered sculpture have been persuasively associated with the temple, and though the pediments have long been bare, they are not entirely without evidence of a sculptural program. Cuttings in their floors have been carefully recorded, measured, and analyzed. Working with evidence from these cuttings and the scattered fragments, archaeologists have hazarded re-creations of the pedimental groups that ancient Athenians would have seen. One end of the building has been conceived as a celebration of the god Herakles. This seems out of keeping with the dedication of the temple to Hephaistos, but it does complement the metopes that represent this god's labors. In the reconstructed pediment, Herakles, who has earned immortality through his labors, is received on Mount Olympus by Zeus, Athena, and others. Evidence for the other pediment is even less clear—its sculptures would probably have had something to do with Hephaistos, but so far cuttings from the pediment floor fail to tell their secrets.

Like the Parthenon, the Hephaisteion was converted to a Christian church during the seventh century. This conversion affected its interior, which was originally divided into three sections, one of which did not communicate with the other two. To create the unbroken open space that Christian worship required, remodelers broke through the wall that separated the two divided chambers and created a new entrance. At the western end of the building, they widened the entry and built an apse into the original porch. The outside of the building was hardly affected, though at some point the cornice above one half of the building's front pediment fell down.

From the Agora, the Panathenaic Way led north toward the city walls. Near the point where it reached the ancient fortifications, it passed through the Kerameikos. Excavations in that area have revealed the exact outlines of the Panathenaic Way, the Dipylon gate that stood at the end of it, and the nearby Sacred Gate, where the road to the important shrine at Eleusis left the city. Traces of the Pompeion, the site where the Panathenaic procession assembled, have also been uncovered and can be seen by visitors to this site. Little remains, unfortunately, of the houses, shops, and work areas that gave the quarter its name and that gave Athens one of its most dynamic industries for local consumption as well as widespread export.

Even today, ancient Athenian pottery, the product of the ceramic workshops, is not in short supply; it is on view—often in mind-numbing abundance—in most major museums throughout the world. Despite this plentiful evidence that Athens produced luxury pieces, the industry was not primarily geared to producing items of aesthetic interest. Pottery was one of the main arts of the Neolithic period: fired clay vessels first appeared in the

Mediterranean sometime in the eighth millennium BCE, and production and use spread with the other technologies that supported domestication and cultivation. Pottery was an essential part of everyday life, and most of what the Athenian workshops produced was consumer ware meant to be useful and durable. Potters produced toys for children, like rattles, toy chariots and horses, dolls, and game pieces. They made baby bottles and booster chairs, as well as chamber pots and portable toilet seats for people of all ages. For the kitchen they produced amphorae to carry water and pots to boil it in, as well as grates for the fire, double boilers, and portable ovens. They produced plates, cups, bowls, and dishes for everyday use and vessels for all sorts of religious rites. They mass-produced votive statues of favored gods and goddesses that were within the price range of virtually any worshipper. In popular shrines, these objects were so abundant that the overflow had to be buried periodically in specially dug pits or tossed down abandoned wells.

Collectible pieces were distinct from these everyday products of the potters' industry. High-quality Athenian wares look more or less the same in outward appearance; they were made from highly processed clay that produced finely textured surfaces, and they were fired at high temperatures that created an extremely strong and durable fabric. Despite that strength, pots did inevitably break. Bits of broken pottery were so common that they were used for casting votes of ostracism, and they were so durable that modern archaeologists rely on them to give an indication of the presence of artifacts beneath pottery-littered soils. Once excavation begins, pottery types are the predominant daily monitor of the age of a site's layers.

The color spectrum in high-quality Athenian vases was limited to two primary shades: a rich terracotta red and a dense and subtly lustrous black. White pigment was sometimes used as a ground or added to the surface of a pot to create detail. The quality wares of Attica were not the inventions of Athenian potters; rather, the potters relied on techniques pioneered during the eighth century BCE in nearby Corinth. Corinthian potters of that era began to decorate their vases using black pigment to create dark figures on the lighter ground of the vase. Figures were often etched to show highlights that defined surface detail, like the folds in robes or outlined eyes and beards. Vases with this kind of decoration are called "black-figured." Sometime during the sixth century, Corinthian potters improved the graphic effect of their paintings by coloring the unpainted part of the vase with a rich red glaze. This glaze hid the pale surface of the clay they used and gave the pot a more uniform luster and starker color contrast.

During the sixth century, Athenian potters successfully imitated Corinthian techniques. For a variety of reasons, the market shifted away from Corinth; that city ceased to be the biggest exporter of quality wares, and Athens took the lead. In the last quarter of the sixth century, Athenian potters made a striking innovation of their own. It occurred to someone that painting dark figures on a light ground did not allow much room for expression, since it reversed the real-world distribution of light and shadow. Instead of scratching highlights into shaped areas of paint, decorators reversed the process, allowing the dark pigment to stand for shadow and the lighter clay to represent light. Then, instead of applying paint in blocks and retouching with awls or etching tools, they used a brush to create shadows, an innovation that improved the subtlety of representations. With this new way of approaching the surface of the vase, painters were able to create a visual art of remarkable complexity and adaptability. It now seemed that anything and everything could be represented on a vase by a skillful painter who had sufficient imagination.

In their images, vase painters represented themselves at work, or carpenters hammering, or shoemakers cutting leather. They showed foundry men casting bronze and sculptors making statues. A great deal of what we understand about daily life in the ancient world has been extrapolated from scenes on Athenian vases. Paintings were by no means limited to scenes from daily life. More important vases might feature paintings of mythological scenes or vignettes from Greek tragedy and epic, and images of the gods were very common.

Generally speaking, the language of representation in all the arts had many shared characteristics and qualities. Though the vase painter's technique was different from that of the sculptor, the stone carver, or the painter of canvases, the commonplaces of representation in one art form closely resembled those in another. This essential continuity among the arts is very useful in the overall effort to understand the broad spectrum of fifth-century Greek art. Ancient writers suggest that painting in the fifth century was very beautiful and widely admired. People saw important paintings by master artists on display in public places. Almost no Greek painting survives today, so scholars turn to vase painting for clues about this important and influential art form. Vase painting is also useful in cases like that of the Hephaisteion pediments, where all that survives of a sculptural installation is bits and pieces of worked marble and carved sockets in the pediment floor. Representations on vases depicting the arrival of Herakles on Mount Olympus allow scholars to guess with a little more certainty how the scene might have been displayed on the building.

Some vase types were associated with particular events. The winners of the Panathenaic games received their prizes in special vases, and symposium guests enjoyed their wine in vessels of a particular kind. Pottery also marked particular moments in daily life: the major landmark in a woman's life was her wedding, and the domestic object most closely associated with weddings is a specially shaped oil flask called a *lekythos*. Though these came in many sizes and in various forms, the most widely used *lekythos* was a slim, footed jar with an extended cylindrical body, abrupt shoulders, and a narrow neck. It was usually about a foot high and often had handles attached to the neck. Figurative painting was common on the body of the flask, which was meant to hold a small amount of olive oil to be used as an ointment for the skin. The *lekythos* that symbolized a bride on her wedding day was also used in other ways; when girls or women died before marriage, a *lekythos* was often buried with them. Larger *lekythoi* might even serve as grave markers.

While potters worked inside the walls of Athens, the name Kerameikos also designates an area beyond the walls. This was not a working neighborhood but a cemetery. The ancient Greeks believed that the safe burial of bodies could occur only beyond the sacred limits of the city, but in order for relatives to reach family graves for ceremonies of commemoration, they tried to group burials as close to home as possible. Burial was another of the ways in which Athenian families displayed their wealth, and like every other public expression of prestige, burials fell at various times under political control. From the eleventh century until the eighth century BCE, graves of the wealthy were often marked by large, elaborately decorated terracotta vases. During the sixth century, ceramic monuments became less sought after, and stone monuments replaced them. Before the democratic reforms of Cleisthenes were enacted, rich families spent lavishly on funerals and on monuments for their dead. These monuments were likely to be quite expensive when they were commissioned to commemorate young nobles who died in warfare or young women who died before marriage. Under Cleisthenes, the rules were tightened, and monuments were limited to those that could be produced by a team of ten laborers over three days of work. This restriction led to the widespread adoption of simpler grave markers, of which many examples can be seen in the Kerameikos Museum. During the fourth century, laws restricting the cost of monuments were relaxed; tombs from that era, massed along the Street of the Tombs in the Kerameikos, testify again to the wealth of aristocratic families. War dead were honored at public expense by monuments and annual commemorations.

Like the symposium, death involved a good deal of private ritual. Preparing the body for burial was typically the work of family members and household slaves. Corpses were washed and anointed, dressed in new clothes, and placed in a coffin. A coin was placed in their mouths to give to the god who ferried the newly dead across the River Styx. The body lay in the entryway to the house until the morning after death. At this moment, the ceremony changed from private ritual to public display. Once the corpse left the house, males of the family carried it through the streets of the city to its final resting place outside the walls. A woman carrying a *lekythos* headed the funeral procession. Behind her came the men in gray or black clothing. There were no professional funeral directors or embalmers, but professional mourners—experts at wailing and weeping—were often added to the procession. Flute-girls also took part. Athenians practiced both inhumation and cremation; in both cases the body was honored with libations of oil and wine. A libation is an offering that is poured onto the ground as a symbolic form of nourishment, in this instance for the dead, though they were also common offerings to the gods. After the graveside ceremony, mourners returned home to a funeral feast. The corpse was a source of pollution, so mourners needed to be cleansed before they were able to participate. The house where the death occurred—and where the corpse was prepared—required a ritual bath of seawater and herbs to set it right.

Athenians have generally preferred the north slope of the Acropolis, which enjoys some relief from the summer sun, thanks to the shadow cast by the promontory. The south slope of the Acropolis is brutal in midsummer, but during the colder months, its warmth can be very welcome. Located on the sunny south slope and sheltered from the north wind, the Theater of

The Theater of Dionysos, with the Acropolis in the distance, 1869. William James
Stillman, photographer. (Fine Arts Library, Harvard University)

Dionysos was a comfortable place to sit during the all-day theater performances held in honor of the god. Climate may have played a major part in
the choice of locations, but the Theater of Dionysos may also owe its location
to an accident. In the mid-sixth century BCE, the people of a small town on
the borders of Attic territory asked to join the Athenian community. The
fruits of this new alliance included an ancient wooden statue of the god
Dionysos. Once the alliance was concluded, this statue was carried in procession to Athens and installed in a small shrine on the south slope of the
hill. This was hardly a place of honor for the newly imported image, but the
god made the best of it. From this small beginning, one of the most celebrated features of Athenian worship developed.

March, when the coldest days of winter are over and the ground is ready for tilling, was sacred to the god. Sometime around the tenth of the month, Athens held a parade and sacrifice in his honor. The processional included impersonators of the original servants of the god, the half-man, half-animal figures called satyrs. Songs were sung and little skits were performed to recall the story of Dionysos's birth and rise to power. As in all sacrifices, the meat of the sacrificial animals was shared with the crowd, and, of course, the god of wine could hardly be worshipped without drinking. Like the private symposium that honored the god, this public display, called the Dionysia, must have included a good deal of officially sanctioned public drunkenness and wanton behavior.

In the final third of the sixth century BCE, the satyrs, the skits, and the singing were organized into something more formal and complicated. According to Greek tradition, in the year 534, Thespis—who has given actors their formal name, thespians—recast the entertainment in ways that we recognize as dramatic. A principal actor played a part or multiple parts, and a group of singers responded. From this beginning, the tradition of the Greek theater, with its chorus representing an anonymous crowd and its principal actors representing the heroes and gods of the Greeks, came gradually to maturity.

The main developers of Greek tragedy were the trio of playwrights still known to us today: Aeschylus, Sophocles, and Euripides. Aeschylus was born just a few years after Thespis made his mark, and he lived until the middle of the fifth century. Sophocles, born a quarter century after Aeschylus, outlived him by nearly fifty years. His lifetime of nearly ninety years spanned almost the entire fifth century. Euripides, the last of the great tragic poets, was born in 480 BCE and died in 406 BCE, the same year as Sophocles. Though these three poets were very different in political points of view, they were alike in their handling of language and dramatic characterization, as well as in their understanding of the underlying structure of the genre that they together perfected and epitomized.

Under their guidance, Greek tragedy displayed a number of common characteristics. Traditional legends and stories formed the basis for most plays. While we are able to read and reread their printed texts or see their plays in multiple performances, each of these dramatists had to assume that his audience was seeing a play for the first and perhaps only time. Rooting their work in traditional stories helped the audience follow along. A second and perhaps more substantial reason for their choice of well-known material was the structure of the tragedy itself; only certain story patterns fit the underlying themes that guided their dramas.

Generally speaking, Greek tragedies have a moral or spiritual dilemma of some sort at their core. That dilemma is almost never clear to the characters in the play until a certain amount of action—often of an irrevocable kind— has unfolded. The dilemma at the heart of Sophocles's *Oedipus the King* is a paradoxical obligation that Oedipus must accept: as king of Thebes, he must do everything in his power to rid his city of a spiritual pollution brought on by the murder of the city's former king. Every Athenian, indeed every Greek, would have understood that obligation. What Oedipus does not know, however, is that he himself is the murderer, and that the victim was his own father. The more obsessed Oedipus becomes with investigating the crime and punishing the wrongdoer, the more he is forced to confront terrible truths about his own identity.

In Aeschylus's play *The Libation Bearers,* the hero, Orestes, faces an equally sinister paradox. A divine oracle requires him to avenge his father's murder, but as he learns more about the perpetrator of that crime, he comes to realize that in order to avenge his father, he has to murder his mother. To avenge a parent's death, he must himself murder a parent. Aeschylus's play about Orestes came at the center of a trilogy of plays. Greek tragic presentations often involved a trio of plays followed by a farcical satyr play, but only one trilogy survives: the cycle by Aeschylus called *The Oresteia.*

The hero of tragedy did not act alone, nor was the hero always a man. Even though women played a very subordinate role in the social and political world of the ancient Greeks, living their lives largely segregated from men, strong female characters were objects of fascination onstage. The *Oresteia* is set in motion by King Agamemnon, Greek commander at Troy, but it is his wife and queen, Clytemnaestra, who is the most compelling presence onstage and the driving force of all the action in the cycle of plays. In the *Eumenides,* the third play of that sequence, the goddess Athena and female deities charged with avenging Clytemnaestra's murder occupy center stage. The sorceress Medea, heroine of plays by a number of dramatists and best known to us from Euripides's portrayal, is among the most complex and dynamic characters created by any ancient author. Hecuba, wife of

Priam and mother of the Trojan hero Hector, was also a dramatic force and focus. Even though dramatic performances gave starring roles to legendary women, the actors who portrayed these characters were always men. Prominent women attended dramatic performances, but it is unclear whether this privilege extended to the majority of Athenian women.

The major character in tragedy, whether a man or a woman, interacted not only with other masked principal actors, but also with a troupe of performers known as the chorus. Onstage, the chorus was headed by a figure who stood somewhere between principal actor and anonymous chorus member. Often the chorus spoke all at once, but sometimes it was useful for a spokesperson to represent its point of view. This dramatic role belonged to a character called the *chorephaios* or chorus leader. Offstage, the play was in the hands of the *choregos,* who was the impresario or producer. We associate ancient dramas with their authors, but in fifth-century Athens, that association was secondary, as it is in modern filmmaking, where directors and producers overshadow writers. Athenians had a similar view: they recognized and honored the producer of the play first, and the author second. The choregos was necessarily a wealthy and prominent man who served his city by underwriting the production of a drama to honor the festival of Dionysos. The choregos hired the playwright, enlisted the principal actors, chorus members, and musicians, and rehearsed the play.

While these acts seem like commendable public service and an undying contribution to the artistic heritage of Athens, admiration of the plays and those who underwrote them was not universal. As Plutarch noted in *De Gloria Atheniensium,*

> A Spartan not ineptly remarked that the Athenians were making a great mistake in wasting their energies on amusements, that is to say, in lavishing on the theatre what would pay for great fleets and would support armies in the field. For, if we reckon up the cost of each tragedy, the Athenian people will be seen to have spent more on productions of *Bacchae, Phoenissae, Oedipuses,* and *Antigones,* and the woes of Medea and Electra, than they spent in fighting for their supremacy and for their liberty against the barbarians. For the generals often ordered their men to bring along uncooked rations when they led them forth to battle; and the commanders, I can swear, after providing

barley-meal and a relish of onions and cheese for the rowers, would embark them on the triremes. But the men who paid for the choruses gave the choristers eels and tender lettuces, roast beef and marrow, and pampered them for a long time while they were training their voices and living in luxury. The result for the defeated *choregos* was to be held in contumely and ridicule; but to the victors belonged a tripod, which was, as Demetrius says, not a votive offering to commemorate their victory, but a last offering from their wasted livelihood, an empty memorial of their vanished estates. Such are the returns paid by the poetic art and nothing more splendid ever comes from it.

Whether or not it was fed on eels and lettuce, the chorus was always made up of young Athenian men who, in every tragedy, played roles distinctly unlike themselves. In *Oedipus,* they play citizens of Thebes ravaged by the plague. In *The Libation Bearers,* they are the serving women of Agamemnon's household. In Euripides's *Bacchae,* they are female worshippers of the god Dionysos. The most characteristic speeches of the chorus were odes or hymns. The ancient chorus sang and danced; its odes were divided into passages called "strophes" that alternated with passages called "antistrophes," meaning "movement" and "countermovement," and these names suggest that the chorus danced back and forth across the stage while chanting or singing its hymns to the gods. The Greek audience must have been familiar with this pattern, but audiences today have a hard time with it, and modern producers are forced to do all sorts of things to adapt the chorus to contemporary taste and understanding.

While the hero or heroine at the center of the drama is falling into the typical downward spiral of tragic action, the chorus becomes alienated from him or her. This alienation leads the chorus to focus its attention increasingly on the gods. Though Aristotle paid little attention to the chorus, its distinct plot trajectory is one of the great constants of Greek tragedy. It is one of the principal keys to understanding what the plays were about and how they contributed to the celebration of the god Dionysos. In *Oedipus Rex,* for example, the chorus begins by looking toward the king as its main ally in battling a plague that ravages the city. As the play progresses, however, the slow unraveling of Oedipus's self-confidence becomes more acute, causing the chorus to turn away from him and begin to put its trust in the power and goodwill of the gods. In most plays, the pressure of events acting upon their own internal contradictions proves too much for the heroes of tragedy. As these heroes crumble and fall, the chorus abandons faith in them and rediscovers faith, however challenging, in the god.

Scholars have related this plotline to the patterns of Greek sacrificial ritual. The chorus represents the community for whose benefit the sacrifice is performed. The tragic hero is the fictional representation of the sacrificial animal. As he experiences disgrace, dismemberment, or death, he becomes the victim. In the Athenian theater, the space set aside for the chorus included a functional altar. So while the chorus represented a community of worshippers pretending to offer a symbolic sacrifice, they were at the same time celebrants in a genuine sacrificial ritual. Like all the great communal activities of the Athenians, and the ancient Greeks in general, the tragic theater was religious first and foremost, and only secondarily an artistic performance.

Aristotle, who described Greek tragedy in his *Poetics,* was not very interested in religion. He thought that the tragic hero and the plot that revolved around him were the elements of the drama that mattered. In analyzing tragedy, he paid no attention to its role in celebrating Dionysos, and little to the distinctive role of the chorus. He may have liked the *Oedipus Rex* in particular, because Sophocles's hero is a rationalist and a riddle solver, two traits that Aristotle recognized and valued in himself. Whatever the reason, Aristotle represented Greek tragedy as a triumph of rational investigation and an unmasking of the fatal contradictions its heroes are forced to confront. It was not until the nineteenth century that these prejudices were exposed. The German philosopher Friedrich Nietzsche countered Aristotle by rethinking the role of the chorus: he concluded that the plays were a struggle between two points of view. Only one of these, the one that Aristotle gave exclusive attention to, was represented by the principal actors. Nietzsche associated it with the god Apollo, who values reason and clarity. The chorus that Aristotle ignored represents the dark and irrational concerns of the god Dionysos, who presides over the mysteries of sex, euphoria, and death. In Nietzsche's view, tragedy forced these two contending points of view into a revealing dialogue.

Built on the sunny south slope of the Acropolis, and useful only for daylight performances, the Theater of Dionysos may seem like an odd place to

The Theater of Dionysos.

celebrate the dark, obscure, and irrational concerns of the god. But the plays began at dawn in semidarkness and ended as the sun was going down. In the Athenian theater, there would have been no escaping the fact that Dionysian darkness encircles and embraces Apollonian light. Other structural details of the theater, which separate it from our own stages, also accommodated the peculiar traits of Greek tragedy. The Theater of Dionysos was not the first Athenian locale where plays were staged. Like so many other parts of Athenian public life, the theater had begun in the all-purpose open space of the Agora. As the plays grew longer and the staging infrastructure became more elaborate, performances there came to an end. Even after the stage moved to its new location, theater practice continued to change and with it the structure of the theater building. Though fixed in its new location, the theater was remodeled many times, and later structures repeatedly overwrote older ones.

The principal excavation of the theater began at the end of the nineteenth century under the supervision of German archaeologist Wilhelm Dörpfeld.

Like Schliemann, in whose excavations at Troy Dörpfeld took part, the Athenian excavator disregarded material he considered of secondary importance and focused on what mattered to him—the fifth-century theater of Aeschylus, Sophocles, and Euripides. The theater he teased out from among the remains of what is substantially a fourth-century ruin with later additions remains the subject of scholarly controversy. Some of its basic elements are clear, but others remain obscure. One feature that is agreed upon is the space set aside for the chorus. The earliest identifiable choral space was a flat circle with a surface of beaten earth outlined by a ring of stones. This structure took its form from a staple of rural agriculture that was familiar to every Greek: at harvest time, farmers brought their crops to areas exactly like this, called threshing floors. On these flat, circular spaces, flails or the hooves of oxen separated the ripe grain from the stalks that supported it, then freed it of its husks. Drawing on this familiarity, the chorus used a similar space to perform the odes and dances that celebrated the god of fertility and abundance.

The chorus remained onstage throughout the performance, but the principal actors came and went as their parts required, so they needed a place offstage where they would be hidden from view. Since most of these characters were kings and queens, their place of retreat was represented as a palace, though at first it was anything but regal. In early performances, the principal actors sheltered in a temporary shed or even a tent at the back of the dance floor. In this era, the audience was accommodated on impermanent benches made of wood. The move away from the Agora had been prompted not only by the wish to create a more permanent and suitable performance space, but also to replace temporary stands that had at some point collapsed and caused injury and loss of life. The permanent theater faced a hillside where the audience were accommodated on benches more solidly anchored in the earth.

Today visitors to Athens will see a very different theater from the first one on the site. Its orientation is the same, and its constituent parts are the same, but important changes have taken place. The chorus's space has been transformed: what was once a circle traced on the earth has become a semicircle paved in marble, and the tent or shed to which principal actors once retreated is now represented by a large, permanent stone structure. Stone benches rise up the hillside, occasionally interrupted by aisles and fronted, on their lowest round, by throne-like chairs intended for the most distinguished members of the audience.

The part of the theater that is least understood and most stridently debated among scholars is the scenic backdrop behind the performance space. It is usually imagined as a stoa on a reduced scale that had significant additions at either end. The columns of a theatrical stoa are closer together than on other structures, and the colonnade, instead of opening directly into a building, stands before a blank stone wall pierced by an unknown number of doors. At each end this stoa extends toward the audience in two wing-like projections, rendering a stage setting that resembles a scaled-down version of the Stoa of Zeus in the Agora.

What was concealed behind this fictional colonnade is also a matter for speculation. It probably held dressing rooms for the actors and a place for them to wait for their entrances. It certainly held some kind of stage machinery. At the end of Euripides's *Medea,* the sorceress soars above her husband's head in a magic chariot. Ropes moved by some sort of mechanism must have held her in the air. In the *Poetics,* Aristotle insisted that the complexities of a tragic plot should never be resolved by a god descending magically onstage. A figure like this is still called a *deus ex machina*—a god from the (stage) machine—referring to the Greek and Roman practice of lowering actors on cables from above. It is also clear from the language of some plays that characters could appear on a rooftop, so there must have been both roof access and some kind of performance space above the colonnade.

The ruins of the Theater of Dionysos are easy to identify, but an equally substantial and important building that once stood next to it is hardly apparent at all. The Odeon of Pericles was a large, square, enclosed and roofed concert hall built in a four-year period beginning in 446 BCE. Because traces of the building are few, and because the ancient sources that describe it are confusing (if not themselves confused), its exact character and appearance are hard to imagine or reconstruct. The building fulfilled a number of purposes, some ceremonial and others quite pragmatic. As an *odeon,* its primary role was to house public performances and recitations of poetry, both new writing and well-loved classics. Lectures might also have been given there. The roof would have been supported by multiple rows of columns, so the interior space was by no means wide open. Sight lines would have been blocked from many angles, and it is likely that only a portion of it could be used effectively as a performance space. A stage or at least a dais would have elevated the performers. There may have been some form of seating—perhaps movable benches—for the audience.

The informal roles of the Odeon of Pericles were multiple: participants in the Panathenaic processional and other public ceremonials rehearsed there; the choruses of tragedy learned their lines and dance moves there; and props, such as they were, used for dramatic performances might have been kept in the Odeon. The city also used the building as a place to store the overflow of votive gifts made to temples on the Acropolis. In fulfilling these multiple and seemingly inconsistent roles, the Odeon was not unlike many other structures in the classical city. It was big, more or less without definition, and able to offer shelter from the rain, wind, and sun, so it became a general-purpose space that accommodated all sorts of activities.

5

Hellenistic and Roman Athens

Athens was at its most autonomous and most successful during the fifth century when its prominent role in resisting and, ultimately, defeating the Persian invaders catapulted it to leadership among Greek cities. As the century advanced, Athens leveraged its prominence among equals into a position of dominance over its neighbors, and transformed a system of alliances into a self-serving empire. Old allies became heavily taxed members of a regional confederacy with Athens at its head. As the foreign policy of the city expanded from a relatively narrow focus to a more ambitious scale, Athens stumbled.

The rise of Athens to imperial dominance within the Greek world was by no means uncontested. Sparta, a sometime ally but more frequent antagonist, assembled a coalition of willing partners in the Peloponnesos region of Greece to resist Athenian dominance. After a long truce ended in 431 BCE, the contending sides erupted in episodic open warfare lasting nearly to the end of the fifth century. The Peloponnesian War, chronicled by the great Athenian historian Thucydides, began as an asymmetrical conflict between Spartan-led land armies and Athenian naval forces. Sparta and her allies repeatedly invaded Athenian territory, and Athens raided coastal cities in the Peloponnesos. The Spartan goal was to starve out the Athenians by depriving them of access to the Attic countryside where their grain was harvested. These Spartan campaigns were typical of early warfare and lasted only about a month at a time. Their armies repeatedly returned home before much damage was done. Athenian freighters kept the city supplied during these brief periodic sieges while their warships harried enemy coasts.

Pericles was the mastermind behind this Athenian strategy. He counseled Athens to avoid direct engagement with the Spartan army. His plan was working in 430 BCE, when a plague began to infect the besieged city. Ancient statistics are notoriously hard to pin down, but Athens may have lost one-half to two-thirds of its manpower as a result. Pericles and his sons were victims, and leadership passed to men with different ideas of how to conduct the war. After ten years of inconclusive struggle, in 421 BCE both sides signed a treaty.

Five years later, hostilities broke out again. Though weakened by the manpower deficit created by endemic plague, Athens decided on a bold campaign, not against Sparta but against the island of Sicily. Sicily was home to a number of colonies planted by cities in the Greek mainland. It was rich in resources of all kinds, but especially in grain. The Athenian plan was to capture these resources for itself and turn Sicily into the granary of a new and larger empire. The brilliant but very controversial Alcibiades, who had long-standing ties to the enemy city of Sparta, was the most prominent of three men chosen to lead this invasion. Even before the fleet sailed, Alcibiades was accused of mutilating the Herms in the Agora. Whether he was guilty or, instead, the destruction was a plot to implicate him, the pressure of war forced Alcibiades to leave Athens before standing trial. When he arrived in Sicily, the judicial authorities called him back; rather than obey, he defected to the Spartans. The war, carried on by other Athenian commanders, ended in destruction of the Athenian fleet and the capture and enslavement of its armies.

This overwhelming failure should have foreshadowed the eclipse of Athens, but it did not. Having kept a fleet in reserve for just such a rainy day, Athens fought back. Meanwhile four hundred antidemocratic, rich, and noble Athenians seized control of the government. The fleet, again headed by the dizzyingly versatile Alcibiades, refused to join the oligarchic revolution and carried on the fight against the Spartans and their allies. The oligarchs were ousted and replaced by a democracy, and from 410 to 406 the Athenian military more than held its own. Alcibiades was driven from his command in 408, and left Athens for good. Meanwhile the Spartans selected as their warlord Lysander, a commander who understood how to coordinate naval and land-based forces. He mounted a blockade of the Athenian grain fleet coming from the Black Sea, forcing the Athenians into a winner-take-all engagement. This battle ended in a rout in which Athens lost nearly two hundred ships. Facing starvation brought on by a blockade it could not break,

Athens surrendered to Sparta in 403. Corinth and Thebes urged Sparta to level Athens and enslave its citizens, but Sparta resisted and instead incorporated the city, once again under dictatorial rule, into its own empire. Another democratic revolution followed, and within less than a decade Athens had joined other cities in opposing their Spartan conquerors.

Though historians have looked inward for the roots of the city's fourth-century decline, the more plausible reasons are external and international. It really was a fluke that the Greeks had been able to defeat the Persians—in numbers and resources, the Persians vastly overpowered the Greek alliance—but distance was the Persians' biggest enemy, aggravated by the technological superiority of Greek ships. Greece's winning strategy was to cut the Persians' supply chains and force them to retreat back to their base. This strategy succeeded in wars against an antagonist whose resources were remote, but when the enemy was closer at hand and better prepared militarily, the results were bound to be different.

During the fourth century BCE, King Philip of Macedon succeeded in uniting the northern Greek realm under a single kingship. Unification required a good deal of political savvy and no small amount of good luck. He fought enemies on multiple fronts, using diplomacy when possible and armed force when necessary. Finally, having consolidated control over a large contiguous kingdom in the north, he headed south to fight a Greek coalition. The battle of Chaeronea in 338 BCE pitted experienced professional Macedonian soldiers against Greek volunteers. A onetime hostage of the Greeks, Philip had carefully studied their characteristic fighting technique. Homer's *Iliad* had celebrated a kind of warfare that was little more than man-to-man combat multiplied across two armies. One soldier called out another across the battle lines and engaged him in a duel to the death. The cumulative result of all these clashes made up the balance of victory or defeat. Greek fighting in the recurrent intercity wars or in the campaign against the Persians was nothing like this; discipline and coordination were its keys, not individual valor. Courage was certainly called for, but it was the courage to hold a position, not the courage to step out of line and face a powerful opponent alone.

Real Greek armies fought in a tight formation called a phalanx. They marched toward the enemy as a coordinated block of troops several rows deep. Each man in the front ranks held a long spear pointed forward. This tactic ensured that the advancing edge of the phalanx bristled with spear points two or three times greater than the number of men in the first row. From the third or fourth row back, soldiers held their spears upright to avoid stabbing a man ahead as the phalanx jogged forward. Each soldier also held a shield, and the combined work of the shields was to create a barrier that protected all the ranks.

The Macedonian soldiers of Philip's youth also fought in the phalanx formation, but the king introduced a clever innovation: he gave his soldiers spears that were much longer than those used by the Greeks, and this simple change gave the Macedonian formations a disproportionate advantage. On the attack, their spear points reached the enemy and began to inflict wounds before the Greeks with their shorter spears could begin to counter. This small imbalance translated into an enormous strategic advantage, since the strongest and most experienced Greek soldiers were assigned to the front lines. The Macedonians killed these men before they were close enough to retaliate. As the front ranks crumbled, the weaker second and third ranks were left to fight on alone. Longer spears also meant that more spearheads would project from the front of the phalanx, increasing the chances that a spear deflected in one rank would find a target in another.

Two years after his success at Chaeronea, Philip was assassinated, and the political situation in Macedonia reverted to what it had been before his rise to power. The neighboring peoples he had conquered rebelled, and the Greeks, who considered the Macedonians barbarians, reassessed their options. The Eastern Mediterranean would certainly have gone back to the way it had been before Philip's rise to power, had it not been for his son Alexander. Though still an adolescent at the time of his father's death, and evidently estranged from him, Alexander was ready to step in and repair the damage. Indeed, he may have been preparing to step in even before his father's assassination. Near the end of his life, Philip repudiated his queen Olympias, Alexander's Greek mother, and took another wife more acceptable to his Macedonian supporters. This repudiation threatened Alexander's future and legitimacy, and Philip's assassination may have been carried out for his benefit, if not at his instigation.

Like his father, Alexander understood the complex tasks to be accomplished before his kingdom could become reunited. He began by killing his rivals at home; then he marched against rebellious neighbors and drove the fiercest and most fractious of them northward beyond the Danube. Neighbors to the immediate south were his next concern: heading south, in two weeks Alexander's soldiers covered more than two hundred miles in a forced march. They arrived before the walls of Thebes, where they met a large and well-disciplined force determined to protect the city. According to the historian Diodorus of Sicily, fighting went on all day, without either the Macedonians or the Thebans gaining the upper hand. Late in the day, Alexander's spies discovered that a small gateway had been left unguarded. When Alexander sent a detachment of troops through this gateway into the city, the Theban army broke ranks to protect their families inside the walls. In the narrow streets of the city, the defenders abandoned their formation. A garrison of Macedonian soldiers stationed in the city since Philip's victory in 338 left their citadel and joined the fight. When the two Macedonian forces linked up, they overwhelmed the disorganized Theban army and destroyed it. In the aftermath of this victory, Alexander's soldiers ran amok. Diodorus Siculus describes the scene in his *World History:*

> All the city was pillaged. Everywhere boys and girls were dragged into captivity as they wailed piteously the names of their mothers. . . . In the end, when night finally intervened, the houses had been plundered and children and women and aged persons who had fled into the temples were torn from sanctuary and subjected to outrage without limit. Over 6,000 Thebans perished, more than 30,000 were captured, and the amount of property plundered was unbelievable. (Diodorus Siculus, *World History* 17:14.1, C. Bradford Wells trans.)

The pillaging of Thebes may have been the work of soldiers on a rampage, but most authorities consider it a deliberate action on Alexander's part. Conscious that the rest of the Greece was waiting to see what happened at Thebes, the Macedonian leader displayed a power and determination that could not be misinterpreted or ignored. In the cold light of day he ordered his soldiers to burn Thebes to the ground. Only the temples of the gods and the house of the fifth-century poet Pindar were to be spared. The effect of this demonstration of brutal resolve was all that Alexander could have wished for. The rebellion collapsed, and the Greek cities renewed their vows of obedience.

For the Athenians, Alexander was a much easier pill to swallow than his father. Philip had been a Greek hostage in Thebes for ten years, and so he was Hellenized, a characteristic that was reflected in his choice of Olympias, from a Greek royal family, to be his wife. Alexander was Olympias's son, which made him less of a barbarian in Greek eyes. He was also extremely well educated; his father hired the Athenian philosopher Aristotle to be his son's tutor. Though he quarreled with his tutor as he had with his father, Alexander retained the style, opinions, and language of a cultivated Athenian.

Alexander spent little time in the Greek mainland. In 335 he set off with an army of some thirty thousand troops, primarily Macedonian but with a significant contingent of Greek fighters, to conquer Asia. It is not entirely clear what he had in mind. Popular notions of Alexander are based on his total record of conquest, which seems to reflect an underlying aim to bring the entire eastern world under his control. In the minds of Greeks— with whom he shared a language, a culture, and perhaps a worldview— Alexander's first goal must have resonated in a more specific way. The power in western Asia that Alexander first set out to confront and conquer was the Persian Empire. Greeks could only think of that empire as the enemy who had threatened them repeatedly during the fifth century. And although this was the titanic enemy they once successfully repelled, the Greeks had never been able to turn their defensive success into a campaign of aggression and attack the Persians in their home territory. Alexander's plan to make this his immediate purpose must have inspired both admiration and jealousy, but it was not a campaign that Athens could ignore.

Once Alexander began his conquests, neither Athens nor the Greek peninsula would ever be what it had been before. Alexander's campaign against Persia was successful, and this success was soon followed by the liberation of Egypt from its Persian overlords and a replacement of its traditional rulers by Alexander and his heirs. A line of pharoahs with Egyptian names like Ramses and Amenhotep was replaced by a dynasty with names like Ptolemy and Cleopatra. Though these men and women seem quintessentially Egyptian to us, they were not ethnic Egyptians but noble Macedonians. Cleopatra shared her name with the wife for whom King Philip repudiated Alexander's Greek mother. Ptolemy was the name of one of Alexander's most important generals.

From Egypt, Alexander campaigned still farther eastward and reached the borders of India before turning back to Persia. In each of the countries he conquered, he replaced native rulers with Macedonian ones, and—more significantly and more lastingly—he replaced indigenous languages of administration and commerce with Greek. Macedonian, the language of Alexander's troops and his own native language, was apparently not a Greek dialect but an isolated language very different from it. Greek was the language of Alexander's education, and Greek was the language that came into regional prominence because of his conquests. Athens became a part of a Greek-speaking Eastern Mediterranean culture zone with a new kind of pan-regionalism called Hellenism. This new order was distinct in many ways from the political world and especially the worldview of pre-Alexandrian Athens.

Athens had a long history of accommodating outsiders within its boundaries and an equally long tradition of treating them as undesirable aliens. It would be wrong to call them second-class citizens; they had none of the benefits of citizenship. Resident aliens had no right to vote or to participate in major festivals like the Panathenaia. They paid taxes that locals did not pay. Even the rights they retained were not nearly so easy to defend as those of birthright citizens. When it came to the treatment of people far from their borders, the Athenians, like Greeks in general, appear to have all too easily leaped to the characterization "barbarian" for people who were different from them. That word reflects their deep disdain for the foreigner's inability to speak Greek. Though we would probably think of "savage" as the most apt synonym for "barbarian," an ancient Athenian might have come up with the word "babbler." People are unlikely to appreciate the culture or respect the abilities of those they think capable only of meaningless blather.

Alexander's conquests united the Eastern Mediterranean and much of its deep interior within a single political system and gave it a unified cultural foundation. This new order changed dramatically immediately after the conqueror's death, when his most important generals began fighting for shares of conquered territory. In the course of a few generations, the broad eastward-tending swath of captive lands shrank as peoples in the extreme east freed themselves of Macedonian dominance. The remnant broke ultimately into four kingdoms: a northern realm including Macedonia; a second on the western coast of Anatolia; and two much larger interior kingdoms.

The first of these two was the kingdom of the Seleucids, named for Seleucus, one of Alexander's generals. This realm included Mesopotamia as far east as a line joining the Caspian Sea with the Persian Gulf. Egypt and the southern Mediterranean coast as far west as modern Libya became part of the second, the kingdom of the Ptolemies, named for another general, Ptolemy. Despite political fragmentation, these four realms had much in common. In all of them Greek was the language of politics, culture, law, and business. The dress and customs of those in command were entirely Greek, and the region was united in a single trading community. Hellenism remained a unified idea across territories that were politically divided.

Alexander's legacy put a very different complexion on what it meant to be Greek. It created a broad expansion of Greek identity—both geographical and cultural—that challenged the prejudices of Athenians. They saluted the triumphant expansion of an approach to the world that they respected and of which they regarded themselves as founders. They were also forced to recognize that innovation in the arts was passing away from the mainland and taking root in new centers like Alexandria in Egypt or Antioch in Syria. At the heart of this new culture was a tradition of literature and art native to Athenians but foreign to most of its new devotees and practitioners. A scholar in Syria or Egypt would have been deeply devoted to the Greek classics, but for him they represented a collection of great books, not a cultural memory.

Hellenistic culture located its core in the Greek language and in the corpus of Greek literary texts. This centrality prompted a great deal of critical effort to collect, preserve, and study that body of works. The greatest and most concentrated effort in this direction took place at a study center of fabulous name and reputation, the Library of Alexandria. Alexandria was a new coastal city in Egypt with a name that honored the Macedonian conqueror, just as many other towns and cities did. The Egyptian Alexandria, however, had more than a name to keep it going. It quickly became the primary port for the export of the enormous Egyptian grain crop. It also developed a strong scholarly community and an intellectual tradition built upon a collection of books housed in a building dedicated by the first Ptolemy to rule Egypt.

No one knows how many volumes the library contained—estimates range from a half million to 750,000. Better known is the work carried out by the library and its hundred or so professional scholars. With the help of the ruling dynasty, they collected versions of all Greek authors, from Homer and Hesiod through the later Greek poets and dramatists, to the philosophers of nature and the metaphysicians. They collected the works of geometers, astronomers, and pure and applied mathematicians. They did not simply preserve and consult these works; they labored to correct errors in the texts by comparing as many versions of a single work as they could find, purging them of mistakes and, where possible, filling in the blanks. The upshot of their work was to provide an authoritative body of Greek texts, many of them Athenian, to represent the heritage of Greek culture. This semiofficial literary culture became the core of Hellenism.

While Alexandria became the literary and scholarly capital, Athens remained the homeland of Greek philosophy and rhetoric. Eager to learn the methods of the philosophers, young men—and perhaps women too, though the evidence is unclear—flocked to Athens to be educated. Thus Athens became the first university town. As the world around them changed, Athenians adopted a measure of cosmopolitanism that contrasted strongly with their traditional contempt for strangers. They also changed politically. Macedonian regimes throughout the region were resolutely hierarchical and monarchical. The ancient world had always been resistant to Athenian democratic ideals, and the new rulers of the city were no exception. Athenian aristocrats welcomed the death of a form of government that had denied them privileges they felt their wealth and prestige should have guaranteed. Politically, Athens settled into a mode of uneasy acceptance of the preferences of foreign overlords.

Athens fell within the sphere of influence of the Macedonian Antigonid kingdom within Alexander's divided empire. While the city's fate was in the hands of Antigonid overlords, it found champions and protectors in rulers from other Hellenistic kingdoms. Among the most consistently supportive of these monarchies was a succession of leaders based in small, independent coastal states in Anatolia. Generation after generation, rulers of the great coastal city of Pergamum were benefactors of the city and backers of Athenian efforts to maintain their traditional rights and privileges as a free and autonomous political community.

In the nineteenth century, enthusiasm for all things Greek finally overtook the long-established veneration of the Roman heritage, but that enthusiasm was not without its limitations. Classicists were firmly convinced that the period of Athenian—and indeed Greek—history that mattered was the so-called Age of Pericles, the fifth century BCE. This was the classical era in culture, history, art, philosophy, and law; it was the era to be admired, studied, and resurrected in any way possible. The era of Macedonian conquest and its aftermath, on the other hand, struck these same enthusiasts as a period of decadence rather than an era of continued cultural development and expansion. J. B. Bury's much respected *History of Greece* sounds evenhanded in the short title commonly used to reference it, but that is a mistaken impression—its full title is *A History of Greece to the Death of Alexander the Great*. In other words, Bury's is a history of the fifth century and its immediate aftermath; what happened after that era was judged unworthy of inclusion.

Attitudes toward the Athenians of the postclassical age were particularly harsh. A scholar like Theodor Mommsen could fault them for losing their independence and for their ready acceptance of foreign rule and foreign visitors. In his mind, these were weaknesses indicative of misrule and cultural decay. At the same time, Mommsen blamed the Athenians when they rebelled against their overlords and attempted to reestablish political autonomy. In the historian's paradoxical but characteristic view, when Athenians welcomed foreigners, they were toadies. When they rejected them, they were ungrateful to those who had treated them well.

Modern scholars are far more willing to recognize the virtues of the Hellenistic world, and agree that the history and archaeology of ancient Greece did not come to an abrupt halt in the era of Alexander. Though an excavator like Dörpfeld cut through Turkish, Byzantine, Roman, and Hellenistic layers to get to the fifth-century material that his era valued, modern excavators are far more evenhanded. As a result of their methods, the history of Athens has expanded, and monuments from every era are now recognized. These include many in the most prominent Athenian locations, including the Acropolis hill, the Agora, and the Panathenaic Way. These excavations point to a city that continued to live and evolve as the classical era waned.

The neighborhood of the Theater of Dionysos was one of the first areas to benefit from the largesse of foreigners. Eumenes II, who reigned in Pergamum during the first half of the second century BCE, funded a long and impressive stoa linked up with the theater and probably intended to serve its patrons as a kind of de facto lobby. The stoa, the arcaded foundations of which survive, stood next to the circuit road that ringed the Acropolis. It was a two-story building with no internal divisions. Visitors to the theater could shelter in it before or after performances or take refuge inside when the weather turned nasty.

Hellenistic Greeks from all over the Mediterranean came to visit, admire the monuments, and study in Athens. They might have regarded the city as a living monument to the gods of art and knowledge, but its buildings and their scheme of organization looked shabby and disorganized. In an era when new towns were springing up around the Eastern Mediterranean, an unplanned and shopworn city like Athens began to look decidedly out of step. Some of the most conspicuous efforts to give it an overhaul occurred in the Agora. Around the year 180 BCE, Athenians erected a huge new building that blocked off the south end of the Agora. Called the Middle Stoa, this Hellenistic building was almost five hundred feet long from end to end. Its scale dwarfed the older buildings in the Agora, and its extent effectively divided the Agora into two sections. The new structure was made of limestone and lacked internal subdivisions. In this way it resembled the stoa that Eumenes funded near the theater, but its function was different. Rather than a retreat from the weather, this long, shed-like building was a vast market. An older stoa to the south was torn down and replaced by a longer one that ran parallel to the market. By connecting it to the Heliaia, this complex formed an isolated, semi-enclosed area called the South Square.

Two other stoas completed the Hellenistic transformation of the Agora. Its classical character as an agglomeration of disparate buildings haphazardly gathered at the fringes of a vast open area became submerged in a cohesive architectural plan. The Stoa of Attalos, perpendicular to the Middle Stoa and nearly as long, closed off the western end of the Agora. By the time the building project was completed, the Hellenistic Agora had become more uniform in layout and uniformly monumental in its scale. Its buildings created a nearly rectangular space with regular and easily identified entries and exits.

The Stoa of Attalos commemorated another of the Pergamese benefactors of Athens. Attalos II was the younger brother of King Eumenes II. At his brother's death, Attalos married the widowed queen and assumed control of the kingdom in place of his nephew, Attalos III, who was still a minor. Attalos

The Stoa of Attalos.

was educated in Athens, and he supported the city both militarily and culturally throughout his lifetime. His gift, the stoa named after him, and re-created on its original foundations between 1953 and 1956, now houses the Agora Museum. True to its ancient form and incorporating some surviving ancient elements, the building is a two-story portico. Its multiple colonnades make use of three different architectural orders. On the ground floor the outside row of columns are Doric and the interior ones Ionic. On the second floor, the columns visible from the outside are Ionic, and the interior ones Pergamene, a name that commemorates its West Asian origin. Stylized palm leaves decorating their capitals distinguish these columns from the common Greek orders. The entablature separating the two stories is decorated with triglyphs and metopes, and there are stone balustrades between the upper-story columns. Lion masks decorate the roof support, and acroteria punctuate the roofline. Exterior stairs at both ends of the building lead to the second floor.

At the same time that these public buildings were changing the appearance of the city's most prestigious areas, more practical modernizations also occurred: temples were renovated and repaired; new aqueducts increased the water supply to the city; the city's walls were fortified; and cemeteries outside those walls were enlarged. Along with the creation of public buildings and the improvement of amenities, foreign patrons were also recognized in symbolic ways. The number of eponymous heroes honored by statues in the Agora was increased to include two Hellenistic kings on whose goodwill the fate of the city depended. Presumably with greater enthusiasm, the city honored its Pergamese benefactors with sculptures on monumental plinths. One of these plinths can still be seen outside the Propylaia on the way to the Acropolis (a statue of the Roman emperor Agrippa replaced the original dedicatee), and a monument in front of his stoa honored Attalos II.

During the Hellenistic era, two new powers vied for prominence in the Mediterranean. Just to the west of Egypt was a former colonial outpost of the tiny kingdom of Phoenicia on the eastern coast of the Mediterranean. Like Greece between the eighth and sixth centuries BCE, Phoenicia was a trading culture that sent ships throughout the length and breadth of the Mediterranean and outward into the Atlantic. Phoenician ships brought tin from Britain and, according to the Greek historian Herodotus, circumnavigated the African continent. Like the Greeks, the Phoenicians created colonies that served as trading posts. There were Phoenician colonies in Spain and Italy, on Sicily, and elsewhere. One of their colonies, the kingdom of Carthage, planted in North Africa, eventually grew beyond the limits of a simple port city to became a leading regional power. By the time the Phoenician homeland was absorbed by more aggressive neighbors, its former colony had become a dominant force in the Western Mediterranean. In the center of the Italian peninsula, an entirely different kind of culture was slowly gathering territory and power to itself and increasing its regional influence. It was not long before these southern and northern kingdoms expanded to a point where they began to get repeatedly into each other's way. Sicily, midway between the two rivals, was one of the flashpoints, along with Spain, where the territorial creep of the Romans threatened Carthaginian colonies.

Italy had not escaped Greek influence. From the sixth century BCE onward, colonies planted by Greek cities sprang up in Sicily and in Southern

Italy; in fact, Naples was originally a Greek city. Roman expansion in the peninsula troubled the parent cities of these colonies, and Greek armies were dispatched to support them. The Romans were very wary of the sea and did not venture on it without deep misgivings. They were essentially a land-based culture, and their method for establishing and maintaining contact within their increasingly large territory was to improve communication overland by building roads, not ships. Even though Rome and Carthage were separated by a narrow belt of sea, the majority of fighting between the two rivals was carried out by armies rather than navies. Hannibal attacked Rome via Spain and the Alps. Scipio marched the other way to attack the Carthaginians.

When the wars with Carthage finally ended in Roman triumph, the victors turned their attention to conquest throughout the Mediterranean. The Greeks had intervened briefly and unsuccessfully to support colonies in Italy, but the Macedonian successors of Alexander had actively supported Carthage. Rome did not take their partisanship lightly: at the turn of the second century BCE, it launched a series of military campaigns against them that eventually led to Roman conquest and occupation. In 196 BCE, Rome declared that the Greek cities had been liberated from Macedonian control. For the next fifty years, the Romans intervened in Greece, but throughout this era, Greeks continued to maintain their own political stance. Romans would step in when there were attacks or provocations, but they refused to annex Greece or to assume political control.

Fifty years after giving guarantees that they would protect Greek sovereignty, the Romans were ready to change tack. Sparta had appealed to Rome to protect it against an aggressive league of other Greek city states. Rome promised support, but instead of sending troops, the Senate sent ambassadors of high rank to address the league of cities threatening Sparta. These very distinguished representatives were shouted down in the assembly. Their bodyguards were killed, and the ambassadors themselves were chased through the streets of Corinth in fear for their lives. The Roman response to this mistreatment was not what the Greeks had come to expect after a half century of indulgence. Rather than making a show of aggression without follow-through, Roman soldiers landed in force and ordered the people of Corinth to assemble. When the crowd in the Agora grew quiet, Rome's representative, Mummius, announced that all would be exiled. Roman soldiers would round up municipal objects of art to be sent to Italy. Corinth would be dealt with as Alexander had dealt with Thebes: the city would be leveled and would not be rebuilt.

From 146 BCE, Rome controlled not only Athens but every other part of the Greek mainland and islands, with different parts of the country serving different purposes. Sparta, which had a long and colorful military tradition, became something of a military theme park—its warrior customs made it an object of ethnographic curiosity for international visitors. Athens continued to be the university center. Affairs went along well enough until 88 BCE, when Athens tried to free itself from Roman control and restore its democratic traditions by siding with the yet another West Asian monarch, Mithridates of Pontus. This revolt led to a swift Roman counter: in 86 BCE, the Roman general Sulla and his troops laid siege to the city. Intent on cutting the food supply, they focused on the port of Piraeus. Without a navy of their own, the Romans were unable to seal off the port. Sulla sent his troops inland to cut the corridor that linked the port and the city, building a wall between the two that made it impossible for supplies to reach the defenders. When the Athenians refused to negotiate, Roman sappers undermined a weak and poorly defended section of the fortifications, and a huge portion of the wall collapsed. Sulla sent in troops who ran through the city killing, raping, and looting. These soldiers were only brought under control after prominent Romans took the city's side and convinced Sulla to spare what had not already been destroyed. After this episode, Athens remained under Roman control.

One of the best documented acts of destruction associated with the attack was not the work of Roman invaders but of the Greek defenders. Sulla's troops had been pelting the city with stones lobbed from catapults. To prevent Roman soldiers from building war machines using the roof timbers of the Odeon of Pericles, Greek defenders burned it. Long after the war was over, Ariobarzanes II, a king of Cappadocia, paid for the building's complete restoration. This act, typical of the Hellenistic period, had become an exception during the Roman era, when Roman patrons and Roman funds were almost universally used.

Damage inflicted during Sulla's era took a long time to repair. In the area surrounding the Odeon, the Temple of Asclepius suffered damage, as did the Theater of Dionysos. During the first years of the empire, Roman rulers repaired both buildings; at the same time, they rebuilt the porch of the Asclepius temple, with a new entry, and rededicated it to the god of healing. This same dedication included the god of health, Hygeia, and also Augustus Caesar. In the theater, Romans added a front row of throne-like chairs to be occupied by priests in the service of the deified city of Athens, as well as the gods of arts, the Muses. Alongside these traditional and local dignitaries sat priests of the goddess Roma and the deified Augustus. Nero replaced the old scenic backdrop during the first century CE and rededicated the theater to honor both Dionysos and the deified emperor. This stage building thrust forward into the old orchestra and forced a change of shape from the traditional circle to the extended semicircle visible today. During his mid-second-century rule, the emperor Hadrian added kneeling figures of Sileni, the mythical companions of Dionysos. (When invaders sacked the city in 267 CE, the theater was again badly damaged. When it was rebuilt more than a century later, these Sileni were moved to the front of a new stage.)

These recovery projects suggest a pattern typical of the way Romans approached the city during their long period of control over it. They repaired and rebuilt ancient monuments, but always with an important addition. They respected the original identity of structures they repaired, and their architects learned a great deal in the process—a knowledge that was put to use elsewhere in Roman imperial buildings. At the same time, they expanded the dedications of these historic buildings to include new deities. Invariably these new gods represented the Roman Empire and the emperor-made-god at its head.

Evidence of a growing Roman presence—and ideology—in the city was reflected by more than Rome's official policy to reshape Athens. Following a pattern set by generations of powerful and wealthy men before them, many Roman notables preferred life in Athens to life in Rome. Marc Antony, one of three men sharing power over the nascent Roman Empire, settled in Athens in 39 BCE and lived there for almost a decade. Hadrian, one of Rome's most peripatetic sovereigns, preferred Athens or Alexandria to his imperial residence on the Palatine Hill in Rome's center, or his magnificent villa in the foothills outside that center. Where important men led the way, others were sure to follow.

Though there is piecemeal evidence of the damage Sulla's troops did to particular buildings, there is no clear sense of its cumulative effect, nor of how long it might have taken the city to recover. There are signs, though, that things took a long time to return to normal. When Marc Antony moved into Athens more than forty years after Sulla's rampage, a planned commercial extension of the Athenian Agora still remained incomplete. The work was restarted by Julius Caesar, and after his death it was completed by Augustus. In Rome, both Julius and Augustus added similar structures to the edges of the Forum, and the land that these projects required was enormously expensive. That land of equal centrality at the edges of the Athenian Agora was more readily available suggests that damage inflicted by Roman soldiers was quite extensive and that the pace of recovery was very slow.

Roman efforts to transform the Athenian Agora were by no means a neutral act. The prestige of the Agora buildings was tremendous, so when the site's political symbolism is also taken into account, this Roman restructuring seems cataclysmic. The most obtrusive Roman monument introduced in this historic political center was the Odeon of Agrippa. Built sometime around 15 BCE, when the prominent general visited Athens, this building was plunked down in the Agora with an intention that no one could mistake: though it was cousin to such buildings as the Odeon of Pericles, which had just recently been restored, it had a distinctly Roman look, and it was built on an imperial scale (its roof was one of the largest in existence at the time). Building this Roman auditorium in what once had been the center of Athenian democratic government effectively announced a new political and cultural order with a new scale of power and influence. Sometime around 400 CE, the Odeon was replaced by a rich urban residence that probably housed the region's governor during that era. Statues of giants and tritons on large pedestals were gathered to decorate its façade. These statues, re-erected by excavators in the nineteenth century, are now the clearest marking of the site once dominated by the Odeon of Agrippa.

When the Agora was transformed into a showcase for Roman power, there was no need to create alternative spaces for Greek political institutions that had been suspended, but business activities still needed to be accommodated. To house the commercial exchanges a new Roman marketplace was built—it linked up to the Athenian Agora at the southern end of the Stoa of Attalos by a ceremonial roadway flanked with columns. The Gate of Athena Archegetis, the formal entrance to the Roman market, still stands. Four Doric columns support an entablature with triglyphs and metopes and

The Gate of Athena Archegetis.

a pediment. A statue of the grandson of the emperor Augustus once stood on a small platform at the roofline. This grand doorway leads into an open square once embraced on all four sides by a colonnade with shallow buildings behind. Buildings on three sides were wide-open sheds like the South Stoa in the old Agora. Small rooms with individual entrances lined the fourth. The remains of a stairway on the south side indicate that the building had two stories. This site must have imposed some limits on the builders, because its corners do not meet at right angles. Paving stones on the open courtyard were added during the reign of the emperor Hadrian. Scholars agree that the Roman market was meant to house all business operations that had for centuries transpired among the political and ceremonial monuments of the Athenian Agora. Athens did a big business in oil and other commodities, so this new marketplace must have made the life of buyers and sellers easier.

On the eastern edge of the Roman market, a second gateway not quite on axis with the Athena Archegetis leads eastward out of the complex.

The remains of a Roman-era public latrine lie just outside this gate to the north. Public facilities of this kind did not exist in the classical city; they were introduced in the Hellenistic era and continued to be an important part of the Roman city as well. Nearby was the Agoranomeion or Market Inspectors' Office. Parts of this building are still buried, but the visible portions include its façade with three doors topped by arcs of marble. Portions of its limestone walls are also visible.

Both public latrines and offices for the men who ensured fair weight and measure in the market were important practical adjuncts to the new commercial center, yet another of the surviving buildings is far more unusual and, in fact, somewhat enigmatic. That building, the Tower of the Winds, was built in the first century CE. Its sponsor and creator was Andronicus, a Syrian astronomer, and his building is evidence that non-Romans continued to endow the city with monuments, even during the Roman period. The monument takes its popular names from winged personifications of the winds depicted on the frieze that encircles it. A weather vane at the top of the building has long since disappeared, but it would have signaled the wind direction and identified the particular wind blowing at any moment. On each of the eight marble walls, etched lines below the figures of the winds trace sundials. The monument was not just a wind indicator, then, but also a solar clock. Two doors under shallow pediments lead into the tower, and a cylindrical bulge juts out from its south side.

There is general agreement that inside the monument there was a clock powered by springwater brought down in pipes from the slopes of the Acropolis. The cylindrical bulge may have been a storage tank that was constantly refilled and so maintained a steady pressure on the mechanism of the clock. Clocks of this type typically register the hours by measuring the height of water captured in a vessel of some sort. If water pressure varies, the fill rate varies and the clock does not keep accurate time.

Early imperial building was not confined to the Agora, nor to the south face of the Acropolis. A temple of Roma and Augustus, twin deities that represented imperial power, was built on the Acropolis itself. Though the Romans treated that area sacred to Athenian religion and tradition with respect, it was important for them to give their political ideology a religious anchor on this spot. To fail to do so would have been unthinkable. The Roman temple to the two state deities was a round colonnaded building, a type

The Tower of the Winds.

of building already familiar to Greeks. The circular temple was not common in Roman architecture before the first century CE, but there was a very important example in Rome that this new temple intended to recall. The sacred fire that once burned on the hearth of the Roman kings and which, through time and political mutation, had become a symbol of the Roman imperial household, was tended by Rome's Vestal Virgins in a round colonnaded building. This building was the Roman model for the temple on the Acropolis.

In defiance of the respect that Augustus and his immediate successors had generally shown on the Acropolis, Nero had the Parthenon rededicated to himself. While he did not have the Athena Parthenos removed and replaced with a giant self-portrait like the one that stood outside his Roman palace and eventually gave its name to the Colosseum, he did glorify himself through an inscription in bronze letters on the outside of the building. The dedication was taken down after his death. Though Nero's interventions reflected his own megalomania, his tactless interference with the city's most treasured building suggests that over time Roman sensitivity to the feelings of their Athenian hosts might have become less acute. As the occupation became prolonged, the Romans seem to have grown more determined to remake the city in ways that suited them.

Despite the public building campaigns carried out by Roman officials, there was still room for private men of wealth to enrich the city they loved. The astronomer Andronicus, who built the Tower of the Winds, was one such figure. Another was Titus Flavius Pantainos, a wealthy Roman with no political office, who funded and built a library for the city in the late first century CE. Its remains have been uncovered at the south end of the Stoa of Attalos, and one of its sides ran along the Roman road linking the two agoras. Pantainos dedicated the building to Athena, to the city of Athens, and to the deified emperor Trajan.

Trajan's successor, Hadrian, rivaled Augustus in his transformation of the Athenian Agora, but he outpaced him when he expanded the city's limits and created a Roman New Athens next door. Inside the old city, Hadrian's most important building project was what is generally known as his library. Unlike the Library of Pantainos, which was nearby, Hadrian's building was what in Rome would be called an imperial forum. Similar in layout to the enclosed Roman Agora, and located just to the north of it, the project included a library, but also much more. Excavations have uncovered its ground plan, portions of its back wall, and a short length of its monumental western wall and main entrance gate. The surviving features show that the façade was a long unbroken marble wall ornamented with columns of a wavy textured green marble called cipollino. The columns are raised on pedestals and topped by sections of the building's entablature that jut out over each one. Statues may have been placed on the platforms formed by these extensions. At the center of the west wall was the monumental entrance to the complex. All that remains today is one fluted Corinthian column standing far apart from the façade.

Excavations have exposed the original ground plan of this complex, but it is overwritten in confusing ways by successive buildings that include a reconstruction of the library that began after the Herulian sack, the remains of two or three churches, and traces of the Ottoman-era market once held here. Hadrian's complex featured an open courtyard with a shallow pool at its center that was shaded by trees. This area was surrounded by a colonnade

The west wall of Hadrian's Library.

that offered shelter from the weather. Opposite the grand entrance stood the library building, a two-story structure with a central room where written scrolls were stored in cabinets, and rooms at either side that accommodated readers. Beyond these reading rooms, at each end of the building, were lecture halls. Statues of the emperor and altars dedicated to his cult have been found, but there is no temple dedicated to his worship, although such a monument might have been expected.

Hadrian had an even greater impact on an area beyond the city's ancient boundaries. In the region that is now covered by Syntagma Square, the National Gardens, and the Zappion Gardens, a New Athens or "Hadrianopolis" sprang up. The dividing line between the old and the new towns is still marked by a free-standing symbolic gateway dedicated to the emperor. An inscription on the Athenian side of the gateway describes the city as the one either anciently or formerly founded by Theseus. An inscription on the other side is meant to honor Hadrian either as the builder of the new quarter or perhaps as a founder who replaces Theseus as the creator of the city.

Hadrian's Arch.

If there is any justification for the notion that Hadrian not only supplemented but also replaced this mythical founder, it is to be found in his adoption of a centuries-old project. In 515 BCE the Peisistratid rulers of Athens began work on an enormous temple dedicated to "the Father of Gods and Men," as Homer calls Olympian Zeus. This building was laid out on an enormous scale, and it was clearly intended to be the overmastering achievement of a political regime struggling to maintain and to manifest its power. When the regime fell, to be replaced by an Athenian democracy, the temple project was abandoned. There was no interest in carrying through with a monument that could not be disassociated from its antidemocratic originators. The temple site then lay dormant, though not forgotten, for almost three and a half centuries, until Antiochus Epiphanes, a West Asian monarch and ally of Eumenes II (of stoa fame), decided to complete it. A Roman architect drew up plans for the updated temple. This building was nearly complete when Antiochus died and work came to an abrupt halt. After the sack in 88 BCE, Sulla harvested some columns from the site and sent them back to Rome, where they became part of the great temple to Jupiter on the Capitoline Hill.

Between the death of Antiochus and Hadrian's reign, another three hundred years passed for the abandoned temple site. When it was finally completed in about 131 CE, the colossal building stretched nearly 350 feet on its long side and 120 on its ends, and it was surrounded by just over one hundred columns. The sides were ringed by a double colonnade, and the end walls stood behind triple rows of fluted Corinthian columns. Sixteen columns that still stand today on site were part of the triple array on the building's southeastern end. This temple housed an image of Olympian Zeus that was crafted in gold and ivory, like the image of the Athena that the Parthenon sheltered. Statues of Olympian Zeus often show the god seated in a throne, holding a scepter in one hand and an image of victory in the other. He is typically bearded and nude with a cloth draped over his shoulders and across his lap.

Like all Roman monuments, the Temple of Olympian Zeus—known as the Olympieion—made an unambiguous political statement. Hadrian may have dedicated it to the ruler of the Greek pantheon, but he did so at a time when he had added the epithet "Olympian" to his own titles. To underscore the association between the chief god and the Roman ruler, statues of the

The Temple of Olympian Zeus (the Olympieion).

emperor were erected in multiple locations on the wide paved plaza that surrounded the massive temple; each was the gift of a city that had been brought into a newly organized Panhellenic League with its symbolic headquarters in the new temple. This political confederation, which recalled the multiple alliances among cities that peppered the Greek past, had a dedicated building for its actual meetings. There between the temple ruins and the banks of the Ilissos River, the foundations of a shrine to Zeus Panhellios and Hera Panhellios have been identified. Delegates gathered here under the direction of the Olympian chief couple and the emperor who had also added Panhellios to his imperial name.

Hadrian's new town was not just a religious and political center; it has been described as "one of the most beautiful parts of the city with gymnasia, bath houses, and luxury villas" (Korres, 181). What was true of the suburb became true of the city as well: under imperial and other benefactors, the city flourished as it had never done before. While the Athens of the fifth century may have been a scene of great political, artistic, and intellectual creativity, the Athens of the second century CE was urbane, cultured, wealthy, and comfortable.

Athens's last great benefactor was active during and after the Hadrianic era. Herodes Atticus was in many ways the example of what it meant to be a prominent and successful Athenian in the era of Roman rule. Though he traced his ancestry to Zeus and Theseus—twin threads that identified him as both a Greek and an Athenian—his lineage also included among a long list the names of two Roman emperors: Tiberius and Claudius. As his namesakes suggest, Herodes Atticus's life was divided between his native Greece and Italy, and his career reflected his twin nationality. As a prosperous Roman, he held a succession of political offices, while he also enjoyed a career as a philosopher of some standing, which his political appointments came to reflect. Hadrian appointed Herodes Atticus as prefect in the Asian provinces of the empire. Hadrian's successor, Antoninus Pius, appointed him as tutor to Marcus Aurelius and Lucius Verus, the two men who succeeded Antoninus as emperor. While Aristotle's influence over Alexander the Great may have been uncertain, Herodes Atticus is responsible for training the last two of the five Roman emperors generally recognized as the most dedicated and effective.

Herodes Atticus's first contribution to Athens was an update of an older building. Sometime around 330 BCE a stadium had been built across the Ilissos River from the Temple of Olympian Zeus, which was then in a state of abandonment. Almost exactly four centuries later, sometime around 140 CE, Herodes Atticus financed construction of an improved stadium built along Roman lines. In Greek athletics, the stadium was a venue for track and field events. Romans used this same kind of structure for horse racing. The new stadium of Herodes Atticus—called the Panathenaic Stadium, in honor of the league established by Hadrian—combined Roman architecture that was typical of the hippodrome with the staging of Greek athletic contests. Roman horse races were held on a long track with a sharp turn at one end and starting gates and finish line on the other. The distinctive architectural feature of this plan was the semicircular rank of seats that ringed the turn on its outer edge. Since the most intense action in the race, including deadly collisions, took place at this turn, these were the most sought-after seats. Long ranks of seats also flanked both sides of the course.

In 1870, the Panathenaic Stadium was excavated and restored by one of Greece's great modern benefactors, Evangelis Zappas, and Olympic Games

Panathenaic (Kallimarmaro) Stadium.

were held there in 1870 and 1875. The success of these games inspired the effort to create the modern Olympics, which were first celebrated in Athens in 1896. At that time the partially remodeled Panathenaic Stadium was brought to completion with a grant from George Averoff, a Greek entrepreneur active in Egypt. During the first modern Olympics, most of the events were held in the stadium. In the Athens Olympics of 2004, the Stadium of Herodes Atticus served most significantly as the finish line for the marathon.

Herodes Atticus must have been a very lucky man: contributions by hundreds, perhaps thousands of benefactors of the ancient city have disappeared with hardly a trace, but his stadium is not only remembered but used. As if that weren't enough, the Odeon that Herodes Atticus built on the south slope of the Parthenon also survives, and since 1954 it has been used for performances each summer. The Odeon was built between 160 CE and 175 as a memorial to Regilla, the patron's Roman wife. Sometime before it was built, the roof on Agrippa's Odeon in the Agora had collapsed, putting

The Odeon of Herodes Atticus.

that building out of commission and leaving only the rebuilt Odeon of Pericles to serve the city's concertgoers. The new Odeon now looks a great deal like the nearby Theater of Dionysus, with a three-story wall at its flat end. This wall, pierced by Roman arches, was not a scenic backdrop, as it might now appear, but an enclosing and supporting wall in what was originally a roofed structure. Odeons were enclosed, while theaters were not. The Odeon suffered significant damage during the Herulian sack, but it was not destroyed.

Another conspicuous benefactor was lucky in a different way. None of the architectural commissions of Gaius Julius Antiochus Philopappos remain to be enjoyed or even remembered, but this Syrian benefactor of Athens received the unusual privilege of a highly visible tomb. At the top of the Hill of the Muses, the lower flanks of which were a cemetery in Roman times, a commemorative monument was constructed in his honor (and no doubt at his expense). The Philopappos Monument was in essence a billboard set in a prominent spot on a hill southwest of the Acropolis and designed to

The Philopappos Monument.

advertise its eternal occupant to the most significant audience. It is a curved marble wall directed toward the Acropolis and the city. A bas-relief on its lower level is topped by images in framed recesses. The relief shows Philopappos being inaugurated as Roman consul by Trajan. Statues in the niches above—identified by their inscriptions—represent the entombed occupant with images of his ancestors, King Antiochos IV and King Seleucus, founder of the post-Alexandrian Seleucid kingdom.

6

Late Antique and Medieval Athens

Within a hundred years of its completion, the Odeon of Herodes Atticus, and most of Roman Athens with it, was wrecked by Herulian pirates. The Heruli were Goths, a people whose homeland on the perimeter of the Black Sea had never been incorporated into the Roman Empire. Centuries of uneasy coexistence with these and other unruly neighbors broke down in the third century when tribes who had once been cowed by overwhelming Roman force began to surge across the borders that had long kept them out. The Heruli were a little different from the norm: most invaders came overland, but the Heruli had ships—in fact, an impressive fleet of ships, numbering perhaps five hundred. They embarked from the coast of what is now Ukraine and sailed southeastward toward the outlet of the Black Sea, marauding as they went. Their raids had mixed success—some cities were able to repel them, while others, like Byzantium, not yet the eastern capital it would become, were not so lucky. Ships of the Roman navy engaged them in the Dardanelles and reduced their numbers, but they were not able to stop the fleet's outbreak into the Mediterranean. They reached Athens in 267 CE, attacked, and overwhelmed it. They then moved on to the Peloponessos, where they did further damage. They were repelled at last by a Roman fleet and a land army organized and led by Athenians.

Evidence of their destructive path through Athens is abundant. The focus of their attack may have been the Kerameikos, where they breached the gates and entered the city. The city's outer defenses at that time were an old encircling fortification called the Themistoclean wall. It had been repaired and reinforced under the emperor Valerian a few decades before the attack (and it was from then on referred to by his name), but its perimeter was too great to be effectively manned. A layer of ash and debris across the Kerameikos and its buildings commemorates the attack; the same measure of destruction has been found in excavated homesites and villas of the era scattered throughout the city. There is no evidence that the Heruli were able to take the Acropolis, and it may be that the luckiest of the city's inhabitants took shelter there.

Though the ash layer that commemorates their attacks is especially eloquent, the best evidence for their impact on the city is indirect and much after the fact. Sometime after the Heruli had gone away, the city regrouped and organized itself for defense. The Valerian wall had proven to be of no value in repelling the invaders. It was repaired, but no longer relied on as the city's chief protection. Instead, a new wall with a much smaller perimeter was built well within the old limits of habitation. Constructed in six or seven years, that wall was more than ten feet thick at its base and incorporated architectural materials collected from prominent buildings throughout the city. The availability of material from historically important structures gives eloquent evidence of the devastation the city had suffered. Leaving the Greek Agora outside the perimeter of the new defenses also speaks to the Herulian impact.

Called the Late Roman wall by archaeologists, the new and much reduced perimeter incorporated not just bits and pieces of broken monuments but entire structures that were then diverted from civilian to military use. The Stoa of Attalos became part of the defenses; the Library of Hadrian with its massive perimeter became a bulwark jutting out from the circuit of the walls. The triage of space and architecture, much of it deeply historical, gives a measure of the city's suffering, but the purpose of the new perimeter is not entirely clear. Many scholars have assumed that it surrounded a city shrunken in ambition and population that was small enough to be accommodated within a very confined area. Rebuilt houses outside the perimeter, however, which date to the era after the Herulian attack, suggest that the city eventually stretched beyond the limits of the Late Roman wall. Scholars have argued that what the wall enclosed was a citadel within the city intended to shelter essential civil and military services in periods of conflict. Whatever its original purpose, the wall outlived its creators by centuries. In medieval Athens it became a significant part of the urban skeleton and helped to give shape to the minor city that grew up among the scattered ruins of the ancient one. Its outline formed a significant boundary in the nineteenth-century city plan.

Late antiquity saw the city return to something like its ancient glories. It remained a goal for travelers, especially those throughout the Mediterranean interested in philosophy, rhetoric, music, literature, and art. But the indomitable Roman Empire was no longer what it had been: political instability, in part brought on by the very success of the empire in its periods of expansion, became an increasing problem. Rome had colonized an enormous territory, roughly triangulated by Hadrian's wall on the Scottish border, Morocco on the North African coast, and Petra in modern Jordan. The challenge this gigantic landmass presented was an essentially logistic one: how could Romans communicate quickly and effectively between such widespread frontiers and the center of power and government in Rome. The famous system of Roman roads was meant to solve this problem, which is why all of them led to Rome. In the Eastern Empire, the imperial road network was augmented by ships. Peripatetic emperors like Hadrian represented another approach. In the late third and increasingly in the fourth century, the imperial power was parceled out among officeholders who held the title of Augustus, but not Caesar, and coleaders whose title was the reverse. Sometimes there were two of each denomination, making for a total of four more-or-less emperors. These emperors could be located in different parts of the empire and govern more locally.

Predictably, co-emperors spent a good deal of their time attempting to eliminate their partners and consolidate control over the empire as a whole. Civil war, typically on a fairly limited scale, broke out again and again. News of such internal conflicts, however, always seemed to reach the encircling hordes, who repeatedly took advantage of the empire's periods of instability to raid. It turns out that the very roads that enabled news of instability to circulate widely and quickly also served the invaders as convenient highways to major urban targets, ultimately including Rome itself.

During the fourth century, the Roman Empire experienced a shift in political organization that had enormous effects not just on the Mediterranean world of that era but over the long term as well. The emperor Constantine, a onetime partner in an imperial tetrarchy, overcame his final rival, Maxentius, in a battle outside Rome in 312 CE. He attributed his victory to the intervention of the Christian god, and during the rest of his long reign he fostered the religion. At that time, Christian communities were scattered throughout the empire, but Constantine gave them official support. He avoided building churches in the center of Rome but constructed vast and conspicuous buildings to house worshippers on the city's edges. He recognized that Rome could never be divorced from its pre-Christian past, and for this reason, as well as for reasons of logistics and personal preference, he moved the capital of the Roman Empire from Rome in the Western Mediterranean to Byzantium in the East.

Constantine's successors eventually made Christianity the official creed of the empire, and this act had enormous consequences for the future of the region and for every locality in it, including Athens. Re-centering the empire around an Eastern Mediterranean capital was just as consequential. The most obvious effect was to turn the city of Rome into a second-tier government center, and then to bypass it altogether as the host city for imperial overlords shifted to coastal Ravenna in Northern Italy. This new site had no significant past and no recalcitrant, wealthy elite to oppose imperial policies, as the nobles of the city of Rome continued to do. From this weakened center, the lines of communication and the allocations of troops that might hope to guard the Western Empire from invaders and political opportunists spread out with diminished effect. The success of barbarians in the West—and their ability to carve out kingdoms for themselves within the corpse of the abandoned empire—shaped the future of the region until the Renaissance.

Athens at first was part of the far more vital and more centralized Eastern Empire. Even this region, however, suffered its share of hardships in the centuries following the conversion and the displacement of the imperial capital. Like Rome, where patrician families resisted both imperial policy and the new religion, Athens, too, was a religious holdout. Philosophy, the arts, and worship of the Greek gods seemed to be natural partners—their influence remained strong in Athens. It was felt most directly in the reign of the emperor Julian, called the Apostate, who, probably because of his Athenian education, tried to reverse the Christianization of the Roman Empire and restore the worship of the old gods. He was, of course, unsuccessful. Even recalcitrant Athens had its Christian community. Two very prominent defenders and definers of Christian orthodoxy, Gregory of Nazianzos and Basil the Great, were both trained in the city where the Panathenaic processional continued to be celebrated until 500 CE.

In the fifth century, new centers of Christian worship began to appear. Remains of five basilicas have been uncovered in scattered excavations around the perimeter of the old city. The remains of a church of the same era with wonderful floor mosaics, now preserved in the Byzantine Museum, have been uncovered on what was then an island in the Ilissos River, not far from the Olympieion. The most conspicuous Christian structure of the era was built in the open center court of Hadrian's Library. The contours of this building are outlined on the ground. Architectural historians refer to this as a quatrefoil building, or a tetraconch, to describe its clover-shaped linking of four unequal lobes. In the center was an aisle lined on one side by columns and on the other by an arcade; this aisle ended in small protrusions at each end. Behind each line of supports was a small, semicircular colonnade enclosed within a larger, encircling wall. The underlying form of the building, like that which was to give definition to the majority of later Athenian churches, was a cross traced out by the interconnected lobes.

The sixth century brought an end to the late imperial city, with its complex mix of ancient and modern, of Christian and pagan. Some sources report that in 529 CE the emperor Justinian closed the philosophical schools and banned the teaching of ancient philosophy. Though the date and the extent of the abolition are hotly debated by historians, there is no disputing the fact that the teaching of philosophy and rhetoric in Athens came to an end within the century. Imagine the effect on Boston if all its colleges and universities shut down, dismissed their faculties, and sent their students home. Athens suffered a parallel blow to an economy that had for centuries been based on its ability to attract foreigners to the city's multiple educational and cultural institutions.

At roughly the same time, the cultural patrimony of the ancient city was itself converted to Christianity. The architectural segregation of Christian and traditional worship sites that had been the norm for centuries was reversed. Monuments that had represented Athenian civic religion since the fifth century BCE were stripped and refashioned for use as Christian places of worship. The Parthenon was the most prominent of these. The ancient temple of the virgin goddess Athena became a Christian church dedicated to Mary the virgin, mother of Christ. The Erechtheum was remodeled as a Christian basilica. The Temple of Hephaistos in the Agora and the Temple of Asclepius on the south side of the Acropolis also became Christian churches.

The seventh through the ninth centuries were not kind to Athens, the Byzantine Empire, or the Eastern Mediterranean as a whole. Slavic invaders struck the city just on the cusp of the seventh century and destroyed old and new monuments alike. By mid-century, the Byzantine Empire was under constant attack by an entirely new force in the area. In 634, an Islamic army overcame Byzantine forces at the battle of Ajnadayn. The victors followed up their unexpected success with a march of conquest through the Byzantine province of Syria. Driving north along the Mediterranean coast, they conquered Damascus by 636. Victory in the east was quickly followed by a western campaign against Egypt, the granary of the Byzantine Empire. By 643, Byzantine Alexandria, though it was well fortified, heavily garrisoned, and easily resupplied by sea, had fallen to the attackers.

A new political and military rivalry divided the Eastern Mediterranean. Arab privateers challenged the Byzantine navy and made repeated raids on coastal cities. Though not on the sea itself, Athens was close enough to become a frequent target. So intense and constant was the pressure from Arab attack that the Byzantine administrators of Greece moved their center of operations away from Athens to the inland city of Thebes. Already suffering economically and socially from the interruption of its trade and the decimation of its population, Athens suffered a significant loss in prestige and influence when the Byzantine governors abandoned it.

Recovery began sometime in the ninth century. Byzantium regrouped internally, and its navy once again controlled the Mediterranean. Naval security restored trade, and political stability created a climate for expansion and normalization. The imperial bureaucracy moved back to Athens early in the century. The bishop of Athens gained the rank of archbishop, and the Parthenon was his cathedral. There is evidence that new churches were built in the city, but none from this early period survive. As the era of prosperity and stability went on, however, building continued, and from the eleventh and twelfth centuries churches survive in many parts of Athens and in the region around it.

By the time church building resumed in the ninth century, the architectural traditions of the Eastern and Western Mediterranean, despite their common foundation in Roman imperial architecture and the shared tradition of Constantinian Christianity, had diverged. Typical Western churches of the ninth to the twelfth centuries were recognizable offshoots of the first basilicas that Constantine had commissioned on the Roman periphery. They were open-plan buildings with a central nave separated from one or two aisles by an arcade or colonnade. The nave arcade supported high walls pierced by openings that lit the center area. Windows on the outer walls of the single-story side aisles lit the rest of the church. At its eastern end, the nave opened into a perpendicular transept that led from one side wall to the other. Eastward, beyond the transept, was an elevated platform where the altar stood and the officiants said Mass. This area, called the choir, was enclosed within a semicircular outer wall—an apse—that reflected the words of the liturgy toward the congregation.

The first churches in Athens fit this mold. The church excavated on the Ilissos island, the remains of the five basilicas that archaeologists have uncovered, the Parthenon restructuring and that of the other converted ancient temples—all reflected it as well. But by the time churches were again being built in Athens, a new architectural tradition had become established in the Byzantine world to support a significantly different ideal of Christian worship. Even in the fourth century, when Christians first used the basilica, it was an old-fashioned building type. Fourth-century Roman architects were doing far more imaginative things with space, and the best new buildings were bold and adventurous. The Byzantine tradition preserved far more of that creative spirit than the Western tradition.

The oldest surviving churches of Athens are all more or less of a piece in their structure and organization of space. Each is a Greek cross—a cross with four equal arms—inscribed in a cube and topped with a dome. The pattern is called "cross-in-square." A porch at the western end of the church, the narthex, leads into the building. Inside there is a nave-like center space looking toward the altar in the eastern end. This space is cut off from an area on the north side of the nave called the prothesis. In this special area the priest celebrating the Eucharist prepares the bread and wine. A similar area to the south of the nave—called the diaconon—is roughly equivalent to the sacristy or vestry in a Western church, where the celebrants put on their vestments and where liturgical objects are stored. In front of the nave is a raised platform called the bema. On it are a bishop's throne and a lectern.

The most striking difference between a contemporary Western church and a historical or contemporary Greek Orthodox church is the relationship between the nave and the space surrounding the altar. In a modern Western church, the congregation has an unobstructed view of the altar. In an Orthodox church, the two are separated by an altar screen called an iconostasis. Until the Council of Trent in the late sixteenth century abolished it, Western churches had an analogous structure separating the two areas and screening the altar. The iconostasis has three doorways, often closed by curtains: two smaller ones at the side, and one large central door. During the liturgy these passages are used by the officiants as they move between the sheltered altar and the public space on the edge of the bema.

The barrier takes its name from the sacred images, the icons, that decorate it. Images have a role to play in the Orthodox Church very different from that of any of the arts employed over time to embellish Western churches. In the Byzantine world, icons came to prominence after a prolonged controversy about their nature and use. During the eighth and ninth centuries, when the Eastern Mediterranean was still convulsed by the warfare between Christian and Muslim states, the Byzantine Empire also fought a bitter and violent civil war about icons. Controversy over representing holy figures, especially Christ, divided it. Sometime around 730 CE, the Byzantine emperor Leo III banned the creation or preservation of any image of Christ that represented him as human. For the next hundred years, icons were smashed by iconoclasts and defended by those who continued to believe in their propriety and efficacy. Finally, in the mid-ninth century, the conflict ended when prominent theologians arrived at a theory of iconic use and representation.

The historical overlap between Muslim advances and the iconoclastic controversy was no coincidence. Leo III apparently believed that icons had violated the Mosaic prohibition against the worship of images. The rise to power of Islam struck him and others as divine judgment against this practice—his iconoclasm was an attempt to assuage God's wrath.

The theological issues, though obscure, were certainly not superficial. Resistance to representing the human nature of Jesus implied an argument about that human nature. Man, the book of Genesis says, is made in "the image of God." In effect, then, humans are icons of God, though as they fell from perfection, they became damaged representations. As a human, Jesus was also made in the image of God, and he possesses both a divine nature like God and an "image of God" nature like other human beings. Since he is perfect, his two natures are present simultaneously in some mysterious balance. Arguing that an icon can or should do the same involved a host of misconceptions about the two natures of Christ and their coexistence. Theologians eventually decided that the icon did not embody the two natures of Christ. It was a representation with no substance that referred to Jesus and his mysterious substance. Like a signpost, the icon led the viewer closer to its subject, but it was not that subject, and so it was not an idol. Veneration of icons was an acknowledgment of their link to the sacred, not an assertion of their status as independent sacred objects.

The images on the iconostasis of the contemporary Orthodox Church, like those that decorated the screens in twelfth-century Athenian churches, are placed in a fixed order. Images of Christ and John the Baptist are arranged on the right side of the iconostasis. Images of the Theotokos, the mother of God, stand on the left, along with images of the saint or the event for which a particular church is named. An image of Mary holding the infant Jesus is common in the semi-dome of the apse behind the altar. In the central dome of the church, it is most common to find an image of the risen Christ, the Pantocrator who rules over heaven and earth. One of the things that may strike a visitor to the Orthodox churches of Athens is their very diminutive scale. This may be a reflection of the small population of medieval Athens, but it is also a characteristic of Greek Orthodox worship. The church interior is meant to be intimate, to bring the community of worshippers close together within a small space. The building may be decorated to delight and impress, but its scale is never meant to overawe.

Despite significant differences in some details, the exterior of Athenian churches of this era share some identifying features. The Church of the Holy Apostles (Agii Apostoli) in the Agora, which was restored in the mid-1950s and is one of the earliest surviving churches in the city, shows most of them. The building very clearly declares its interior shape on its spare exterior. From its eastern corner, the four arms that intersect beneath its dome are clearly visible, as are the inset pieces that define a larger cubic volume. Together these shapes identify the cross-in-square form of the church. On the western end, a narthex obscures the shape somewhat, though it can still be worked out by looking at the rooflines. The ornamentation of the exterior is very spare: most of it is concentrated around the windows and doors. The only other form of decoration is an ornamental brickwork called "dog

The Church of the Holy Apostles (Agii Apostoli).

tooth" that outlines the door and window, surrounding and creating horizontals that unite the wall surfaces.

Another building of the early eleventh century, the Church of the Savior, became a Russian Orthodox church in the nineteenth century. Like Agii Apostoli, it is a cross-in-square church, though its scale is greater. The exterior shapes are similar and almost as easy to read. The decoration of the exterior focuses around the windows, and there are bands of dog-tooth brickwork. These bands alternate with bands inscribed with letters in Kufic script. This incorporation of Islamic decorative motifs is fairly common in churches of this era, though its meaning is difficult to sort out. It may suggest imitation of a motif for purely decorative purposes. More likely, it is meant to be an appropriation of a Muslim artifact and a rededication of it to Christian worship.

The interior of the Church of the Savior was redecorated in the nineteenth century, but the architecture remains unchanged. The area beneath the dome is its most significant and most complex part: there the rectilinear side walls and the circular opening of the dome meet in a series of structural accommodations. The dome is supported on a series of arches: one springs from the flat center of each supporting wall, and four others create arcades that bridge the corners. Beneath these corner arches are complex spherical shapes rounded at the top and squared off at the bottom. The walls beneath have two sets of openings—one at floor level and a second higher up that creates a balcony.

All the most characteristic features of this church are well represented in the smaller church of St. Theodore. Its actual dimensions are somewhat obscured by the fact that over the centuries it has sunk into the soil. On its south side this church has an added carillon. The Kapnikarea presents a very different face to the world: its narthex is roofed by a series of gables that give the impression of a group of bungalows built side by side rather than a continuous façade. A side entrance behind a shallow porch on the south further complicates the picture. The simple interior, more spare than that of the Russian church, was decorated in the same period with frescoes in a Byzantine revival style.

The church called Gorgoepikoos dates to the end of the 1100s. Like its contemporaries, it has a cross-in-square plan, but the exterior is strikingly different from every other Athenian church of the era. Rather than using the stone- and brickwork typical of other churches, the Gorgoepikoos was built of marble. And rather than articulating the internal layout clearly on the outside, the wall surfaces here are continuous. The sides unite the cross arm, the corner spaces, and the end of the narthex behind an unbroken wall. The typical long windows with their characteristic horseshoe-shaped upper curve have been restricted to the gable ends of the cross arms and the dome. There is a slit-like opening with no frame on the south side. The doors are even more striking: arched openings have been replaced by doorways that are rectangular in outline, with arches in shallow relief set in the wall above them. All these features give the building a distinct classicizing character that no other Athenian church of the era possesses. This impression is confirmed by the incorporation of salvaged cornices at the top of each wall, borrowed Corinthian pilaster capitals, and inset panels of ancient stonework forming a continuous frieze at the top of the narthex wall and a broken one elsewhere. The architect of this extraordinary building has not been

The Church of the Savior.

Kapnikarea.

identified, but it has long been associated with Michael Choniates, who served as archbishop of Athens at the end of the twelfth century.

The history of medieval Athens is very sparsely documented. Choniates, who was trained in Constantinople and sent from there to Athens to be its archbishop in the late twelfth century, is one of the few writers who reports on what it was like in his day. His first experiences of Athens were vastly disappointing. He did not find the level of erudition he anticipated among the heirs of Pericles and Demosthenes. Nor did he find the city very attractive. Quoting from his letters, the historian of medieval Athens Molly Mackenzie has summarized his shocked reaction:

Michael arrived in Athens, his mind filled with visions of its splendid and heroic past, and the present reality came as a shock: all around him he saw grinding poverty and material decay . . . the glory of the city had "wholly perished." It was no longer a "city of learning, hospitable and surpassing other cities," but had become a "hell of sorrows, a vale

Gorgoepikoos.

of tears and lamentation," where the "sheep graze among the ancient buildings, little trace of which still remains . . ." No one, he wrote, could "look upon Athens without tears." (Mackenzie, 3)

Choniates referred to Athens in another of his letters as "one of the vaults of Hell." These reactions did not keep him from being a strong advocate for Athens to the Byzantine authorities who held power over the city and its region. He wrote to all of them time and again and urged them to treat the city and its people with greater care and respect than was then the habit of corrupt, self-interested, provincial administrators. Kenneth Setton, the great historian of medieval Athens, summarized his complaints: "The grandees of Constantinople were unwilling, he claimed, even to peep outside the walls and gates of their capital. The provinces were drained of their resources to keep the city of Constantinople in luxury. They were paid in pillage and injustice" (Setton, 203).

As revealing as Choniates is about the historical currents running through the city in his day, he is stubbornly silent about the condition of the city's architectural heritage: "He never refers to the [Library] of Hadrian . . . the Tower of the Winds, the Odeum of Herodes Atticus, the Theater of Dionysos, the Arch of Hadrian, The Olympieion, the Philopappos monument, or the huge Stadium. He does not refer to the aqueduct of Hadrian and Antoninus Pius. We learn nothing from him of the remains of the Academy. . . . The choragic monument of Lysicrates he refers to as "the lantern of Demosthenes" (Setton, 204).

Within the narrow confines of medieval Athens, there is no surviving church that retains its original program of interior decoration. The nearby monastery of Daphni, however, is one of the most striking examples of Middle Byzantine church decoration to be found anywhere. (Unfortunately for visitors, the monastery is currently closed indefinitely.) During the sixth century CE, the same era that ancient monuments in the Agora and on the Acropolis were being converted to Christian worship, a temple of Apollo along the Sacred Way to Eleusis was transformed into a monastery. Well outside the city walls, this structure was targeted by invaders, and the site was abandoned for centuries. In the eleventh century, the monastery was re-inaugurated, and columns from the old temple of Apollo were used in the reconstruction. (All but one of these columns, along with the far more significant Parthenon marbles, were among the artifacts Lord Elgin's agents collected and shipped to England in the early nineteenth century.) The monastery church was built from the ground up in this era, and its form is typical of the cross-in-square plan. Seen from the east, the plan is clear and familiar. The west end of the structure is a more complex puzzle that reflects the interventions of the spiritual predecessors of Lord Elgin.

The church is dedicated to the dormition of the mother of God. This miraculous event, which is commemorated in the Orthodox Church on August 15, refers to the manner of Mary's passing from earth to heaven. At the end of her life, the Virgin fell asleep; after three days, she passed alive into heaven. The decoration of the church explores the life of Mary and her divine son and sets those events in a proper theological context. In a standard Byzantine decorative program, the narrative of the life of Mary and her son would be described in images on the walls of the church, while the broader theological framework that these events underpin would be illustrated in the vaults, apse, and dome. Daphni carries this plan through to some extent, but it is not a place where architectural space and theology always interact precisely as theory would dictate.

The mosaic technique was used throughout the Roman Empire primarily for floor decorations. Byzantine artists transformed both its use and its primary material to create religious images of great beauty and durability. Rather than use colored stone, as Roman mosaicists had done, these artists created tesserae of colored glass. The glass caught and reflected the light, which made the colors more vibrant. The surrounds of richly colored portraits were typically made from glass pieces backed with gold. Tesserae were not set with their faces parallel to the wall surface; they were typically tilted at slightly different angles so that changing light or even the movement of a visitor through the church would bring different reflective faces into play. There is a kind of restlessness about images of this kind; the active play of light reflects the spiritual vitality Byzantine theologians exalted after the end of the iconoclastic controversy.

The life story of Mary is not narrated in any of the canonical writings of the church, East or West. The source is a pseudo-gospel attributed to Jesus's brother called the Protoevangelium of James; its first eleven chapters tell the backstory of Mary's life before the Annunciation by the archangel Gabriel that marks her first appearance in the canonical tradition. At Daphni,

Mary's story begins where the visitor enters the church in the narthex or porch. At its south end, there are three scenes. In the first of these, Mary's parents, Joachim and Anna, receive separate visitations from angels who assure them that their prayers have been answered and that they will be blessed with a child. In the second scene, Joachim receives the blessing of the high priest as further assurance that his prayer will be fulfilled. He pledges that the child will live a sacred life. After Mary is born, Anna keeps her for three years in a shrine she has built in her bedroom. At the end of this period, her parents present Mary to the priests of the Temple in Jerusalem, where she lives until she is twelve. Her Presentation in the Temple is the subject of the third mosaic in the narthex. These scenes set the stage for the birth of Christ. The three scenes at the north end of the narthex—the Last Supper, Christ washing the feet of his disciples, and the betrayal of Judas—in turn pave the way for the Crucifixion. As the narthex prepares the worshipper for entrance into the sacred space of the church, these scenes prepare for the Incarnation and Passion of Christ.

The narthex narratives fit their place in the church, but inside there is a confusion of scenes and images. A number of narrative scenes are present, including a beautiful Annunciation in one of the conical wedges of wall called squinches that support the corners of the great dome. There is no background scenery, and some of the figure of Mary has been lost, but despite its fragmentary state the mosaic is striking. The two figures are on surfaces perpendicular to each other, and the empty space between them, broken by the complex intersection of the two walls, suggests the gap between the human and the divine. Architectural details—an arch, for example— often separate the two figures in this common scene, but this is an unusually subtle positioning.

Another squinch represents the birth of Christ. Christ lies in a manger inside a cave, rather than a stable as is more common in Western representations, and three beams of light shine down on him from above. Mary reclines, as she usually does in Byzantine images. The elderly Joseph sits alone and at a distance, reminding the viewer of Jesus's divine conception. On the hilltop above the cave mouth, three angels look on at the birth, while a fourth announces it to a pair of shepherds.

The third scene under the dome is a magnificent representation of the baptism of Christ. With a crowd of men behind him, John the Baptist stands on the left pouring water over Jesus's head. On the right wall are angels, like those who look on at the Nativity. Christ is naked and visible through the veil-like waters of the Jordan. He is crowned by a nimbus with the cross inscribed in it; a dove appears above his head, and two beams of light lead downward from the hand of God. Here Christ bridges the interstitial space that separated the divine and the human in the Annunciation scene. His union of divine and human natures is also symbolized by the twin streams of light that strike him from above.

The confirmation of Christ's divine nature is represented in the final squinch, in a scene called the Transfiguration and described in the Gospels of Mark, Matthew, and Luke:

> And after six days, Jesus took with him Peter, and James, and John his brother, and brought them up into a high mountain apart: and he was transfigured before them; and his face did shine as the sun, and his garments became white as the light. And behold, there appeared unto them Moses and Elijah talking with him. And Peter answered, and said to Jesus, Lord, it is good for us to be here: if you wish, I will make here three tabernacles; one for thee, and one for Moses, and one for Elijah. While he was yet speaking, behold, a bright cloud overshadowed them: and behold, a voice out of the cloud said, This is my beloved Son, in whom I am well pleased. (Matt. 17:1–5)

Jesus, suspended in midair with both feet visible as he will be at the Crucifixion, is fully dressed in a Roman toga; he holds a scroll in one hand and with the other makes the sign of benediction. He is surrounded by a mandorla, an almond-shaped full-body nimbus that symbolizes his radiance. Beams of light reach out from the mandorla to strike both the prophets on either side of him as well as the disciples beneath him. His head is ringed by a cruciform halo. Though the scene acknowledges his divinity, his image is again placed in the mid-ground of the squinch along the seam that represents the union of the human and divine. Other scenes from the life of Christ in the church include the raising of Lazarus from the dead, the triumphal entry into Jerusalem, the Crucifixion, and the descent into hell.

The apse mosaic, which is much damaged, shows, as tradition prescribes, an image of the mother of God and her child. The dome mosaic is an immensely powerful vision of the risen Christ in his fully divine form as the Pantocrator, the All-Powerful. Christ appears on the gold ground of the dome within a multicolored frame like a circular rainbow. He is dressed in a blue toga and holds a bound and closed Bible in his left hand. With his right hand he reaches toward his chest and reveals the garment beneath. He is crowned with a cruciform nimbus, and the abbreviation of his name appears in letters to either side. His face is the most striking feature. He has long dark hair and a trimmed dark beard. His brow is furrowed in concentration, and his lips unsmiling. His eyes, like those of many Byzantine images, are wide open and staring. He seems to be looking down through the rainbow at things on earth and to be severely critical of what he sees.

Much that has happened at Daphni since its eleventh-century foundation has been destructive. Since the final decade of the nineteenth century, it has been damaged three times by earthquakes, most recently in 1999, when both the church and its mosaics suffered serious harm. In 1204, during the episcopate of Michael Choniates, the Byzantine Empire was targeted by West European Crusaders. Rather than march on the Holy Land, which had not been yielding good results in recent campaigns, the Crusaders, under the direction of the blind octogenarian doge of Venice, Enrico Dandolo, decided to restore a banished Byzantine emperor. This entailed an attack on Constantinople, the city's occupation, and ultimately the division of its territories among Italian and French nobles. Athens and Thebes became the property of Otto de la Roche of Burgundy. Otto moved the Orthodox monks out of Daphni and replaced them with Cistercians.

The imported monks went to work to put their architectural mark on the monastery they had inherited. On the western end of the church, they added a second narthex, which completely blocked the first. Rather than continue to build in the Byzantine style, they created a monumental entry with unmistakable Gothic features. Their unknown architect created three grandiose doors with pointed arches at their summits more suitable to the style and scale of a French cathedral. Above the entrance, they added some rooms to the monastic complex. At some point, the roof that linked this second narthex to the building collapsed. What a visitor to the monastery sees now at its western end is the skeleton of the Gothic entryway standing out from the west front of the building. Like a postmodern addition, it refers learnedly to a historic style, but it bears no functional relationship to the building it introduces. The French dynasty that installed the Cistercians at Daphni made far more drastic changes within Athens itself. Among their first acts after taking control of the city in 1204 was to drive out Michael Choniates, its Orthodox archbishop. Choniates settled on the island of Chios off the coast of Attica. From there he continued his pleas for relief of the Athenians. He returned to Athens briefly and at some danger to himself in 1216. He died in exile in 1222.

The Burgundian overlords of Athens replaced Choniates with a Roman Catholic bishop. In a letter of 1208, the pope thanked God that St. Paul's unsuccessful mission to Athens in 62 CE had finally borne fruit. The Catholic bishop took over Choniates's Parthenon cathedral, along with his personal library forcibly abandoned at the moment of exile. The church was hastily remodeled to fit Catholic orthodoxy, and the bishop was installed in the Propylaia. Choniates's library, with books in a language that the new bishop could not read, was dispersed. The Burgundian overlords joined the bishop on the Acropolis. They threw up high defensive walls all around it and obstructed the Panathenaic Way so that a once broad roadway became again what it had been in the Mycenaean era, a narrow and easily defensible path.

There were no Gothic doorways to mark their possession, like those that decorated the façade at Daphni and labeled it as defiantly un-Orthodox, but their westernization of the city was just as complete without them. Athens now resembled a European fortified town: like Rome, it had a circuit of ancient walls that ran through open country far beyond the real city limits. Well inside them was a second wall, the Late Roman wall, within which the houses of its small population clustered. At the center of the town—marked out by its elevation, its crenellated fortification walls, and a tall castle keep— was the segregated citadel of the ruling dynasty. Separation between the fully fortified Acropolis and the lower town would remain a feature of Athens until the nineteenth century.

Burgundian rule was successful in promoting trade and contributing to the international reputation of Athens as a center of European medieval culture. In other ways it was oppressive. Greeks were without civil rights; they could not own property or sell it. Greek ceased to be the language of government, and Orthodoxy gave way to Catholicism as the official religion. Latin bishops controlled the Greek Orthodox priests ministering to a people who consistently resisted conversion. In 1311, control of the city abruptly passed from one Western European nation to another. Byzantine emperor Andronicus II had hired Spanish mercenaries to fight against the Turks. Dissatisfied with their employer, the troops had attacked the Byzantine colony of Thrace. From there they continued on into the Greek peninsula, raiding and looting. They asked for permission to settle in Attica, a ploy that such bands often used to legitimize their depredations. When permission was predictably denied, they fought a battle near Thebes against Burgundian troops. The result was decisive. Not only were the Burgundian forces overwhelmed, but every member of the ruling family was wiped out. With no legitimate claimants to rule of the city, the Grand Catalan Company became the city's rulers. They moved into the fortified Acropolis, changed the official language of Athens to Spanish, and continued to impose Roman Catholicism.

In 1378, Italian adventurers led by a member of a prominent Florentine banking family drove out the Catalans. Conditions improved, and Greek once again became the official language. Some Athenians became citizens and gained political office. Intermarriage between Orthodox and Catholic was permitted, and an Orthodox archbishop returned to Athens after nearly two hundred years. In 1456, three years after the fall of Constantinople, Athens came under the control of the Ottoman Empire. From this date until independence in 1830, Greece was a province in a vast Muslim state.

Like all the foreign occupiers since 1204, the Ottoman overlords of Athens found the fortified Acropolis perfect for their needs. A force of soldiers garrisoned there could control the city, though they had little prospect of holding out against a rival army. Muslim troops lived on the Acropolis in a village of huts thrown up among the ancient monuments. The military governor had his headquarters there; civil government was housed in the Library of Hadrian. Some but not all of the Parthenon was remodeled to serve as a mosque. The Orthodox archbishop who continued to serve the Greek community was, along with all Christians, excluded from the Acropolis. His Parthenon church changed with the times: frescoes of saints and holy scenes painted on its marble walls during the Catholic years were simply whitewashed over. No significant structural modifications were made to a building that had already been reconfigured in a way familiar to Muslims who had, over the centuries, been heavily influenced by Roman and Byzantine architecture. A minaret was added at one of its corners. Both the Propylaia and the Erechtheum had gone through extensive changes that made them adaptable for multiple uses. The Propylaia became the military governor's residence, and his wives moved into the Erechtheum. The Athena Nike temple was used for a while to store gunpowder before it was dismantled and its pedestal outfitted as a gun emplacement.

The Ottoman Turks were old hands at ruling subject peoples. Since the seventh century CE, Muslims had been conquering and governing countries with very different cultures, laws, and religions from their own. Over time they had evolved an approach that was harsh in some ways, but also generally respectful of local customs and ideals. They always placed their governors and leaders in the top administrative, judicial, and military positions, but they preferred to have local men of influence fill all the lesser offices. Turkish was the language of the upper administration only, not of daily life. Though there were restrictions on the public performance of Christian rites, and church bells could never be rung, Muslims tolerated the faiths of conquered people and did not coerce them to convert. They did impose disproportionate taxes on non-Muslims, which in many parts of the empire led to widespread voluntary conversion. Non-Muslims were not allowed to wear the same clothes as Muslims, their houses could not stand higher than those of Muslims, and they could not carry weapons or ride horses. Non-Muslims were also subject to a terrifying form of taxation in kind. At irregular intervals, collectors from Istanbul would visit the city to seize young boys between the ages of ten and twelve. For the rest of their lives, these children would be members of an elite corps of soldiers called Janissaries. Units could be posted to any part of the empire; a member's lifetime allegiance would be only to his fellow soldiers and his commander. At times young girls would be taken to join the imperial harem. Children taken for either of these purposes would never return to their families.

Evliya Chelebi, an Ottoman Turk who traveled through much of the empire during the seventeenth century, was favorably impressed not just by the remains of the ancient city, but by the Turkish settlement of his own day. He described three residential areas along the northern fringes of the Acropolis where Muslims concentrated in sufficient numbers to support three large mosques and a number of smaller ones. There were two primary shopping areas—one in the old Roman market and another nearby. The shopping area and the administrative center in the Library of Hadrian formed the core of

Fethiye Mosque.

the Turkish town. There was a madrassa for religious instruction, and three schools for Muslim children. And there were three public baths.

The main survivors of Turkish Athens are the three large mosques and the ruins of the madrassa. Traces of the Turkish use of other areas have, for the most part, disappeared as sites were excavated. The Fethiye Mosque is typically dated to 1456, the date of the conquest of Athens—its name means "victory." While the name commemorates the triumph of one nation and religion over another, the architectural style of the building asserts kinship rather than dominance. The building, which has long been used as a storage area for architectural materials uncovered in the Agora excavations, is a multi-domed cubic construction that bears more than a superficial resemblance to an Orthodox cross-in-square church. There are two rows of large windows on its side walls. Rather than a closed narthex at the front of the building, an open arcade supported on reclaimed columns leads into a shaded porch. From there a number of windows open into the building on either side of a wide central door.

Across from the Fethiye Mosque are the ruins of the madrassa. This was an advanced school focused, like all Muslim education, on the Qur'an. At the madrassa, students improved their Arabic and learned some of the complexities of interpreting the foundational text. They also learned anecdotes about the Prophet and his sayings that supplement the Qur'anic tradition. Since traditional Muslim law is also grounded in those twin sources, the student might also have learned some aspects of legal doctrine and interpretation. Not every town would have had such a school, and it is not hard to imagine that the madrassa students in Athens saw themselves as successors of the ancient philosophers.

Little of the building survives beyond a bit of broken wall and a monumental gateway. Nothing about the architecture of that gateway identifies the building as belonging to an architectural tradition that is separate in any meaningful way from buildings that medieval Athenians created for themselves. A peaked roof crowns a barrel-vaulted porch and encloses an arched doorway. There is some use of classical architectural detail at the edges of the pillars supporting this arch. Most surprising is the bas-relief decoration on the surface of the pillars and pediment. Small circular target- or shield-like decorations are arranged here and there on them. They must have appeared to the builders to be neutral, decorative objects. In the ancient Greek architectural vocabulary, they had a particular meaning: they are stylized *pateras*, shallow wine cups for pouring out ceremonial gifts to the gods.

In Monastiraki Square sits the best preserved and most visible of the city's Turkish mosques. The Tzistarakis Mosque looks a great deal like the older Fethiye Mosque from the outside, though there are some differences. Its main dome is octagonal and disproportionate to the subordinate domes that surround it. Its multiple large windows, like those of the Fethiye Mosque, let light into the entire building. The porch is fronted by an arcade that was originally carried on columns taken from the Olympieion. This reuse of classical material was a violation of Ottoman law, and the building's patron, the then civil governor of Athens, was fined and removed from office.

The building now houses the Ceramics Museum, so it is open to the public. Its interior is open and well-lit—the entire space was used for worship and study. The galleries that surround the dome may have been reserved for women, although Muslim law does not require women to pray in mosques. The religious identity of the building is fixed by the presence of a *mihrab*, the

Tzistarakis Mosque, now home to the Ceramics Museum.

decorated niche that indicates the compass bearing of Mecca where Muslims direct their prayers. The niche is surmounted by the image of a fountain—water is an important symbol in Islam, as it is in Christian art. Beneath the fountain is a three-dimensional polychrome indentation in the wall that is shaped like an apse. There is a radiating design at its top, then a series of teardrop-shaped figures, and finally a series of brightly colored columns descending to the floor. The design appears to represent light emanating from the divine and being dispersed into the multiple colors of the rainbow. There are remnants of paintings on the drum of the central dome.

The other great reminder of Turkish rule is of course the Parthenon, which suffered its most severe damage during this period, though not of course at Muslim hands. In 1686, a Holy League uniting Rome, Venice, Austria, and Poland declared war against the Ottoman Empire. The campaign, which recruited a mixed bag of international soldiers of fortune, was led by a Venetian admiral with long experience fighting the Turks. Francesco Morosini had been the commander of a Venetian fortified colony on the island of Crete, which held out against Muslim attack for an incredible twenty-five years. Morosini made good use of his knowledge both of the Greek terrain and of Turkish tactics. He led his troops through the Peloponnesos at a quick pace, and by 1687 gained control of the region. His next goal was the conquest of Athens. Threatened with reprisals from both sides, Athenians gambled on the Venetians and welcomed the attackers when their fleet reached Piraeus.

Once the Venetians had landed, the Turks of Athens took refuge on the fortified Acropolis, as rulers of the city had done for thousands of years. Morosini could see the risks of attacking the fortified hilltop, and he was equally aware that little was to be gained from subduing a garrison that had sealed itself off. Still, when Turkish defenders refused to submit, he decided to attack. Accounts of the bombardment are contradictory and suspect. There is no doubt that on September 24, 1687, a Venetian cannon began to fire on the Acropolis. After two days of steady but unsuccessful bombardment, word reached Morosini—perhaps from an escapee from the citadel itself—that the Turkish defenders had transferred the bulk of their powder reserves to the Parthenon. Because the building had once been consecrated as a church, they believed that Christians would not attack it. With the same trust in Christian piety, women and children had been lodged there as well.

Whether that information also reached Morosini is unclear. It is certain that the attackers responded to whatever intelligence they received by redirecting their fire on the Parthenon. During the night of the twenty-seventh, what Morosini described to the Venetian government as "a lucky hit" somehow passed through the thick marble roof of the Parthenon. When the explosive shell struck inside the building, the powder magazine ignited. A building that had survived more or less intact for nearly two thousand years was instantaneously transformed into a ruin. The roof was completely blown off. Interior walls and colonnades were shattered. Concussion knocked more than half the building's sculptures and friezes to the ground. Falling blocks of marble crushed the women and children sheltered inside and others gathered around it. Marble reduced to shrapnel sprayed out in every direction. Three hundred men, women, and children died. By all accounts, the attackers were exultant: they greeted the "lucky shot" with shouts of "Long Live the Venetian Republic."

The cisterns of the Acropolis were short on water to fight the fire, and the Parthenon burned through the rest of the night and the following day. But even with the heavy losses they had suffered, the defenders continued to resist. They were pinning their hopes on a Turkish relief force that did indeed arrive, only to be repelled by the Venetians. With no hope left, the garrison gave in. Four hundred soldiers and more than twice as many civilians were granted safe passage to Izmir. Morosini immediately reported to the Venetian authorities that the ancient city of Athens was in his hands. In a follow-up message, he acknowledged the destruction of the Parthenon and the three hundred Turkish deaths. Despite complete military triumph, the Venetians were unable to hold the city. The certainty of a Turkish counterattack and an outbreak of plague prompted Morosini to order his troops to withdraw. The majority of the city's Greek population, terrified of what vindictive Turks might do on their return, left with them. The city was nearly deserted until 1691, when the sultan offered amnesty, restoration of property, and exemption from taxes to Greeks willing to resettle it.

In Europe, the Renaissance, which began in the fifteenth century, took hold in the sixteenth, and became an international phenomenon in the seventeenth, brought a new appreciation of classical culture. For most of that era, however, the ideal of the classical was a distinctly Roman one. What artists, the educated, and the well-to-do concerned themselves with primarily were the remains of Roman art and architecture and the works of Latin poets, historians, and orators. Throughout the same period—and spurred in part by the fall of Byzantium, which brought Greek scholars and books to the West—an interest in ancient Greece was slowly taking root. While most of the focus was on recovering Greek texts, there was also a slight but perceptible growth of interest in Greek artifacts and Greek architecture; in fact, a trickle of European visitors had made their way to Athens before Morosini's attack. (The information we have about the state of the Parthenon before the bombing comes from a series of drawings done in 1674 for the Marquis de Nointel, French ambassador to the sultan.) By the end of the eighteenth century, there was a noticeable European presence in Athens.

The travelers who came to Athens collected information: they drew and measured the ancient monuments still visible aboveground, and they did what they could to cajole the authorities into granting access to the Acropolis. As an Ottoman fortress, it was off-limits to Christians and, especially, to those whose interest in sketching and measuring antiquities might be construed as intelligence gathering. Occasional visitors gained special privileges. Not only were they permitted to draw and measure, but they might be allowed to excavate and to carry away bits and pieces of the art and artifacts that they uncovered. In 1788, Louis Sebastien Fauvel, who was then the French consul, won from the Ottoman authorities the exceptional privilege of digging on the Acropolis. Along with the permission to excavate, he was granted the right to ship fragments back to France, where they would become the property of a noble collector. The timing was poor for the Count de Choiseul-Gouffier: his collection was seized by the Revolution, and then, after 1802, a portion of "his" Parthenon frieze, a damaged metope, and other fragments were exposed for public view in the Louvre, where they remain to this day.

The far more successful and far more controversial collector Lord Elgin followed a similar path. Like Fauvel, Elgin had powerful connections at the Ottoman court. The French played a passive but significant role in his depredations. By 1801, when Elgin was negotiating with the sultan's representatives, the French and the English were political rivals in the Mediterranean. Elgin believed that the French might beat him to the punch and secure all the best materials from Greece. A few years earlier, on July 21, 1798, Napoleon's army had overwhelmed an elite Muslim cavalry unit and seized control of Egypt, which was then a territory within the Ottoman Empire. This unexpected victory caused great consternation in the Muslim world in general, and it put an end—for a time—to French influence in the Ottoman court. Not only was the sultan angry with France, but he was grateful to England. It was an English force, not an Ottoman one, that later drove the French army out of Egypt. On the strength of that seemingly generous act, the sultan granted to Elgin and his agents permission to excavate and to export what they dug up.

Giovanni Battista Lusieri headed Elgin's team of excavators and recorders in Athens. Even before Elgin obtained permission to remove objects, Lusieri and his assistants had been at work describing and sketching artifacts. Once Elgin had his document in hand, their work changed dramatically. Though the permit was not very different from the one granted to Fauvel a decade before, Elgin's interpretation of it was bold and unprecedented. His men did not limit themselves to exporting a few broken pieces from the dirt and the litter of architectural fragments created by Morosini's blast. They did this of course, but their major focus was the more intact sculptures still attached to the building. For the next decade, they seized everything they could. In 1810, they received official permission to ship the artifacts they had collected to Great Britain.

Elgin had intended to give his collection to the British nation, but as he began to suffer financial reversals, he offered the collection to the government for a price. A special committee of the House of Commons was charged with setting a price and at the same time determining if Elgin did indeed have legal possession of the artifacts he had gathered. Even in that era, there was concern about the right of one man or one nation to seize the cultural heritage of another. In the end, the House committee ruled that Elgin had a clear title and that the works could be transferred to the government, though at a price far lower than his lordship had hoped for. In 1816, the Parthenon sculptures went on display in the British Museum, where they can still be seen. The New Acropolis Museum has space set aside for them, and the argument over repatriation, which recently celebrated its two hundredth anniversary, shows no sign of resolution.

7

The War for Independence and the Creation of a National Capital

The Greek War for Independence was an extended one, and when even a few of its tangled roots are traced, its history becomes especially complex. A logical place to begin is with the Orlov Revolt of 1770. An unsuccessful and precocious prelude to full-scale revolution, this revolt owed its origins to the Great Power politics of the era. Its inception and fate both reflected the precarious international context in which political actions in the Eastern Mediterranean have always been set. The Orlov who gave a name to the revolt was not a Greek but a Russian admiral. He and his agents inspired Greek fighters from the Mani region to rise in revolt against their Turkish overlords and promised them support from Russian soldiers on land and from the Russian navy at sea.

Since the era of Peter the Great at the very beginning of the eighteenth century, Russian foreign policy had been directed toward the goal of linking up with Europe—not just intellectually and culturally, but physically. In that era, when overland transportation remained precarious and unreliable, access to Europe meant access to European waters. Peter the Great founded St. Petersburg on the Baltic Sea and opened what he called "a window on Europe." But this northern window was seasonal; during the long winter, its harbor iced up, and commerce with Europe came to a halt.

This half-open window whetted Russia's appetite for a year-round ice-free port with European access. The only place to find a warm-water port was on the Black Sea. But access to that sea was blocked both by the surviving vestiges of Genghis Khan's kingdom in the Ukraine and by the Ottoman Turks who controlled passage between the Black Sea and the Mediterranean. In the Russo-Turkish warfare of the 1770s, Greek rebellion promised to be useful to the Russians as a diversion. If revolt could be stirred up, the sultan would need to commit ships and troops. These forces would not be available to engage czarist troops. In the end things worked out very much as the Russians had hoped. Treaty negotiations gave them control over the Muslim kingdom in the Ukraine and all-important access to the Black Sea. From this time on, Russia had a Mediterranean interest and an official role as the protector of Orthodoxy in territories under Ottoman rule.

For the Greeks, the Orlov Revolt, though crushed by the sultan's forces, showed very clearly that the spirit was willing. It also demonstrated some of the hazards of the international political situation that Greece would have to navigate if a revolt were to be successful. And after the 1770s that situation took on a new dynamic. The American Revolution showed that countries dominated by Great Powers could prevail against their overlords. The political debate in France that would lead to Revolution in 1789 was galvanized by this event; during the lead-up to revolution, French philosophers and political theorists laid a strong foundation that justified violent liberation from oppressive rule.

French writers did not confine their polemics to their own domestic political situation. Voltaire urged the empress of Russia, Catherine the Great, to liberate Greece. In a separate campaign, he appealed to the monarchs of Europe to do the same. A French stage play of the period celebrated the liberation of ancient Athens by the tyrant slayers Harmodius and Aristogeiton. Far more important than these specific texts, however, was the prevalence of revolutionary debate and theorizing among educated men and women. Two Greeks were especially affected by this atmosphere: Rigas Phereos and Adamantios Korais. Both were founding spirits of the Greek War for Independence, though their contributions were largely intangible. Rigas, born in Greece but active for most of his life in Vienna, has been credited with linking justifications of the French and American Revolutions to the Greek cause. Even more significant in the end than these intellectual foundations was the fate of Rigas himself. Austria was in its own way just as repressive as the Ottoman Empire. Thought and expression there were carefully monitored. Rigas and his correspondents knew the risks and took precautions. Preparing for a trip to Trieste, Rigas wisely sent his subversive writings on ahead to avoid having them found on his person by customs officers. Unfortunately the documents were opened not by their intended recipient but by his business partner, who turned the seditious writings over to the authorities. Rigas and seventeen others identified through the captured texts were arrested and transported to Vienna for trial. None was an Austrian subject, and all were repatriated to their home countries. Unfortunately for Rigas and a handful of others, their homeland was the Ottoman Empire. Rigas attempted suicide before being turned over to Turkish officers in Belgrade. During the night of June 24, 1798, Ottoman agents murdered him and seven others and threw their bodies into a river. Their killers declared that the prisoners had drowned while trying to escape. Rigas's friend and biographer, Perrevos, reported his last words: "This is how brave men die. I have sown; the time will soon come when my country will gather the harvest."

Korais, born in Izmir, spent most of his adult life in Paris. His contribution to the revolutionary impetus was indirect, but very significant. As the translator of ancient Greek texts into the language as it was spoken by men and women in the eighteenth century, Korais provided the independence movement with an accessible heritage in a language that he helped to regularize and dignify. A national language has sometimes been facetiously described as a dialect with an army. Korais had no army to offer, but he was one of the founders of a national language that became a significant tool for unification of thought and action.

The most mysterious of the early organizations favoring revolution was the Philiki Eteria—the Friendly Association. The founders of this organization were, like Rigas, well aware of the dangers of subversion. They were also inspired by the eighteenth-century vogue for secret societies, the most important of which were the Masons. In emulation of the Masonic hierarchy, they organized their new association into a series of obscure rankings that included "brothers" at the lowest level of membership, then "priests" who acted as recruiters. Above this rank were the "shepherds," who were expected to fund the organization. At the top echelon stood the Supreme Council or Invisible Directorate. The obscurity of this body allowed its members some protection from detection and arrest. It also allowed the founders of the organization to pretend that their secret society was ruled by men of great power and influence, though in its early days this was by no means the case. The name they had invoked from the start as their unacknowledged director was that of Ioannis Kapodistrias. Kapodistrias was born in Greece, but like so many talented Greeks of his era, he found his opportunity to excel beyond the borders of the Ottoman realm. Recruited into the Russian foreign ministry early in the century, in 1815 he became its codirector. Despite their best efforts to associate themselves with the real powers in the Greek émigré community, the founders of the Friendly Association had few connections and little status. Kapodistrias's affiliation, to say nothing of his guiding hand, was pure illusion.

In 1814, the founders regrouped in Istanbul and reorganized the society. They began to have some success raising money from prominent donors, and they could finally send representatives into Greece to recruit and to plan for active revolt. Their most important achievement was their ability at last to attract the prominent leadership they had always claimed. By asserting for so long that Kapodistrias headed their society, the founders had created a significant hurdle. If they could finally bring him in, then all would be well. They made repeated attempts to have him accept the leadership, but he remained adamant. When this became clear, the problem shifted. Now they needed Kapodistrias to give his blessing in some way to the search for an alternate leader. In 1819, with Kapodistrias's tacit approval, they chose Alexander Ypsilantis, a prince with hereditary rights in Romania. Ypsilantis was born in Istanbul, but during a newly erupted Russo-Turkish War at the beginning of the nineteenth century, his family fled the Ottoman Empire and found asylum in Russia. Ypsilantis joined the cavalry, and during the Napoleonic invasion of Russia rose to the rank of colonel. After the war he was appointed aide-de-camp to the czar, promoted to the rank of major general, and given command of a brigade.

By the time Ypsilantis agreed to head the Philiki Eteria, it had become in fact what it had always pretended to be: it had gained the support of powerful and wealthy families in the widespread Greek émigré community; it had built a network of sympathizers and recruiters inside Ottoman territory; and it had the ability to coordinate activities between the two groups. Ypsilantis gave it experienced military leadership, an air of glamour and prestige, along with the expectation of Russian support when rebellion broke out. The major members of the group met in Bucharest in May 1820 to forge a plan for action. That plan was a bold and ambitious one, and it embraced territories far beyond what the modern nation of Greece would claim.

"What is Greece?" has long been, and in some key places remains, a subject of debate. For Greeks today and for the people of Macedonia and

Cyprus, the question is still a hot-button issue. For men and women of the nineteenth century scheming to carve out a nation from the Ottoman Empire, the question was even more pressing, and its answer far less clear. Was Greece the Greek mainland, or the mainland plus most of the Eastern Mediterranean islands, which is more or less what the nation is today? Or was it something bigger, as it had been at many times in the past? Ancient Greece had embraced the mainland, the islands, the shores of the Western Mediterranean and Black Seas, substantial parts of Southern Italy, and most of Sicily. The Hellenistic empire of Alexander the Great and his successors included West Asia and the conqueror's Macedonian homeland. The Byzantine Empire ruled these territories and more.

The fluid identity of an entity not yet born and not yet thoroughly thought out is evident from the scale of the plans that the revolutionaries of 1820 discussed in Bucharest. Their aims embraced revolution in Serbia, Montenegro, and parts of Romania—not because these were thought of as part of Greece necessarily, but because they had large Greek communities and because, as Ottoman subjects, all these countries shared a common plight with Greece. The Balkans were a place where loyal and hardened soldiers could be recruited in a common cause of emancipation, and this was Ypsilantis's home territory, where his power and influence were at their peak. In what was evidently a strategic rather than a nationalistic campaign, the insurrectionists also hoped to stir up trouble in the Ottoman capital, Istanbul. They intended, if they could, to burn the Turkish fleet. The main event, of course, would be rebellion on Greek territory. Ypsilantis was to follow up his campaign in the Balkans with a march through the Peloponnesos.

Events did not follow the program. When Ottoman spies learned of the organization's plans, the conspirators accelerated their schedule. Ypsilantis pushed into Romania. Among his officers there were many Russian subjects of Greek origin, and all imagined that the czar, as the recognized protector of the Orthodox community, would welcome their campaign of liberation. At any other time, he probably would have done so, but at the moment of the eruption into Romania, Russian foreign policy was leaning uncustomarily toward peaceful coexistence with the Turks. The czar dissociated himself from Ypsilantis. Kapodistrias, his loyalty to Russia in question, denounced the incursion, and stripped Ypsilantis of his rank and his command. But it was too late for Kapodistrias. Though unwilling to link himself to the

Philiki Eteria, he could not sidestep their actions. He lost the support of the czar and with it his ministerial position. Meanwhile, despite the lack of international backing, events on the ground were not going badly for Ypsilantis's troops; political control of Romania seemed within their grasp. Then a large Ottoman force marched against them, which they failed to cut off when the opportunity presented itself. The advantage passed to the other side, and the would-be liberators suffered a massive defeat in June 1821. By this time, revolt had broken out on the mainland.

March 25, 1821, the feast of the Immaculate Conception, is the traditional date of the beginning of the Greek War for Independence. Inspired by Ypsilantis's early successes in Romania, rebels in the Mani region declared war on May 17. The uprising Ypsilantis was slated to lead in the Peloponnesos took off on its own, ignited by a moment of opportunity. The Ottoman governor of the region, Hursid Pasha, and his troops were out of the territory campaigning not against Greek rebels but against an Ottoman official, Ali Pasha. Ali, who had built a power base for himself in Northern Greece, felt strong enough to refuse allegiance to the sultan. Hursid Pasha and his troops were dispatched to bring the rebel to justice. Hursid's absence was an opportunity not to be missed, and the rebels of the Peleponnesos took up arms.

The Peloponnesos and especially the Mani had a long history of resistance to Turkish authority. During the abortive Orlov Revolt and in sporadic campaigns thereafter, fighters had gained experience of the tactics and abilities of the occupying power. Their willingness to go to war against the Ottoman Empire increased in the decade following the final defeat of Napoleon. In the aftermath of pan-European war, a period of economic depression struck the Continent. The Ottoman authorities were powerless to reverse it, and the people under their domination suffered hardship and hunger as a result. Widespread want gave an extra spur to revolution.

The efforts of the Philiki Eteria to coordinate the efforts of multiple combatants in different parts of the peninsula were insufficient and ultimately unsuccessful. The Greek War of Independence played out as a series of parallel initiatives at best, and often as a conflict not of Greek against Ottoman but of Greek against Greek. Between 1821 and 1823, however, the history of warfare was more or less a single narrative. Multiple successes by forces acting on their own added up to a campaign that seemed to be moving in a single direction. Towns and cities in the Peloponnesos and in central Greece were liberated, and a number of new leaders emerged, most notably Theodoros Kolokotronis. Athens was liberated in April 1821, though an Ottoman garrison continued to occupy the Acropolis. Not only was the rebellion successful on land, but Greek ships scored victories over the Ottoman navy. The uprising inspired international respect. European sympathizers, known as Philhellenes, raised money and garnered widespread support for the cause of Greek independence.

In the first blush of military success, the insurgents met in congress to create a national government. When this government dissolved under pressure not from the Ottoman Empire, but from rival factions in the independence movement, a second congress in 1823 formed a new national government with Petrobey Mavromichalis at its head. The victories won in the first two years of warfare proved to be short-lived. For his counterattack, the sultan planned a pincer movement to envelop the rebels. Ottoman troops invaded from the north, while Egyptian troops under Mahomet Ali, sultan of Egypt, landed at Messini in the southern Peloponnesos. As the two armies marched toward each other, they swept up the insurgents and recaptured the majority of towns and cities that they had lost. By 1826, Muslim troops had retaken Athens.

Though individual Philhellenes like Lord Byron were deeply involved in the struggle, the Great Powers of the era, Britain and France, remained aloof. Both nations had long-term interests in the Eastern Mediterranean; both were troubled by Russia's increasing influence there and reasoned that a successful Greek campaign would further increase it. What propelled the two to more direct action was the involvement of Egyptian troops. It was one thing for the Ottoman Empire to intervene in the affairs of its own territories, but neither France nor Britain was ready to accept Egyptian influence in Greece. Through treaties and diplomatic action, the two powers tried at first to guarantee the future of a semiautonomous Greek state within the Ottoman Empire. The sultan was unwilling to accept their terms, and the issue was ultimately decided not diplomatically but militarily. At the battle of Navarino in 1827, a combined British and French fleet destroyed the Ottoman-Egyptian navy.

Their victory confirmed European control over the Eastern Mediterranean, and it might have set the stage for the semiautonomous state that

France and Britain had imagined; however, the Greeks had stolen the march on their reluctant sponsors, and at the Assembly of Troezen in May 1827 they had created yet another national government. As president, they had elected none other than Ioannis Kapodistrias—the man who refused leadership of the Philiki Eteria had remained equally aloof from every revolutionary faction and so was acceptable to them all. As a former foreign minister, he had the trust of the European diplomats whom he would have to influence if Greece were to thrive in the political world of its era. Unfortunately, the job proved too much for anyone to accomplish. Despite diplomatic opposition and a resounding naval defeat, the sultan continued to press his claims. The country, which had been ravaged by almost a decade of warfare, had no money to raise troops or to repair infrastructure. When Kapodistrias overstepped his constitutional powers in an attempt to meet these challenges, veteran revolutionaries assassinated him.

Continuing political instability in Greece was a major concern of the Great Powers. Any point of conflict in the region threatened the balance of power, which was the governing diplomatic strategy of the era. Britain, France, and Russia made repeated attempts to negotiate a final solution to the issue, and in a series of diplomatic conversations and conventions over the period of Kapodistrias's government, they worked to achieve a compromise that they could live with. Whether it was something the Greek people could live with was a matter of secondary importance to the powers. Democratic self-government, which the Greeks had repeatedly chosen for themselves, was not something that the powers were prepared to institute. Both Britain and Russia were long-established monarchies, of course, and in the post-Napoleonic era, France, despite its recent revolutionary past, was governed by a succession of revanchist kings. The first choice of rulers was Leopold of Belgium. He lost interest when the boundaries proposed for the new kingdom were shrunk.

The next proposal, and the one that finally took hold, gave the Greek throne to Prince Otto, the son of King Ludwig I of Bavaria. The line of succession was to pass through Otto, his heirs, and siblings; Bavaria and Greece were never to be united under a single ruler. The young king was required to pledge that he would not make war on the Ottoman Empire. In further deference to the sultan's sensibilities, Otto was named King of Greece, not King of the Greeks. The boundaries of his new realm were drawn in such a way that it included less than half of the ethnic Greeks living under Ottoman rule. The sultan collected a large indemnity from the Great Powers, who also underwrote the Greek government with loans.

Otto was only seventeen when he arrived in Greece with three Bavarian ministers to serve as regents during his minority, as well as thirty-five hundred Bavarian troops. His transport was a British frigate. The regents made most of the decisions until 1835, when Otto assumed power in his own right. In 1843, after a peaceful demonstration of political unity and discontent, Otto, who had long been known by the Hellenized name of Othon, granted a constitution. These demonstrations took place in the square outside the Royal Palace. The crowd's demand for a constitution—in Greek, *syntagma*—gave the square the name that it still has today. Otto ruled as a constitutional monarch until a coup put a new government in place in 1862. The British urged the monarch to accept the fait accompli, and he left the country as he had entered it thirty years before, aboard a British warship.

The war had not spared Athens. In 1821, Athens had a population estimated at about eleven thousand people. They were a mixture of Greeks, Turks, and Albanians, who had settled in Greece in large numbers during the Ottoman era. The city was not big by world standards, but in the Balkans, it was larger than most. In Greece it stood behind Tripolis, the Ottoman capital, and Nauplion. The liberation of Athens in 1821 had been quick: the Ottoman garrison had holed up on the Acropolis, and the liberated town went about its business while the garrison waited for a change of fortune. Not much damage was done on either side. The recapture of Athens by Egyptian forces in 1826 was a far more destructive event. This time the Greeks took shelter on the Acropolis, and the enemy response was far more aggressive. Determined to capture the stronghold, the Egyptian army carried out a devastating six-month siege. When they prevailed, Ottoman forces again occupied the stronghold. They finally left it in 1833, some time after Otto's arrival in his new kingdom. By then the town was a pale reflection not just of its ancient character but even of its immediate prewar state.

The population was drastically reduced. Houses, churches, mosques, and other public and private buildings had been abandoned, and many were heavily damaged. In August 1832, Ludwig Ross exclaimed:

> This is not the violet-crowned and famous Athens. This is just a massive heap of rubble, a shapeless gray mass of ash and dust, from which

emerge a dozen or so palm and cypress trees, the only things opposing a universal desolation.

Around the same time (1832–1833), another observer, J. L. Lacour, part of the expeditionary force of General Maison, described his impressions:

> The heart tightens on arriving in Athens. New ruins cover the ancient, which are buried in the earth. . . . Narrow, dark, muddy, erratic paths. Filthy, sooty and foul-smelling shops, with goods that would be held in contempt even by the traveling merchants at our village festivals, and all of this surrounded by a crude wall. (Korres, 327)

The state of desolation and confusion on the ground was echoed in the legal status of properties within the city, an issue that would have an important effect on the new capital that was soon to be developed.

Though the Ottoman Empire still threatened, and Ottoman troops occupied the Acropolis, in 1831 plans were already on the drawing board to create a national capital in Athens for the still precariously independent nation. In November of that year, two architects, Stamatios Kleanthis and Edward Schaubert, who were both associates of the noted Bavarian architect Karl Friedrich Schinkel, began surveying the city, its monuments, and buildings in preparation for designing a national capital. In spring they were commissioned by the interim government that succeeded Kapodistrias to design a city that might or might not serve in that role. Resistance to Athens as the capital, a sub-current that would run through much of the nineteenth century, was not just a matter of intercity rivalry. The major objection to Athens as capital arose from the perennially recurring question of the identity of the Greek nation. This issue was commonly referred to as "the Great Idea," a concept of Greek nationhood that embraced the ancestrally Greek and Greek-speaking community that was widely dispersed through the Ottoman Empire and beyond its borders. For the proponents of the Great Idea, Athens, though evocative of one climactic period of Greek life, was not the best representative of the Greek community in its most inclusive definition. Many imagined Constantinople, former capital of the Byzantine Empire, as the more fitting capital for the Greek people as a whole. Athens was eventually accepted when it was reconceived as a capital not only of a newly formed nation but of the Greek diaspora community as well.

By December 1832, a year after their arrival in Athens and three months before the Turkish garrison was to leave the Acropolis for good, the architects delivered the first draft of their plan. Approved by the regency government soon after, the plan was accepted as the blueprint for the seat of the newly minted monarchy. Though modified within the next few years in significant ways and changed again bit by bit throughout the nineteenth century, the city plan they designed is entirely recognizable in Athens today.

The plan was based on careful analysis of the site, and built into it from the start were a number of givens, some particular to the geographical situation and others more broadly representative of city planning in the early nineteenth century. The axiom of axioms was clear: the new city would be oriented toward the Acropolis. It would embrace that monument from the north and point directly toward it through the creation of a central ceremonial avenue. To achieve these goals, the designers created a triangle of avenues at the center of their map. Though their function has changed, these avenues still define the heart of modern Athens. The avenue that points toward the Acropolis is today called Athenas Street. The avenue that intersects it and defines the base of the triangle is Ermou. Two streets close the triangle: Piraeus Street on the west, and Stadiou on the east. Both streets were designed not just as urban arteries but as scenic vistas. From the apex of the triangle, a viewer slightly above ground level could see the port of Piraeus to the southwest along Piraeus Street and the Panathenaic Stadium to the southeast down sight lines opened by Stadiou. Straight ahead, of course, a viewer would see the Acropolis. In the original plan, the junctions of these arteries with their base in Ermou were to be monumentalized by two great circles. The apex of the triangle was to be a great square. These plans changed along the way. Ermou and Stadiou now meet in Syntagma Square, not the great circle the designers imagined. There is no embellishment at all of the intersection between Ermou and Piraeus.

Omonia Square sits at the apex of the triangle. The prominence of Omonia was no accident: by the time the plan was given the royal seal of approval on July 6, 1833, this urban centerpiece and privileged viewpoint was clearly and unmistakably designated as the site of the Royal Palace. It would be surrounded on the west, north, and east by formal gardens, with an open ceremonial court in front leading into the all-important central axis, not in the original plan a mere roadway, but a long rectangular park, succeeded by a hemicycle and then a short stretch of avenue ending at the Late Roman wall, just where it bulged to encircle the Library of Hadrian.

And just at that point is where trouble began. The new urban grid that presented itself in relation to historical and cultural landmarks was also designed to engage the city of Athens as it existed at that time. Ravaged by war, depopulated, and confused in the assignment of property rights as it was, it still existed, and its boundaries were more or less determined by structural underpinnings of considerable antiquity. Without too much acknowledgment, the Kleanthis-Schaubert plan was designed to mesh with this city. Its principal diagonals traced the old Themistoclean wall, which had been renewed repeatedly over multiple generations, and the inner boundary of the plan corresponded closely to the Late Roman wall.

Pre-independence Athens had been largely but not exclusively bounded by the Late Roman wall. In the Turkish era, some housing had spread beyond it and in the northwest quadrant of the city almost reached the Themistoclean wall. In most parts of the city, though, that wider circuit embraced as much cropland and pasture as it did streets and houses. In the chaotic state of affairs that still governed when the plan was first put together and approved, what to do with this old city embraced by the new was a relatively simple question to answer. What the planners at first thought best was the creation of a large archaeological area within the boundaries of the old town, along with a reorganization of the remainder along strictly modern lines. Within the Late Roman wall, in other words, an archaeological park and an old town with a new, rectilinear street grid were to be created.

Over the course of the next few years, increasing resistance to the plan for modern Athens came from a resurgent old Athens. As families moved back, and as conflicts of ownership surfaced and were resolved, property owners became increasingly sure of their rights and increasingly insistent that they not be impinged on by the new city plan. Their successful reorganization and resistance were reflected in revised plans that followed one another in quick succession. The archaeological area shrank, the wide avenues and streets became narrower, and the most conspicuous change of all came in the projected street grid—the new geometry that the plan would have imposed on the old city was abandoned. The twisting roads and paths of the old town, which in their intricacy captured the complexities of land ownership, would stay. The revised plan put into effect by royal decree in 1833 shows the tight embrace of the tangled network of village streets by the shining grid of the new city. The stainless steel wrench of a European neoclassical capital still grips the rusty nut of the old city, called the Plaka today.

The great triangle was just the skeleton on which a substantial urban fabric was to depend. Anyone familiar with L'Enfant's late eighteenth-century plan for Washington, D.C., would see many similarities with the somewhat later plan for Athens, which is also a reflection of neoclassical ideals of city planning. One major difference stands out: L'Enfant created a complex web of diagonal avenues intersecting, as they do in the Athens plan, in monumentalized squares and circles, and beneath this web he placed a modified but still recognizable grid plan where all the lesser streets meet at right angles. The Athens plan is complex by comparison: around the great square, the streets run parallel to its four sides, and while the streets along the diagonal avenues are perpendicular to each other, the grids there are based in the diagonals, and intersect obliquely with streets radiating out from Omonia Square. The purpose of this feature seems to have been to create lines of propagation from which an expanding city could grow in a logical manner. The subsequent history of Athens shows that this was a reasonable but overly optimistic idea.

The other significant modification of the original plan centered on the Royal Palace. Its placement in Omonia Square, where all the great sight lines of the original plan converged to create a privileged point of view, was entirely in keeping with neoclassical principles of expressing power and privilege through urban organization. The forces that argued for the removal of the palace to a less conspicuous and less commanding location held different views. It is not clear what institution, if any, they might have wished to occupy this place; it is also difficult to understand why the monarchy would have been willing to give up this central spot—almost certainly it was a gesture by the new king to accommodate the sentiments of his subjects.

Whatever the reason, plans were soon made to move the palace to the northwest, near the Hephaisteion. They were quickly revised when that area was labeled malarial. The final choice was to move the Royal Palace from the apex of the central triangle to its eastern corner, where Ermou and Stadiou meet. This dislocation did not change the city grid, but it influenced development very dramatically. Like a powerful magnet, the palace drew the

The old Royal Palace, which now hosts the Greek parliament.

growing city toward it. As a result of its relocation, monumental building in Athens is disproportionately located on the eastern extremity of the central triangle. Once the building was sited, the soon-to-be christened Syntagma Square and Amalias Avenue, named for Otto's queen, were laid out by a military architect.

The Royal Palace was one of the first buildings under construction in the new city. King Othon's father, Ludwig I, visited Athens in 1835 and brought with him the Bavarian architect Friedrich von Gaertner. The architect was responsible for introducing to modern Athens a neoclassicism that was already becoming the preferred vocabulary of building in the Bavarian capital of Munich. In Athens, however, it achieved much greater resonance, as it mirrored not just a revered international style but resurrected an indigenous architecture created and perfected on the spot but abandoned during the long period when Greeks were no longer masters of their own fate. By restoring the architectural vocabulary of ancient Greece to the modern capital, the Bavarian architect was enabling Athens to speak in its native idiom again.

The palace was constructed—over a span of seven years—of native materials in an ancient style. During the course of construction, the project served not just as an architectural model but as a trade school for the first generation of Athenian craftsmen, who were learning to work in the style and the stone of their ancestors. To the modern eye, the building is monotonous (as it was to the eye of many contemporaries). Its most distinctive features are clustered together in the center of what could easily pass for a watered-down version of Bernini's Palazzo Montecitorio in Rome. Even in the center bay, the most distinctly classical features are confined to the ground floor and the roofline. A portico in the form of a stoa with a balcony above it shelters the three entrances to the building. The peaked roof over this center section features acroteria at its corners and apex.

While the Royal Palace has classical features, the building does not correspond to any ancient institution. Today, it houses the Greek parliament. Fifth-century Athens had no palace: its tradition of government was democratic, and the architectural representations of its political principles were the Agora, the Pnyx, and the Areopagus. The other identifying structures of the ancient city were those that sustained its role as educator, conservator of the tradition of learning, and patroness of the arts. Though the codification of this trio was more the work of the Hellenistic and Roman eras than it was of the democratic and independent city, still the identification of Athens with these key institutions was ancient and strong. Architectural expression of these ancient functions in the modern capital was essential to its identity.

The most significant and successful neoclassical structures in Athens are the trio of buildings that embody this ancient heritage and house the University of Athens, the National Library, and the Greek Academy. Construction of the university began in 1839, during the monarchy's first decade in power and while the palace was still under construction. Funding came from a number of sources, including the private wealth of the monarch himself. Despite its importance and despite its powerful backers, the building proceeded at a snail's pace—it remained unfinished until 1864. The university was designed by Christian Hansen, who augmented his neoclassical training by working on the reconstruction of the Athena Nike temple on the Acropolis. His building has a far more unified and appealing façade than the palace. Rather than appearing as a generic block with a neoclassical

The main building of the University of Athens.

central bay, the university is unified in composition and linked to ancient models. The overall integrity of the building depends on an entablature that runs completely around its perimeter and echoes an equally classicizing foundation course. The main entrance is a monumental portal—a reimagined Propylaia—defined by two Ionic columns framed by pilasters that support a pediment with acroteria at its corners and apex. On either side of this entryway are colonnades where square pillars springing from a high wall create a stoa-like arrangement of closed and open spaces. Beyond this, the façade is continued by two windowless stretches of wall. The proportions, the stark linearity, and the absence of ornament all give Hansen's university building enormous presence and dignity. The interplay of open and closed spaces focuses attention on its most significant monumental feature, the propylaia.

Some critics at the time of its creation believed that the university was a misstep. They argued that funds devoted to higher learning might be better spent on public elementary education, which was in a dismal state in nineteenth-century Greece. But contemporary criticism of the university project was insignificant in comparison to the dissent sparked by the foundation of an academy. The newspaper *Aion* remarked in 1858, "We have no ships, no army, no roads, but soon we will have an Academy. Turkey, beware!"

Plato's Academy was a philosophical school, a role that was carried on by the university. What the Greek Academy proposed to do was something that Plato would not have recognized or perhaps appreciated. The proposed Academy would reflect a French ideal rather than the classical one. It was an officially sanctioned body that would encourage cooperation among men of science and achievement in the arts, especially the arts of language; it would promote business and commerce. Like the Académie Française that has since the seventeenth century regulated the French language, overseen its dictionaries, and rewarded its notable authors, the Academy in Athens would also watch over the development of the modern Greek language.

The building to house the Academy was designed by Theophil Hansen, the younger brother of the architect of the university. It was financed by Baron Simon Sinas, a Greek of the diaspora who lived in Vienna. Land next to the university was a gift of the city and the Petrake Monastery. The multiplicity of contributors is characteristic of the way the building of the new national capital was financed. The Greek government simply did not have the funds to create national infrastructure out of nothing. Private donors, many of whom were Greeks of the diaspora rather than nationals, were among the most important patrons of the city. Private benefactions had made significant contributions to the cityscape of Athens in the Hellenistic and Roman periods, and this practice was revived and honored in the neoclassical era.

The university building was a new creation in the spirit of classicism that was not specifically indebted to any single ancient building or even to any ancient building type. It had some connections to the Library of Hadrian and some to the ancient stoa, but it was entirely independent of either. The Academy building, on the other hand, was much more literal in its evocation of classical orders and classical building types. Its underlying classical model was the Acropolis, where buildings on different scales were sited together. Its far more apparent structural debt, however, is to the tripartite palazzo plan with center bay and projecting wings, a widespread European style based, ultimately, on the Palazzo Barberini in Rome.

The Greek Academy.

The Academy is an amalgam of temple buildings clustered around a monumental entry. Its constituent parts imitate the Propylaia and the east side of the Erechtheum. Set on a high pedestal and approached by ramps and a central stairway, the building complex links a shallow pedimented Ionic temple front with two symmetrically placed subordinate temples turned to the side and facing inward. The three are strung together by a stoa. On either side of the monumental entrance are two free-standing Ionic columns with images of Athena and Apollo at their summits. The pedimental sculpture on the main temple front represents the birth of Athena. Terracotta sculptures on the smaller façades represent Athena as patron of agriculture, industry, shipbuilding, and the sciences in general; these are the practical spheres of life in which the abstract thought of the academicians was expected to bear fruit. One of the most striking features of the building is the use of paint and gilding to enhance its ornamentation.

The National Library, also designed by Theophil Hansen, is clearly a companion piece to the Academy. It is composed along similar lines, but it is less clearly indebted to individual monuments. At the center of the three-part complex is an unmistakable Greek temple with six Doric columns supporting an entablature with a frieze of triglyphs and metopes. Above is a shallow pediment with no inset sculptural decoration. Acroteria mark the corners and apex of the roof. The temple and its dependencies sit on a high foundation. The central temple is reached by a curving stairway that combines both ramp and stairs and defines a central elliptical void that is focused around a statue of Panagis Valianos, one of three brothers who funded the building. This ellipse is surrounded by a larger partial ellipse that springs from the base of the twin stairways. The curvature of the stairs and the incorporation of an ellipse into the design reflect nineteenth-century rather than classical ideals. The smaller flanking buildings are recognizable versions of Greek temple fronts, but their colonnades have been replaced by a wall with lightly inscribed pilasters and entablature surrounding triple windows.

Some of the opponents of the Academy had argued that funds for that structure would be better spent on a national museum. While the United States Congress at almost exactly the same time was trying to figure out what to do with the unexpected legacy that would eventually fund the Smithsonian Institution, the rulers of Greece had a clearer understanding of the role such an institution could play. The museum would inevitably showcase the material culture that characterized the Greek past in its most significant eras. It would make the case for the modern state as the successor to one of the great civilizations. It would play a clear and valuable role in the assertion of national identity.

Ancient works of art had been on exhibit in Athens long before the museum was opened. After independence, the Hephaisteion—on its hill overlooking the Agora—was quickly transformed from a church into a national shrine commemorating the classical past. It figured prominently in Othon's coronation, and it served in the years following as a public exhibition space for archaeological finds. The building was also the headquarters of the Central Archaeological Museum, established in 1834 by the new king. This national organization was the owner of the collections exhibited in the Hephaisteion along with others exhibited in the ruins of the Library of Hadrian and in the Varvakeion, a girls' school that opened in 1860.

The concept of the National Museum and the collection both preceded, by decades, the building of a structure large enough to exhibit a rapidly ex-

The National Library.

panding collection of antiquities. As was the case with the other significant national monuments, funds for the museum building came from many sources. Helen Tositsa, wife of a diaspora Greek who had made a fortune in Egypt as a producer and trader in cotton, gave the land. Financing for the new structure came from Demetrios Bernardakis. Ludwig Lange was the architect, but important modifications were made to his plans by Ernst Zwiller. Work went on from 1866 to 1889, when the entire project was completed. The west wing of the museum opened in 1874.

The building façade reflects features of all three of the neoclassical trio: its entryway is a version of the Propylaia, its projecting wings are stoa-like, and the wings each end in temples turned end on. Like the similar end pieces in the National Library, these temples have triple windows rather than colonnades. The ground plan of the building is not easy to guess from looking at the façade. Rather than the long and shallow stoa-like building it appears to be, the museum is square in plan, with four courtyards cut out of its enclosed space. The interior is richly decorated with brightly colored murals in traditional designs. The museum collection is enormous and of the highest quality. The theme of the collection is ancient Greek art as a whole, from the beginning of the Neolithic to the end of the Roman era.

Neoclassicism, redefined and reinvented as it was in the city's most significant trio of buildings, was only one of the architectural traditions that builders turned to as they gave definition to the ideals animating the capital of a new nation. Classicism and Hellenism were significant movements in the Greek past, and they grounded a concept of nationhood that was very important, but they were not the only sources of inspiration. Byzantine architecture was also closely attached to the history of the Greeks; it was well understood, and its characteristics were easily identified. There was one feature that gave Byzantine building an edge—its association with the Orthodox religion, which neither Hellenism nor classicism could claim. In the first half of the nineteenth century, neoclassicism was the dominant international architectural trend, but as the century progressed, there was a shift in enthusiasm toward the medieval. Though most medieval revivalism was centered on the Northern European Gothic, Byzantine architecture also enjoyed a renewal, and international architects began to emulate this style. The architectural revival of Byzantine styles in Athens had particular resonances for the Greek capital, but that revival was, like neoclassicism, part of an international movement.

The most prominent neo-Byzantine structure in Athens is, appropriately enough, the cathedral. It was originally going to be placed near the university, but this site was far from the center of the community that the church was designed to serve, and so the location was changed and the building placed within the limits of the old town. Christian Hansen designed a building that had some Byzantine characteristics but that on the whole bore as much resemblance to the Cistercian addition to Daphni as it did to the main body of that or any other Byzantine-era building. The western façade of Hansen's design combined a series of Byzantine horseshoe-arched portals and windows with a round, stained-glass rose window and two sharply pointed towers. It had a long nave and transept, the crossing surmounted by a dome raised on a drum that was to be surrounded by a colonnade. Hansen's plan was modified by Demetres Zezos. Zezos removed the rose window and the steep spires, but the building he created is still eclectic in inspiration and far removed from the surviving Byzantine churches of Athens.

Yet another historical current is represented by the architecture of the building that now houses the Byzantine Museum. Stamatios Kleanthis, co-creator of the original plan for the new city, was also an architect in private practice. In 1840, he designed a villa for the French Philhellene the Duchesse de Plaisance, on a site overlooking the (now buried) Ilissos River. The building is unmistakably Roman in inspiration, with square towers at the ends of its façade joined together by a double arcade of round-topped arches. Though it now serves a national purpose that has been at various times intimately connected with the Great Idea and the broadest concepts of Greek identity, it was built originally as a private country villa. The architect was free to work in an idiom with no political resonance.

The plans for the new capital had always given prominence to the Olympieion and the Panathenaic Stadium. When the Royal Palace moved from its central position to the new location on Syntagma Square, these monuments gained even greater importance. Developing this area and integrating it into the life of the new capital was a matter of urgency, but the way to do it was not immediately clear. Royal gardens were planted at the rear of the palace, and in 1869 land was granted between these gardens and the ancient stadium for the revival of the ancient Olympics. The driving force behind the re-creation of the modern Olympics was Evangelis Zappas. Like so many of the city's patrons in this era, Zappas was a Greek of the diaspora; born in Epiros, he had settled in Romania, where he achieved his business success. Zappas was eager to contribute to the development of his country, and he came up with a novel way to do it. Like many nineteenth-century revivalist notions at work in Athens, his was a combination of an ancient and a modern theme. The ancient theme was that of the Olympic games. The modern theme was inspired by the first World's Fair, held in London in 1851.

Revival of the Olympic games had been a lifelong goal of the Greek poet Panagiotis Soutsos, who had begun lobbying for their reinstitution as soon as the new state was founded. Though Soutsos received a sympathetic hearing, the government provided no funding. Zappas's idea was to create an international event that would bring new technologies to Greece and put on exhibit the achievements in the arts and industry of the new nation. Alongside this trade fair, he proposed to sponsor a series of athletic contests. And to house these contests, Zappas paid for a refurbishing of the Panathenaic Stadium. As curious as this amalgam sounds after a century and more of modern Olympics, where commercial activity is meant to be excluded, Zappas's notion was not entirely foreign to the ancient Olympic spirit. The ancient Olympics, of course, was not a trade fair, but its contests ranged far beyond athletics to include competitions involving literature and the arts. The Olympics had guaranteed a period of peaceful congregation among nations, which Zappas's idea also incorporated and which the modern Olympics strives to ensure.

The first of what have come to be called the Zappeian Olympiads was held in 1859. Zappas died in 1865, leaving an enormous fortune in his will for the establishment of permanent facilities for the Olympiads that he had pioneered. In 1869, the government designated a large tract of public land adjacent to the Royal Gardens and extending toward the Panathenaic Stadium as a home for future exhibits and contests. Two such combined events were held during the 1870s. In 1874, building began on a permanent exhibition hall to house industrial and cultural exhibits, the organizing committee for the Olympiad, and a museum to showcase representative Greek works of art. This building remained incomplete for fourteen years. Problems with funding associated with the management of Zappas's estate were compounded by artistic differences between two architects involved in the project. Finally the Zappeion, as the exhibit hall is still known, was opened in 1888, a year before the final Zappeian Olympiad.

The building is very similar in structure to the National Museum: its long façade combines a massive center block with a temple front, and long porticos and temples turned on end with the now formulaic triple windows replacing the colonnade. The overall plan is D-shaped, with the façade along the flat end, a series of richly decorated exhibit rooms behind them, and a magnificent peristyle enclosing an open courtyard. The overall effect is opulent. The building is set in what is now one of the city's most popular and welcoming public parks, the Zappeion Gardens, now directly linked to the former Palace Gardens.

Zappas's Olympiads were one of the inspirations for the modern revival of the ancient Olympic athletic contests, a movement that began not in Athens, but in England and France. Dr. William Penny Brookes established Olympic games in Shropshire in the 1850s. Largely at the instigation of Pierre de Coubertin, the International Olympic Committee, which still governs the Olympics today, was established in Paris in 1894. The committee

The Zappeion.

set the ambitious goal of sponsoring the first games in Athens in 1896. For those games the Olympic stadium was again refurbished with money from Zappas's endowment, supplemented by funds from George Averoff.

The 1896 games opened on April 6, according to the official calendar of the International Olympic Committee, which was March 25 on the Orthodox calendar and so the anniversary of the date officially recognized as the beginning of the Greek War of Independence. Eighty thousand people attended the opening exercises held in the stadium. Running and gymnastic events were also held there. The Zappeion hosted fencing, as it did in 2004. In 1896, there was no pool in Athens, so swimming events were held in the Mediterranean. Cycling, shooting, and tennis, all without ancient precedents, were included. Greeks did well in discus and shot put, two ancient events in which they had hoped to triumph. In the end, the only Greek to receive a gold medal was Spyridon Louis, who won the all-important marathon.

The international peace and goodwill that accompanied the 1896 Olympics gave way before year's end to public outcry. At issue was the liberation of Crete from Ottoman control and its incorporation into the Greek state. Political parties taunted the king and prime minister and demanded war against the Ottoman Empire. By the beginning of the next year, troops were mobilizing on two fronts: one within Crete, the other on the northern border connecting the two nations. As spring began in 1897, almost exactly one year after the Olympics, the two armies clashed. The Ottomans had the advantage in men and in up-to-date weapons. The war was over in a month, with the armistice, as usual, negotiated by the Great Powers and with no perceptible advantage to either side.

8

Modern Athens

In the years between independence and the first modern Olympics, Athens grew from a modest city of ten thousand to a capital with a population of one hundred thousand. According to some estimates, that number was the maximum that the ancient city and the Attic region together had ever sustained. Though the city's nineteenth-century population had grown tenfold in less than eight decades, nearly 80 percent of its residents could have been accommodated together in a single structure, the Panathenaic Stadium. By the time Athens again played host to the Olympics in 2004, the city of one hundred thousand had reduplicated itself, not just ten times over, but a staggering thirty-five times to reach a second-millennium total of 3.5 million residents.

This explosive growth alone would have been enough to make the history of twentieth-century Athens a turbulent one, but multiplying population and the metropolitan expansion it entailed were by no means the only causes of dramatic transformation. Throughout the century, Athens and Greece were caught up repeatedly in geopolitical struggles on multiple fronts. These conflicts existed on every level—sometimes, though not always, simultaneously—from the internal, through the national and regional, to the international. Internal issues included the deeply divisive "Great Idea"— the vexed question of Greek identity and the geographic boundaries most appropriate to it. Scarcely less venerable in origin was the polymorphic schism within the Greek political community that took different forms in different eras but retained its divisive character whether it set monarchists against antimonarchists, rightists against liberals, or labor against capital. That conflict had its strongest effect within the Greek military, which throughout the century intervened repeatedly in political affairs.

The greatest conflict in the twentieth century of regional origin grew out of the dissolution of the Ottoman Empire, the Eastern Mediterranean's great power for almost five hundred years. Britain and France had long resisted the formal political disintegration of what had been for generations a tottering if not doddering regional superstate. When the First World War ended with the Ottoman Empire on the losing side, the winners agreed to a partition of the carcass. From the time of their first surge toward independence, Greeks had fixed the Ottoman Empire in their sights. The Great Idea saw Ottoman territory as the raw material out of which a nation state would necessarily be carved. Even after independence, Ottoman Turks were regional rivals and the default antagonist for any bellicose leader to provoke. Repeated wars between the two had marked the nineteenth century and continued deep into the twentieth. On the island of Cyprus, divided between the two, there is every possibility of renewed skirmishing today.

Conflict on the international level inevitably involved Greece, either directly as a combatant or indirectly as a nation whose geographical place within the Eastern Mediterranean exposed it to the risks of collateral damage. The British had a long-term vital interest in the Eastern Mediterranean because it guarded the gateway to the Suez Canal, which was in turn the doorway to India and the rest of Britain's eastern colonial empire. Any threat to secure transit in the Mediterranean brought Great Britain to a state of alert. Despite a radical change of government in the early twentieth century, Russia, reborn as the Soviet Union, continued to pursue a foreign policy that demanded a zone of pliant buffer states on its borders and access to the high seas via the Mediterranean. From the 1930s, Greece was repeatedly in the line of fire as the Soviets pursued these ends. Neither Russia nor Great Britain had hesitated to intervene in the domestic affairs of Greece during the nineteenth century. In the twentieth century their involvement was less direct, but it was no less insistent. In the aftermath of the Second World War, Britain acknowledged its inability to carry on the role of regional policeman and urged the United States to step in. With a newly minted international policy dominated by the strategy of containing Soviet aggression and increasingly motivated by the need to guarantee access to Middle Eastern oil reserves, the United States accepted this role and continues to carry it out.

France, Austria, and Germany played different roles in Athens in the twentieth century from those they had played in the nineteenth. After the breakup of the Ottoman Empire, France became a League of Nations mandatory power—a political godparent—to Syria and Lebanon. Despite this, the interest of France in the Eastern Mediterranean and consequently in Greece diminished as its dominance in western North Africa increased. Germany enjoyed a special relationship with the Greek ruling family, a bond that the ups and downs of royal popularity damaged as often as it strengthened. When Greece's anguished and much-delayed entry into the First World War on the side of Germany's enemies broke the long-term bonds of alliance, it created a deep national crisis. During the Second World War, German troops divided control of Occupied Greece with their Italian and Bulgarian allies. Austria, home to a large Greek émigré community, had been an important focus of political action in the liberation struggle, but in the twentieth century its foreign policy was increasingly dominated by Germany.

The first decades of the twentieth century set the stage for a century marked by repeated tragedy. Political divisiveness, repeated, ill-considered wars of aggression, and ineffective leadership characterized the national scene. Early in the twentieth century a charismatic leader, Eleutherios Venizelos, became prime minister. Under his leadership, the government modernized and passed progressive legislation that increased workers' rights and simplified the tax system. Venizelos achieved the nearly impossible combination of creating a powerful Liberal Party without alienating the military. In fact, he increased the military budget and modernized the services. When, in 1910, the Balkan region erupted in a war of independence against the Turks, Greece was among the major beneficiaries of the struggle. Crete—which the Ottomans had long refused to yield—Epirus, Macedonia, and many islands in the Aegean were added to the nation, increasing its territory by almost seventy percent.

The Balkan Wars were a regional prelude to the First World War, which not coincidentally was ignited by an assassination in the Balkan city of Sarajevo. Greece had no wish to enter the war as an ally of Turkey, its long-term enemy, nor on the side of Bulgaria, which continued to dispute territory recently added to the Greek nation—both were allies of Germany and Austria-Hungary. All the same, the queen of Greece when war broke out was the sister of Kaiser Wilhelm; German advisers had played a considerable part in reforming and modernizing the Greek military, and many Greek officers had close ties to Germany, where they had been trained. In this vexed situation, the king urged Greek neutrality. Venizelos pressed for active engagement on the side of Germany's opponents. Reports that Turks were massacring Greeks in Asia Minor increased war fervor. Venizelos's position gained further ground in the second year of the war, when Britain promised in the event of victory to reward Greece—should it enter on the side of the Entente— with *all* Ottoman territory in West Asia.

Venizelos believed that Greeks could never ally with Turks, that Germany could not win the war, and that Britain would keep its promises. He resigned in protest against the king's call for neutrality. For the next two years, Greece fell into a prolonged constitutional crisis that became known as the National Schism. Venizelos's Liberal Party was pitted against the monarchy, which in turn was supported by the army. Elections were held, coups organized, successive governments dissolved. The Liberals made secret international accords that sanctioned a British invasion of Macedonia. In support of a Venizelos-led provisional government, Britain and France launched a three-month blockade designed to pressure the monarch. Supporters of the monarchy rallied around Ioannis Metaxas and a newly created paramilitary force under his command. Metaxas began a campaign of terror that targeted not just Venizelos's supporters but anyone with antimonarchical views. King Constantine eventually gave in to international pressure, which, like the domestic situation, had escalated dramatically. Britain and France, raising the ghost of Admiral Morosini, threatened a bombardment of Athens. To avoid this, the king agreed to hand over the government to his son. Venizelos returned as prime minister and purged monarchists from the government. Greece finally entered the war in July 1917. Despite the late hour, Greek troops pushed German and Bulgarian forces back in Macedonia.

Having dragged the nation into war at extraordinary cost, Venizelos had every reason to expect the promised reward. Like the international leaders of his day—Woodrow Wilson, Lloyd George, and Clemenceau—Venizelos participated actively and at length in the peace talks. Still, the full share of spoils that Greece had been led to expect did not materialize. There was new land in the European part of Turkey, though Constantinople was excluded. Around the coastal city of Izmir a territory was carved out to serve as a homeland for Greeks resident in West Asia. Greece would have mandatory authority over that territory. Though the result was less than he had anticipated, Venizelos had still broadened the country's borders. Preparing to return home, the prime minister was attacked and wounded by a royalist assassin. By the time he recovered, he had lost his hold on the domestic political situation.

An ultra-monarchist government won election. Once in power, it purged Venizelists from the bureaucracy. To solidify its power and popularity, it fell back on the Great Idea. Not content with the territory Venizelos had won at the peace talks, the new government decided on a head-to-head confrontation with the Turks, who, in their new role as a nation rather than an empire, were led by Mustafa Kemal, later known as Atatürk. Justification for invasion came from the threat the Turkish government posed to the Greeks in and around Izmir, where Turkish massacres had occurred throughout the war years. In March 1921, Greek troops began an invasion that developed into a broad, sweeping front stretching across much of Anatolia. Turkish troops yielded ground and carefully avoided decisive conflicts. The mood in Greece was ebullient; confidence was high.

Meanwhile, international sentiment was cooling toward an aggressive Greece. Britain and the United States urged a pullback and offered to broker a settlement. Former Greek ally France, along with Italy, supplied arms to Turkey. Turkey, which appeared to have been getting the worst of the conflict, was actually pursuing a self-aware if dangerous strategy. When the Turks judged that the Greek army had extended itself beyond the limits of supply and coordination, they counterattacked. Their surge shattered the Greek front; Turkish troops mopped up isolated units and chased the remnant of the Greek force back to Izmir. Greek civilians followed in their wake, terrified at the prospect of Turkish retribution. Before the eyes of hundreds of international observers aboard ships in the harbor of Izmir, Turkish soldiers burned, pillaged, and slaughtered. When the massacre ended, thirty thousand men, women, and children—ethnically Greek but citizens of Turkey—lay dead.

The disastrous campaign killed the Great Idea and condemned the monarchist regime. A group of military officers organized a revolutionary committee and staged a coup. They forced the resignation of the royalists and the abdication of King Constantine in favor of his son. They purged the bureaucracy. Their next job was to find scapegoats to blame for the Turkish debacle. Ousted prime minister Dimitrios Gounaris and five members of his government were tried on charges of high treason before a military tribunal.

All six were executed within hours of the trial's conclusion. Their deaths increased the rancor between the royalist and Venizelist factions.

Venizelos himself was not part of the ruling junta, but its members called on him to negotiate a settlement at the end of the war. The Treaty of Lausanne, signed in 1923, reset the boundaries of Greece and Turkey in favor of the latter, but its most significant feature was unprecedented. The motive for repeated conflict between Greece and Turkey had always been the difference between ethnic distribution and national boundaries. The Great Idea accepted as axiomatic that Greeks, wherever they happened to live, had a right to incorporation with the boundaries of Greece. Implicitly the Great Idea equated the Greek nation with the Greek people. The concept embodied in the Treaty of Lausanne was just the opposite: geography defined a nation, not ethnicity. Greeks, wherever they happened to live, should be "repatriated" in their "ancestral homeland."

Repatriation, of course, was a convenient fiction, since the ancestors of many Greeks living in 1920s Turkey had come there long before the Turks took over, or the Romans, for that matter. To make the situation worse, the indicator of national identity that was chosen was not language or culture, but religion. (Religious difference had spurred Turkish massacres not only of Greeks but Armenians as well.) According to the treaty, "Greeks" meant "Orthodox Christians," and "Turks" meant "Muslims." Nearly half a million Muslims went to Turkey, and 1.3 million Orthodox Christians came the other way. The new arrivals in Greece increased the population by about 20 percent. The exchange transformed a multicultural Greece into a more or less ethnically homogeneous nation-state.

Assimilating this many people would have been a daunting challenge under any circumstances. The situation was made more difficult by an accumulation of factors. The refugees arrived at a time when the expenses of warfare had already strained the national budget. Their immediate needs for food, clothing, and shelter were enormous and unquestionable, but resources to serve them were in short supply. Men of working age had been held back in Turkey and sent to labor camps. Women, children, and the elderly predominated among the first waves of refugees who arrived in Greece. Many had escaped with little or nothing. Some moved to areas like the island of Crete, where large numbers of Muslims had lived. Cities like Athens and Thessalonika took them one hundred thousand at a time. Over generations, these newcomers created distinctive neighborhoods, and in time the skills they brought expanded Greek industry to include tobacco, carpet making, and textile weaving. The short-term impact of the migration was far less positive. When the international depression struck in 1930, the situation reached crisis proportions. Turkish massacres of Greek civilians during the First World War, the abortive Greek military campaign in 1921, and the population exchange came to be lumped together under a single rubric, the Asia Minor Catastrophe.

It is no wonder that the decades between the wars were exceptionally unsettled ones. From the time the Treaty of Lausanne was signed until 1936 there were repeated military coups. In the four years between 1924 and 1928, no fewer than ten prime ministers attempted and failed to lead the government. For a four-year period beginning in 1928, Venizelos returned to power. His government was again successful in passing measures of reorganization and reform. National road and rail networks were expanded; agriculture was reorganized, modernized, and shored up with price supports. Protective tariffs encouraged consumption of domestic products. Public housing, spurred in part by the need to house repatriated Greeks, was constructed, much of it in Athens.

The progressive era came to an abrupt end when the government's economic liberality ran headlong into international depression. Heavily reliant on exports that suddenly lost their international market, the country struggled to continue paying its substantial foreign debt. The Venizelos government fell in 1932. Four years of coup and counter-coup, purge and counterpurge followed. Finally the king appointed General Metaxas as prime minister. As an ultraroyalist and former paramilitary commander, Metaxas promised to rule with an iron fist. Antigovernment riots and a general strike in August 1936 gave him an opening. He declared a state of emergency, dissolved parliament, and suspended constitutional provisions guaranteeing individual rights. Modeling himself on Hitler and Mussolini, he targeted organized labor and the political Left.

Metaxas's international bedfellows proved to be ill-chosen, particularly Mussolini, whose expansionist dreams threatened Greek sovereignty. In 1940, Il Duce demanded that Greece accept Italian troops within its territories. Metaxas drew the line at this, and Italy declared war. In the short term, the results were very good for Greece. United behind a common enemy, factions put aside their quarrels, and men volunteered for the army in large numbers. Initially the military situation was equally rosy: Italian troops were driven out of northern Greece and pushed back into Albania. At the time of Metaxas's death in early 1941, the situation on the ground was entirely in Greece's favor and that of its lone ally, Great Britain, which had provided air and ground support to the army.

In the spring of 1941, Hitler stepped in to redeem the failed Italian campaign. He had no territorial interest in Greece, but needed to secure the region on his southern flank before turning his armies eastward to his all-consuming goal of attacking Russia. The combined armies proved too much for Greece and an overstretched Great Britain. The Greek army was forced to surrender; German, Italian, and Bulgarian forces streamed south out of the mountains to occupy Athens and the Peloponnesos. The king and the British, along with a remnant of the Greek army, fled to Crete, which was seized at great cost by German paratroopers. The king then established his government-in-exile in British-held Egypt.

Greece was partitioned among the Axis nations, with the meatiest bits—Athens, Thessalonika, and Crete—going to the leader of the pack. Collaborationist leaders created Vichy-type regimes within the separate zones of occupation. With no strategic interest in the country, no concern for its welfare as a nation or survival as a people, the Nazis stripped Greece of every resource. Medicines were confiscated, and the sick and wounded were turned out of hospital beds to wander the streets. Industrial and agricultural products, including tobacco, leather, cotton, and silk, were shipped to Germany. The draft animals that pulled plows and carts and formed the backbone of Greek agriculture, along with herds of sheep, goats, and cattle, were confiscated. Some fourteen million animals are estimated to have left Greece bound for the Axis homelands. A British blockade of the occupied country cut off imports.

All available supplies of food and gasoline were seized, nominally to support the German army on the march, as well as German, Italian, and Bulgarian civilians back home. In reality, much that was confiscated remained in Greece and passed into the hands of black marketers. The occupiers paid for confiscated goods in debased currency, a practice that quickly led to massive inflation and severe inequities. Better-off people could afford black-market prices; the poor, the unemployed, and those on fixed incomes could not. The winter of 1941–1942 was extremely cold, especially in the Mediterranean. During that first winter of Axis occupation, an estimated one hundred thousand Greeks starved to death or died of exposure. The afflicted were disproportionately poor; the hardest hit were Greeks from Asia Minor, many of whom were still living in slums or temporary housing. The relative good health of those who collaborated and could afford to buy black-market food created a powerful reservoir of class hatred within the country.

German soldiers, at first ordered to treat Greek civilians with courtesy, quickly wore out their welcome. Exploiting intelligence collected by the Metaxas regime, Nazi agents hunted down leftists. The obligation to quarter German soldiers in their homes radicalized many Greeks. Much to the disgust and dismay of Athenians, the swastika had been raised over the Acropolis on April 27, 1941. It hung there as a symbol of the nation's subjection. On the night of May 30, two students, Apostolos Santas and Manolis Glezos, hauled it down. Both escaped into the night, and both were condemned to death in absentia—sentences destined never to be fulfilled. The students' seemingly futile act of resistance had enormous consequences not only in Greece but throughout Occupied Europe, wherever news of their exploit spread. Though they had poked the Nazi beast with nothing more than a pin, they had lived to tell the tale. Their example inspired endless acts of substantial resistance that caused untold damage to the occupiers. It is a tragic irony that those same acts of resistance condemned Greece to cancerous civil strife once the war was over.

Armed resistance groups sprang to life during the first summer of the occupation. The main such organization, called EAM—translated as the National Liberation Front—and its combat-focused offshoot, ELAS, were from the start dominated by a cohesive and savvy minority member-group, the KKE or Greek Communist Party. The KKE had long been targets of Metaxas's paramilitaries, his spies, and provocateurs, so they were well established as a clandestine organization before the occupation. Of course, at the time of occupation Stalin was still allied with Hitler, so the KKE, like Communist parties everywhere, offered no resistance to Nazi attack. Only after Hitler's invasion of the Soviet Union began in June were Communist groups worldwide mobilized to aid the homeland of socialism.

The National Schism played its part in the era of resistance to Nazi occupation, just as it did before and after the war. EAM and ELAS were anathema

not just to the Germans, but to Metaxas supporters. On the right of the political spectrum, EDES was the most important group. Though it was not
the most successful group or the largest, EDES at first got the bulk of international support, particularly from Britain, because of its conservative
political slant. When Britain attempted to change course and throw its
weight behind the stronger EAM, the political situation actually became
worse rather than better. At a conference in Cairo in the summer of 1943,
representatives of the resistance, the British, and the government-in-exile
met to prepare for the postwar world. ELAS demanded that a vote be held
on the future of the monarchy in Greece before the sovereign reentered the
country. It also insisted that in the postwar government, ELAS—meaning
the KKE—would be guaranteed the most powerful ministries: Justice, the
Interior, and War. The monarch refused further negotiation along these
lines, and the British backed him up.

Since it had proved impossible for ELAS to negotiate a postwar political
position commensurate with what it believed its membership and achievements deserved, the group decided to take a different approach. Rather than
continue to fight for the liberation of Greece and hope for the best at war's
end, their orientation shifted. They began fighting for control of territory
and power within Greece, confident that this strategy would result in political dominance once hostilities ceased. Their primary rival ceased to be
the Nazis, who had no political role to play in the Greece of the future, and
became their fellow resistance groups, especially EDES. Britain continued
to back the conservative resistance and tried to keep military supplies from
reaching ELAS. In 1943, Italy abruptly sued for peace, and ELAS captured
the abandoned resources of the Italian army. ELAS established an independent liberated zone in the north of the country and spun off a new organization to govern it, called PEEA, Political Committee of National Liberation.

In the spring of 1944, a "grand revolt" gathered forces inside and outside
Greece in favor of PEEA, and the government-in-exile reorganized in response. Georgios Papandreou, antiroyalist but also anticommunist, became
head of a new government-in-exile headquartered in Lebanon. Under pressure from the Soviet Union—the consequence of a secret deal between
Stalin and Churchill—EAM agreed to support a Papandreou government.
Though ELAS's strategy of territorial control had been successful and na-

tional power was within their grasp, they bowed to the Soviet directive. Athens was liberated on October 12, and Papandreou entered the city on October 18 to national rejoicing. Along with the government-in-exile came British troops, who were destined to play a crucial role in events about to unfold.

The euphoria in Athens and throughout the country was short-lived. The terms negotiated in Lebanon called for ELAS to disarm the bulk of its partisans; a single elite unit was exempted. Just over a month after entering the city, Papandreou called for the total disarmament of ELAS. Already dismayed by the new government's failure to punish collaborators, EAM organized a mass rally in Syntagma Square and a general strike to protest the government's actions. When police fired on unarmed demonstrators, tensions between Right and Left exploded into unrestrained violence. Once again the deeply rooted National Schism had surfaced. The British army was caught in the middle between two factions whose rivalry at first had nothing to do with them. As fighting intensified in Athens, however, a widespread welcome of British troops gave way to fear and hatred.

In the early days of the monthlong conflict in Athens, ELAS snipers kept British soldiers confined under fire in the center of the city. When the troops finally broke out, street battles raged in working-class neighborhoods where EAM supporters predominated. Soldiers on the ground were supported by planes of the RAF. Spitfires machine-gunned apartment buildings and the wooded parks around the center of the city where the snipers were concealed. Even neighborhoods where partisans were in much smaller concentration were systematically strafed. British forces rounded up an estimated fifteen thousand supporters of the Left and sent more than half of them to internment camps in West Asia. ELAS responded by rounding up and killing those they identified as "enemies of the people." They compounded this brutal act by collecting hostages from the "privileged social classes" and marching them in the dead of winter into the mountains. The horror these men endured and the many who died along the way eradicated the respect and sympathy not just of Greeks but of the world in general for the former partisans. When the conflict was finally quashed, an estimated eleven thousand men, women, and children of Athens had perished during the December fighting. Property valued at millions of dollars was destroyed.

The tragic events in Athens hardened attitudes on both sides and turned the National Schism into an unbridgeable chasm. The Left, wounded, disenfranchised, and stigmatized by charges of brutality and excess, was isolated and deeply embittered. The Right was both empowered by victory and confirmed in its contempt for those ex-partisans and their supporters who had subjected the city and the nation to a month of terror and class warfare. Conservatives controlled the government and so had greater scope to punish their enemies. That punishment developed into a systematic campaign of reprisal known as the White Terror.

Nominally protected by a national amnesty, former partisans became the target of concerted action. The Ministry of Justice, the security forces, and extralegal paramilitary death squads made war on resistance survivors, whom it accused of crimes against the Greek state. The Greek state that the Right defended with the full rigor of the law and the zeal of the lawless vigilante was the puppet government that had collaborated with the Nazi occupiers. The number of men and women affected was staggering. In 1946, the government placed an estimated thirty thousand in concentration camps or sent them into internal exile. The Left fought back: guerrillas began attacks against the army and the security services in the winter of 1946. Worn out by the staggering effort of the war and facing the loss of the overseas empire that had made the Eastern Mediterranean a focus of national interest, Britain threw up its hands. In a diplomatic note delivered to the American secretary of state, the British government conceded that it could no longer sustain its traditional role in the region and urged the United States to step in. Determined to counter Soviet expansion, the United States agreed, and American military advisers soon arrived to support the national government. Against all odds, the rebellion continued for another two years. When the conflict finally ended in 1949, an additional eighty thousand Greeks had been killed. This toll was added to the half-million who had perished in the war and the seven hundred thousand displaced during the decade-long era of conflict.

The first years of the war had left Athens scarred emotionally but with little physical damage. That condition had changed for the worse during the mechanized fighting that took place throughout December 1944. The political turmoil of the postwar era compounded the damage, not because fighting continued in the city, but because there were no resources for repair and rebuilding. The Athens population in 1940, at the outbreak of war, had been near the million mark, about 15 percent of the national total. The devastation of the countryside during the war and, especially, during the Civil War, spurred internal migration; by 1950, when the nation could again focus its energies on daily-life issues of food, clothing, and shelter, the need for new housing was overpowering.

Political stability in Greece in the 1950s and 1960s was a relative thing. Politics were definitely more organized than they had been during the Civil War era and considerably calmer than the violent ups and downs of the interwar years, but the National Schism was still in play. The monarchy continued to intervene abruptly and catastrophically in domestic affairs. The military saw itself in a political role, too, and colonels staged a coup in 1967. Their seven-year dictatorship revived Metaxas-era practices of surveillance, torture, and suppression of opponents and presumed enemies. In the intervals between seizures of power by the unelected, the political parties on the right and the left jockeyed for advantage. Generally speaking, not much was expected from the governments of this era.

Meanwhile the population continued to grow, especially in urban centers like Thessalonika and Athens, which continued to draw rural people at a steady pace. Population pressure accelerated, and Athens landowners, builders, and would-be tenants responded. In the complete absence of national, regional, or municipal planning, they contrived a way to meet the demand for living space. The method they came up with was a creative form of financing called the "antiparochi" system, which continues in effect today. The owner of a property would collaborate with a builder and a group of prospective tenants. The owner provided land, the prospective tenants contributed financing, and the builder did the work.

There were no architects; builders worked from a commonly evolved functional plan. Much of what they threw together was graceless and crudely utilitarian. The typical apartment building created under this system was a five- or six-story rectangular prism of reinforced concrete floors and pillars. Outer walls between the concrete supports were filled in with mortar and cheap stone or hollow brick. Since incomplete buildings were taxed at a lower rate than finished structures, it was common to leave rebar sticking out of half-height pillars above a flat roof. Building codes were nonexistent or overridden by well-placed bribes. Houses went up everywhere space and financing could be found. Rough and ready as it was, the system met the immediate needs of a growing population. It failed in organization and integration. Water supply, sewage, and transportation, all requiring higher-level coordination, fell behind. In the first two decades after the Civil War, apartment blocks spewed across Athens and Attica with a force and intensity that no one restrained or directed.

The million Athenians of 1950 became 2.5 million by 1970, and added a further million in the next decade. At an equally quick pace, the city spread outside its old municipal boundaries. At the outset of the Second World War, slightly under half the population lived within the city limits. Thirty years later, two-thirds of Athenians lived outside the old boundaries. By 1971, Athens was a quickly spreading pool of characterless concrete apartment buildings. This mass of housing still represents the majority of greater Athens today.

Within this undifferentiated, unplanned mass, architects did manage to design a few major projects. The first significant public buildings of the late 1950s sounded an entirely new note in a city that during the nineteenth century had re-created itself in the mold of its classical past. Neoclassical architecture was not in vogue in the 1950s and 1960s: the ascendant style was international in inspiration, functionalist and minimalist in approach. Its profile was sharp, its surfaces uncluttered, and design as a whole was largely if not completely devoid of reference to history. Why look back when the past was marked by disaster and death? Significantly, the first two major projects in Athens represented not just a new architectural matrix, but the appearance on the national scene of a powerful new international presence.

Like the rest of Europe, Greece had received enormous amounts of postwar aid from the United States acting through the Marshall Plan for rehabilitation and development. The country's major benefactor had taken over Britain's abandoned role of international big brother in the region, and so when a new United States Embassy and a new Hilton Hotel were created in Athens, they bore a heavy symbolic weight. They were not just architecture; they were declarations of intent, messages from the outside that introduced a new model of nationhood and a new force of political influence. The embassy building is a low, rectangular, glass-walled box designed by Walter Gropius. A colonnade of concrete piers supported on a raised plinth ring the building and anchor its extended roof, which is meant to act as a sun shield.

The United States Embassy.

Beyond its purely utilitarian use of columns, the building makes not a single nod to the architectural heritage of Athens.

Like the embassy, the Hilton Hotel could have been built in any part of the world. While it was still under construction, it began to cause controversy. Designed by a team of Athenian architects, the building fit the international style of the moment. Above a ground-level colonnade, its grid-like façade curves across the face of what from the ends appear to be solid concrete pylons. Before the building went up, the Athens skyline was dominated, as it had been for millennia, by the Parthenon. Once the Hilton, which exceeded municipal height limits, was completed, it rivaled that ancient symbol of Athenian identity. The building's dismissal of all historical reference, its commercial purpose, American brand-name, and, above all, its arrogant usurpation of a place on the Athens skyline made it an all too ready symbol of American overreaching.

Despite adverse reactions to these pioneering structures, the international style became the accepted vocabulary of Athenian building. The Supreme

The Hilton Athens.

Court is very similar to Gropius's American Embassy—it lacks the sun-
shade, and its concrete pillars are integrated directly into its glass-walled
façade—but both buildings present themselves as unwelcoming monoliths.
The Municipal Concert Hall, though sumptuous and gracious on the inside,
presents an exterior nearly identical to that of the Supreme Court building.
Concrete pylons in pairs stand somewhat forward of glass-walled inter-
stices. The impersonal and domineering style of buildings designed to house
and to represent powerful institutions seems especially ill-suited to a building meant to welcome the public. Built in the same era, but with different
international influences, the National Gallery combines permanent and
temporary exhibition spaces with an outdoor sculpture garden. The building's rambling shape and dissected façade owe some debts to Le Corbusier.
Despite isolated buildings like the Hilton, which stood out above the rest,
the municipality of Athens had, like many other national capitals, resisted
the international trend toward metropolitan skyscrapers. During the reign
of the colonels, the Athens Tower was completed. In 1980, after the restora-

The Municipal Concert Hall.

tion of democracy, a second skyscraper, the Atrina Tower, went up. It is unlikely that additional buildings on this scale will be created.

An overview of Athens today shows a city that appears not just to sprawl but to flow like lava over every bit of low ground from the Saronic Gulf to an apex some fifteen miles inland. The steep slopes of Mount Hymettos and Mount Penteli confine it on the east, though a gap between them has made way for a subsidiary eastern outflow toward the airport that threatens before long to merge with dense settlements on the Aegean coast. On the west, the ridges of Mount Egaleo hem the city in. Within this geographically confined mass settlement, a loose coordination is suggested by a webwork of interstate highways and the metro and interurban rail lines. The old center with its nineteenth-century street plan floats within, like the tiny nucleus of an amorphous single-celled organism. It is hardly even discernible in the mass, and would appear to have offered only a limited trajectory to the city's growth. Architect and critic Dimitris Philippidis has described contemporary Athens in these words:

The mountains surrounding the plain of Athens, and the perimeters of the hills that emerge like islands from the sea of concrete are the front line in the running war between the aggressive forces of building development—which are steadily gaining ground up the hillsides—and defenseless nature. The main battlegrounds are the areas around abandoned quarries, which mark the present edge of the city. . . . Northwards from the plain, the city is expanding unchecked. New houses are rising apace, with or without official planning permission, many of them in the few patches of forest that remain. . . . The main roads, described earlier as "arteries and veins," would perhaps be better compared with rivers. There the thunderous roar of traffic never ceases, shattering the peace and raising the stress level of everyday life. . . . The arterial roads help the city to expand outwards, but at the same time they encourage the development of local centers outside the historic city center. The urban carpet covering the Athenian plain is held in place . . . so to speak by a number of nail-like spikes sticking up into the sky. These are the few skyscrapers and tower blocks—very few in comparison with other big cities—built in the 1970's.

While unrestrained growth has been the mode in Athens since 1950, there are increasing efforts today if not to restrain the city's expansion, at least to make the urban agglomerate more livable and more manageable. One of the greatest and most successful of these has been the subway system, which many visitors to the city first encountered during the 2004 Olympics when it did an efficient job of moving masses of people quickly and reliably. The system appears entirely up to date, but in fact its history reaches back into the nineteenth century. An aboveground passenger railway connected Athens with Piraeus a year after the first modern Olympics. By 1904, the line had lengthened, and electric engines replaced coal-burning locomotives. By 1957 the single line had reached far inland to the then village of Kifissia, at the base of Mount Penteli. Within the new Athens subway system, this line, which still runs almost entirely aboveground, is Line 1.

Construction of two additional underground lines began in the last decade of the twentieth century. Their main purpose was to link sections of the city together in a useful way and in the process to reduce its dependence on buses and cars. Levels of atmospheric pollution in Athens are persistently staggering. A grayish yellow smog hangs over the city on most days. Its poisons cause massive amounts of respiratory disease; over the decades, they have damaged buildings and artifacts exposed to the air. Ameliorating this terrible situation came at a substantial cost. Cutting into the subsoil of the venerable city, the plan that offered the greatest chance of success, was a bold undertaking. The geological underpinnings of Athens are a mix of soft, unconsolidated alluvial deposits and submerged ridges of rock that vary in hardness and stability. Each of these vastly different materials requires its own engineering approach. The complexity of the geological environment, however, is nothing compared to the cultural horizons through which the underground tunnels were inevitably to burrow. Some parts of Athens have been settled since the beginning of the Neolithic. Any excavation was bound to turn into an archaeological leap into the unknown.

The Metro project was fully aware that it would strike archaeological material as it bored through the Athenian earth. Project directors made extraordinary and ultimately effective efforts to ensure that every bit of material that was uncovered was not just carefully preserved, but well documented. The best place to appreciate both the complexity of the job and the quality of the results is in the Syntagma Metro Station. An enormous volume of earth was excavated to create this station, and the archaeological dig that preceded it lasted for two years. The vertical dimension of the excavation representing the cultural eras that the dig cut through is revealed in a cross-section preserved on the walls of the station. The cultural horizons exposed are represented through maps and artifacts on display as well.

Peeling back the layers of the site from the top as the dig progressed first revealed nineteenth-century paving on Amalias Street. Beneath that were remnants of an Ottoman-era water supply system. The early Christian and Byzantine eras further down were represented by a small cemetery and a group of houses with vats built into their floors for storing wine or oil. Upscale late-Roman houses and baths were peeled away in their turn to reveal multiple cemeteries with Roman, Hellenistic, and late-classical burials. There were the remains of bronze foundries from the same era, and beneath these were bits of the city's earliest aqueducts. At the site's ground zero, excavators uncovered an abandoned channel of the meandering Eridanos River.

The Syntagma site was an extremely rich field for investigation, because it lay just outside the round of the Themistoclean wall—hence the classical and Hellenistic burials—but inside the limits of Hadrian's New Athens, where Romans built their villas. The Kerameikos, on the opposite side of ancient Athens, was, in the original plan, scheduled to be transected. The archaeological richness there ultimately made it impossible to carry through with the line as designed, and it was diverted around the site. The subway, which was up and running in time for the Olympics, continues to expand. Its ridership is nearly three quarters of a million people per day. Though traffic still flows in incredible volume over the massive interstates that criss-cross Athens, and smog remains a major concern, the subway has done much to improve the city.

The greatest architectural and cultural project of the recent past has been without question the highly successful 2004 Olympic Games. The site chosen for the Olympics already had a sports complex built on it, but one that was inadequate to meet the needs of the games and entirely lacking in architectural appeal and coherence. In 2001, a bare three years before the games were to begin, Spanish architect Santiago Calatrava received the commission to redesign the site. Calatrava relied on two existing structures to anchor the project and created a ceremonial avenue to join them. Along an intersecting axis he created secondary monumental entrances to the site. The entire complex then needed to be plugged into parking, metro, and street access.

The two major structures on the site were an outdoor stadium and a velo-drome—a cycling race course—both open to the air. Since the Olympics were scheduled for August, when the sun beats down without mercy on Athens and daytime temperatures can reach 100 degrees Fahrenheit or more, roofing these arenas was a fundamental requirement of the remodeling. The existing arenas were not strong enough to support roofs. Rather than build them up or somehow reinforce them, Calatrava created self-supporting tent- or wing-like roofs anchored in the ground outside the arenas and floating above their seats and playing fields. The system of support that holds these roofs up is similar to others that Calatrava has designed for his signature suspension bridges. Cables stitched between two great bowed beams support each roof. The beams rise from earth anchors outside the stadium, cross over the structures, and re-descend. These carapaces with their soaring external ribs and webwork of cables identify the twin anchors of the site.

The Olympic Stadium.

The structure that unites the two creates a sheltered passageway, a meeting place, and an outdoor lobby for the crowds entering and exiting the venues grouped around it. Calatrava pared down and reshaped the defining arcs over the stadiums to identify this area. The link to historic architecture is the stoa, an indoor-outdoor colonnade that supported multiple activities by sheltering crowds from sun and weather. The overall look of the structure is similar to a stretched Slinky slithering across the ground or a series of croquet hoops stuck one next to the other in the earth. The arches provide broken shade, and the spaces between them allow for easy entrance and exit, while their directional flow guides and orients the visitor.

An even more dynamic flow of materials is found in one of the site's most inventive features. Called the Nations Wall, the structure is a colossal, multipurpose, mechanized screen of suspended metal elements supported on piers. The wall fronts an open-air amphitheater with room for a staggering three hundred thousand people. One of its primary roles is as a video display in this outdoor theater. At other times it serves as a picket fence that

The Olympic Agora.

casts interesting shadows. Its components are anchored in the middle and powered by motors. They can be animated to create a sinuous wave that runs across the entire surface from end to end. It is a mechanical evocation of the moving waves that stadium crowds can create.

The imaginative playfulness of the Olympic site, its beauty and efficiency combined with the brilliant showmanship of the opening and closing ceremonies, created a powerful international impression. A door seemed to have slammed shut on the hardships and bitter defeats of the previous century, and a new Greece appeared ready to claim a prominent spot on the international stage. Then, within a scant six years, that new Greece was all but eclipsed in international news and the world imagination. It is doubly ironic that the success of the 2004 Olympics and the staggering debt it occasioned played a major part.

The current crisis represents a new direction in Greek politics that threatens everything that has passed for the politically normal during the last

The Nations Wall.

forty years. The National Schism may no longer be virulent, but it has been active, and its legacy has shaped events for the last four decades. During this era, the political process has been a closed competition between Right and Left where victors and defeated alternate, but neither side retires. A life in politics has been a sinecure, and those lucky enough to enjoy it have taken full advantage of their position. Corruption and mismanagement have been epidemic.

Voters have tolerated this imperfect system for a variety of reasons, some altruistic, some not. For the most cynical, the connection has been anything but idealistic. Some electors have chosen parties that benefited them directly through political patronage or indirectly through generalized benefits and entitlements. Guaranteed jobs, wage and price supports, and liberal medical and pension plans are only some of the more visible inducements. The less noted entitlements include favorable regulations for established profession-als like doctors, architects, pharmacists, and, most critically, the trucking industry. Governments have supported legislation that limits competition, fixes prices, and reduces access to the professions. The austerity measures that the national parties agreed to meant that the parties could no longer deliver on these promises. In the first round of the 2012 national elections, neither of the long-term ruling parties came close to a majority.

This crisis in the normal conduct of political business has sparked repeated protests since 2010—as many as two or three per day in Athens—with a clear economic focus. As early as 2008, when the euro crisis was still on the horizon, protests of great intensity but lacking a clear agenda had already begun. In early December 2008, a minor disturbance in the Exarchia district of Athens, a neighborhood of student housing, bars, and restaurants near the campus of Athens Polytechnic, drew a response from armed security police. An officer fired three shots, one of which fatally wounded fifteen-year-old Alexandros Grigoropoulos. Though the officer was charged with homicide, intense rioting broke out that lasted well over a month and impacted not just Athens but cities throughout Greece and beyond. The riots signaled an intense but vaguely focused malaise.

Student unrest has been a fact of life as long as there have been students, and some tolerance of their escapades is not unusual. In Athens, however, students, especially those at Athens Polytechnic, hold a special place in the memory of many Greeks. Student-led protests and demonstrations brought an end to the dictatorship of the Colonels that had begun in 1967. What sealed the junta's fate after seven years in power was the work of a single night. On November 17, 1973, a tank broke down the gates of Athens Polytechnic, which students had occupied and sealed off three days earlier. During a night of violent confrontation between citizens and the police, twenty-four people were killed. In the aftermath of this tragedy, national law was changed to prohibit police from entering campuses. Student protesters continue to enjoy the protection of a safe refuge on any campus and an inherited reputation as defenders of democracy. The police, even when they are attempting to maintain order, are not universally trusted or supported.

The current political protests in Greece are normal expressions of dissent in a nation where the traditional means of communicating with government is through organized marches and episodic strikes. Within this familiar political landscape there are new actors at play—some of these are populist and grassroots democratic. Their protests are coordinated by Facebook and

Twitter. Participants in rallies organized in this way are not necessarily allied with established political parties, and their actions have spurred confusion and even some contempt among political and union leaders. Also present at the protests is an amorphous crew of the what the police and news media habitually refer to as "hooded youth." Noted for their hooded sweatshirts and black clothes, their faces hidden by scarves or kerchiefs, these figures are the ones at fault when peaceful protests turn violent. They are often armed with clubs or metal rods; they throw rocks and Molotov cocktails at helmeted and armored riot police. In the wake of their actions, innocent protesters, foreigners, and businesses have suffered damage. Protesters out of control have burned and looted stores, caused violent deaths, and provoked enormous economic losses.

The agenda of the hooded youth is unclear. Many are simple hooligans. Incidents in the streets of Athens are not different in character or degree of violence from others that have occurred in soccer stadiums. In March 2012, a group of about two hundred supporters of Panathenaikos, the Athens team, set fire to the upper deck of the Olympic stadium, attacked riot police with metal bars, and pelted them with water bottles filled with "gasoline, ammonia and little sticks of dynamite," according to the Athens daily *Kathimerini*. It is more common to label the thugs in hoodies as anarchists, which gives them something of a political identity if not a recognizable political goal. Black is the traditional color of anarchy. Their aim as anarchists is seen as resistance to any form of government.

The identity and purpose of these young men in black is troubling in itself, but what concerns people even more is the blatant inability of the police to do anything about them. Failure to contain or even to identify these men is a combined result of the safe haven provided by the university campuses and a reticence on the part of the police to appear too aggressive. Some analysts have gone so far as to suggest that the police only appear impotent; in fact the hooded youth are actually *agents provocateurs* or other instruments of the police themselves whom police have no desire to contain. Generally speaking, though, people blame the violent turn of the protests on these anarchic young people, and they blame the police for their failure to ensure that political protest remains safe and within bounds.

The other outside force that plays its role in the protests is never seen on the street. This is the representation of the financial industry that has been the nation's creditor and is now the mortgage holder demanding some return on investment. Whether personified in the European Central Bank or the so-called Troika of auditors and negotiators, or, more commonly, as Chancellor Angela Merkel of Germany, these foreign dignitaries in defense of the euro and its economic regime are ever-present in the minds of demonstrators. The ruling parties that were seen as knuckling under to these interests and forcing multitudes of ordinary Greeks to bear the cost of past extravagance, mismanagement, and corruption paid the price in recent elections. Whether any government can reconcile the needs of Greeks who face increasing prices, loss of opportunity, staggering unemployment, and reduced benefits with the demands of their international creditors remains an open question.

Despite the outbursts of violence that have from time to time punctuated the last few years, the contemporary visitor is likely to remain entirely untouched by the city's ongoing crisis. Business as usual is Athena's public face, and tourism remains a bright spot in an otherwise moribund economy. Yet no visitor sensitive to the city's and the nation's struggle can be entirely untroubled by the crisis. Wages and pensions have been deeply cut; unemployment, especially among young people, is high; food and fuel have been scarce in previous winters and will likely prove so again. Hardship and suffering continue even if the public display of anger and resentment is muted. The city's stoic façade and the majesty of its monuments once again fail to tell the whole story of this fascinating and recurrently agonized city.

Further Reading

Aristotle. *The Athenian Constitution*. Translated by Frederic G. Kenyon. http://www.constitution.org/ari/athen_00.htm.

Bastea, Eleni. *The Creation of Modern Athens: Planning the Myth*. Cambridge: Cambridge University Press, 2000.

Beard, Mary. *The Parthenon*. Cambridge, MA: Harvard University Press, 2003.

Brewer, David. *The Greek War of Independence: The Struggle for Freedom from Ottoman Oppression and the Birth of the Modern Greek Nation*. Woodstock, NY: Overlook Press, 2001.

Camp, John M. *The Archaeology of Athens*. New Haven, CT: Yale University Press, 2001.

——. *The Athenian Agora Site Guide*. 5th ed. Athens: American School of Classical Studies, 2010.

Cartledge, Paul, ed. *The Cambridge Illustrated History of Ancient Greece*. Cambridge: Cambridge University Press, 2002.

Curtis, Glenn E., ed. *Greece: A Country Study*. Washington, DC: Federal Research Division, Library of Congress, 1995.

Hurwit, Jeffrey M. *The Athenian Acropolis: History, Mythology, and Archaeology from the Neolithic Era to the Present*. Cambridge: Cambridge University Press, 1999.

Keeley, Edmund. *Inventing Paradise: The Greek Journey, 1937-1947*. New York: Farrar, Straus and Giroux, 1999.

Korres, Manolis, ed. *Athens from the Classical Period to the Present Day*. Translated by Timothy Cullen. New Castle, DE: Oak Knoll Press, 2003.

Mackenzie, Molly. *Turkish Athens: The Forgotten Centuries, 1456-1832*. Reading, UK: Ithaca Press, 1992.

Mazower, Mark. *Inside Hitler's Greece: The Experience of Occupation, 1941-44*. New Haven, CT: Yale University Press, 1993.

Neils, Jenifer, ed. *The Parthenon from Antiquity to the Present*. Cambridge: Cambridge University Press, 2005.

Pedley, John Griffiths. *Greek Art and Archaeology*. 2nd ed. New York: Harry N. Abrams, 1998.

Pollitt, J. J. *Art and Experience in Classical Greece*. Cambridge: Cambridge University Press, 1999.

Servi, Katerina. *The Acropolis: The Acropolis Museum*. Athens: Ekdotike Athenon, 2011.

Setton, Kenneth M. *Athens in the Middle Ages*. London: Variorum Reprints, 1975.

Tzonis, Alexander. *Santiago Calatrava: The Athens Olympics*. New York: Rizzoli, 2005.

Walker, Susan, and Averil Cameron, eds. *The Greek Renaissance in the Roman Empire*. London: University of London Institute of Classical Studies, 1989.

Acknowledgments

In writing this book, I have been helped by many people. I am especially grateful to Margaret Metzger, whose knowledge and fervent love of Athens jump-started the project. As a researcher on the ground, she contributed insights and practical information. Dr. Georgia Sermamoglou-Soulmaidi carefully read each chapter, corrected errors, and suggested additions. I am extremely grateful for her help. Karen Coker proofread the manuscript, smoothed out the language, and corrected errors. After all this assistance, the mistakes that remain are entirely my own.

I am grateful to Susan Wallace Boehmer at Harvard University Press. It has been, as always, a pleasure working with her and with the multi-competent staff of the press. Once again, Cliff Boehmer's photographs have captured the spirit of the text and of the city; unless otherwise indicated, all photos are his. Wendy Strothman again smoothed the way. My family has kept me going with their boundless patience and support. The book is dedicated to the memory of a great Hellenist, my teacher, mentor, and friend, Robert Fagles.

Index